"*Incredibly, Nancy Whitmore Poore c* *ings. Her words retold with exceptioɪ* *– and survived.*"
— Joan McHugh

"*This book transports you smack into the middle of the most riveting arson/ triple murder case and courtroom drama of my career. The author nailed the mood and personalities in the courtroom with uncanny accuracy.*"
—Roger Bourne, Deputy Ada County Prosecutor

"*[Nancy Whitmore Poore] has gone far and beyond what I would conceive an author doing. She understands the crime, the people and the circumstances…and has captured them like I thought no one could. If you want to know what a real homicide investigation is like, this book will tell you.*"
— Sheriff Gary Raney, Former Lead Detective, Ada County Sheriff's Office

"*Homicide affects many lives and its ripple effect reaches far beyond what we can imagine. Nancy Whitmore Poore sensitively gives us insight into how this tragic case affected, and continues to affect, the lives of those involved.*"
— Ellen Freeman, Victim-Witness Coordinator, Ada County Sheriff's Office

"*I never, ever suspected…it was pretty awful for me that my name had been used to trick people and take their money…I was humiliated.*"
— Barbara Fawcett, Former YWCA Director

"*Every day of their lives [Joshua & Tabitha] trusted her, and they were in danger, every single minute of their lives…*"
— Shirley Jackson, Former Amity Elementary School Teacher

"*She victimized everyone here…she played God.*"
— Sue Fellen, Former YWCA Shelter Director

DEADLY CONFIDANTE

Nancy Whitmore Poore

This is a true story. Some of the locations and names have been changed to protect the privacy of certain individuals. The dialog has been reconstructed as best as possible from personal interviews, court documents and transcripts, and police and public records.

Poore, Nancy Whitmore.

Deadly confidante / Nancy Whitmore Poore. -- 1st ed. -- Bothell, WA : Book Publishers Network, 2005.

p. ; cm.

Subtitle on cover: Arson-betrayal-embezzlement... murder.
ISBN: 0-9755407-7-7
ISBN-13: 978-0-9755407-7-0

1. Row, Robin Lee--Trials, litigation, etc. 2. McHugh, Joan.
3. Murder--Idaho--Boise. 4. Murder--Investigation--Idaho--Boise.
5. Trials (Murder)--Idaho--Boise. 6. Trials (Arson)--Idaho--Boise.
7. Murder--Psychological aspects. 8. Murderers--Psychology.
9. Murderers--Mental health--Case studies. 10. Criminal psychology. I. Title.

HV6534.B66 P66 2005   2004115658
364.152/3/09796/28--dc22   0509

Published and Printed by

 Book Publishers Network

Printed in the United States of America

ISBN: 0-9755407-7-7
ISBN-13: 978-0-9755407-7-0

DEDICATION

To Tabitha Cornellier, Joshua Cornellier,
Randy Row, and all other victims whose lives or
peace of mind have been usurped
because they unsuspectingly
came into contact with a
remorseless human being.

LETTER TO THE READER

I clearly remember the day I told Detective Gary Raney that I had never met a sociopath. He looked directly at me for a couple of seconds and then asked, "How do you know for sure?" I stared at him in shock, speechless, thinking back over my life and wondering how many times I had come into contact with a sociopath and escaped – the close calls.

The blind faith and trust I put in Robin Lee Row is something I still wrestle with. Robin's crimes never leave me completely. This was my friend. We worked together, spent time socializing at each other's homes. The trauma of the murders, for me, was compounded even more by the investigation and then the trial. But hard as it was, I would do it all over again. I would still stand up and tell what happened, to vindicate the precious lives that were lost.

The fear of being misrepresented or misquoted was and is an ongoing concern. Most people unfamiliar with the legal system aren't aware that appeals can go on indefinitely.

Anything I might say could be twisted and used as a new defense tactic to drag out Robin's appeals.

Naturally, when Nancy approached me for an interview for this book, my instinct was to say no. But after a couple of meetings, and when Nancy freely allowed me to read what she had written, I slowly began to trust her and to talk about what had happened to me. Nancy was a good listener and my confidence in her grew.

Amazingly, Nancy has managed to describe my thoughts, feelings, and emotions with pinpoint accuracy in this book. My husband Bernie and I not only trust her and her judgment completely, we consider her a friend. In fact, we still marvel at the wonderful relationships that were formed from such a horrible experience. Bernie and I also keep in contact with Roger Bourne, Gary Raney, and the victim-witness coordinator, Ellen Freeman. All of them are invaluable friends who have lent their support throughout this whole ordeal.

– Joan McHugh

CHAPTER ONE

February 10, 1992

"It's my house! My children are in there! My children are in there!" She yelled, yet the tone of her voice sounded flat. Her knees buckled. Joan, her best friend, holding her arm to steady her, felt Robin sag then catch herself in time to prevent a fall; on the other side, a police officer braced her. They were transfixed by the sight before them. Their three pairs of eyes were tiny mirrors reflecting fire-red tongues leaping up against the night backdrop, aggressively licking the eaves of the duplex. Fiery bursts escaped from a window at the rear of the building. Joan tightened a maternal arm around Robin's shoulder, a part of her supposing that if she squeezed hard enough they would both wake from this nightmare.

Robin had been spending the night more and more often at Joan's apartment, sleeping on the couch. Early that Monday morning, Robin had awakened Joan and told her of a premonition that had nagged her all night to go home.

"I know something is wrong," Robin had said with a frown.

It was about 5:30 a.m. when the two women jumped into Robin's cold, silver Mazda sedan and sped through the fog toward her home on Seneca Drive in a subdivision on the outskirts of Boise, Idaho. Turning onto Five Mile Road, Robin drove out of the city limits, through farmland and past scattered housing developments, then slowed as they approached the turnoff to her street.

"You know, the feeling has left me. I'm probably being silly. It's probably nothing," Robin said, her hands relaxing their grip on the wheel.

1

"As long as we've come this far, just for our peace of mind, let's drive by and check it out," Joan, always the voice of reason, urged.

"This is silly, we're wasting our time," Robin balked.

"We can drive by, and when we see that everything's okay, we can go have breakfast so the trip isn't wasted. You'd never forgive yourself if something were wrong with the kids."

They were almost there. Up ahead, signalling the Seneca turnoff, were the low-slung white brick buildings with red tile roofs that made up the Casa Blanca Apartment Complex, a taste of Mexico in the middle of rural Idaho. As they approached the intersection, they became aware of multi-colored, flashing lights bouncing rhythmically off their surroundings.

"That's my house. There's something wrong at my house!" Robin became more agitated. "There's a fire...it's my house!" she repeated over and over.

Joan's heart jumped, then sped up as if keeping time with the met-ronomic flashing of the lights. She took a deep breath, trying to stay composed. Maybe, she thought, her eyes were not as good as Robin's youthful ones. But try as she might, Joan's eyes could not penetrate the hanging fog to make out what Robin said were flames and smoke.

"No, you're just nervous. There's probably a car accident or some-thing." Joan tried to sound calm even though her stomach fluttered with apprehension. She had helped Robin through many frightening ordeals lately and she prayed this wasn't another.

"It looks like smoke to me," Robin insisted.

Was this more of her premonition, or was she just overwrought and jumping to conclusions? "Don't worry, it could be anything," Joan reas-sured her friend.

Past the apartment complex, they crossed a small bridge over a canal, then slowed to a stop at the next intersection. Joan could now make out the contour of a knot of vehicles blocking the street. Robin's left turn signal was blinking when a police officer stepped up to the driver's window. "No one can go down this street," he said gravely. Joan thought his face looked permanently puckered and doubted he had smiled since "1967."

"That's my house – my family is in there!" Robin screamed. "There's something wrong at my house!"

"Pull your car over," the officer barked, directing Robin to turn onto Seneca and park at the curb.

The two women got out of the car and followed the officer up Seneca toward the activity.

Walking haltingly, still unsure about what they would encounter, Joan stopped. The scene floated like a dream sequence in a movie. Voices were garbled and seemed to fade into a vignette with the rest of the background. The immediate area was lit, resembling a stage set. In the pitch black of night, tinted lights careened off buildings and stained trees. Working with purpose, like a community of ants, emergency personnel hustled about.

As the two women moved closer, the formidable reality loomed like a giant 3-D screen in a movie theater. Flames leapt from a bedroom window at the back of the structure where Robin's son slept – red, yellow, shooting flames whipped the inky canvas of night. Black smoke curled from the master bedroom window in front.

"Oh, my God!" A wail escaped Joan's lips. Her heart felt as if it had stopped – time seemed somehow frozen or distorted. It couldn't be Robin's house that was on fire – but it was. Joan had never seen a raging fire up close; it was gigantic and malicious.

Robin panicked and started to run toward the burning structure. She wailed, "I want to go to my children!" The officer restrained her; attendants steered her to an ambulance parked nearby, sitting her down on the metal tailgate. The shock muted all sensation, even the bone-chilling cold.

"Is everybody all right?" Joan croaked, barely able to push the words out. It was difficult to get air. "Did you get them out of the house?" Her heart beat like a cornered wild animal's.

"A boy has been found dead," Paramedic Brian Snyders told them.

The evidence was before them. Knowing it was 10-year-old Joshua, but not accepting it, Joan cried. Robin wailed. Brian explained to Robin that the firemen could see an adult body, her husband Randy's, on the bed, but the floor was too hot to get to him. They hadn't been able to find 8-year-old Tabitha. They didn't believe anyone had escaped, he told her; anyone in the house probably was already dead of smoke inhalation. In a matter of a few minutes, Robin's condition seemed to

3

deteriorate from hysteria to shock. Joan, inconsolably upset, continued to weep.

Emergency Medical Technician Barbara Witte escorted the two women inside the ambulance to evaluate their condition. Inside the ambulance Joan didn't know what to say to Robin; she had no words. How could she help Robin when she herself couldn't comprehend what was happening? What could she possibly say that would assuage the shot in the heart Robin had just received?

Joan couldn't sit still, she felt dazed and helpless. Exiting the ambulance she walked in circles, lacing and unlacing her fingers, clutching her purse. She was oblivious to the tears staining her cheeks and reddening her eyes.

Joan used a cellular phone to call her husband, Bernie, to break the tragic news. Robin sat on the bench seat in the back of Ambulance 49 and answered Barbara Witte's questions.

Robin asked Witte several times if she could see her dead son. "No, you don't want to see him there." Witte emphatically denied her requests. "You'll have to wait until the coroner takes him to the morgue."

A short time later, determined to see him, Robin pleaded again to go over to the duplex. Witte again gave her a firm no. The EMT was certain that if Robin saw her son laid out on the front lawn of her gutted home, burnt and disfigured, she would lose any shred of sanity that remained.

Joan wandered like a lost child in the vicinity of the ambulance, her thoughts a mishmash. How could this be happening? How could a child she had just seen only two days before be dead? She needed to see for herself that Joshua was really gone, to verify that he truly was not breathing. She had gone about half the distance to the body when the coroner stepped in front of her.

"You don't want to do this," he said.

"Yes, I do. I have to." Joan looked up into his face with her most willful stare. She was short in stature but tall in determination.

"I can't let you do this," he insisted, guiding her back toward the ambulance.

EMT Witte joined them and Joan looked to her for support. "I need to see him," Joan pleaded. "Robin is going to want to know about him."

She couldn't explain exactly why, but she just knew it was something she had to do. She wanted to know for herself and be able to tell Robin that he had a peaceful expression on his face, which would mean he died in his sleep and didn't suffer. But the coroner told Joan it would not be in her best interest to see the boy.

Maybe the coroner didn't understand; apparently neither did EMT Witte. Joan was annoyed with both of them. Robin's son was like a grandson to her. When Joan was seized with a righteous purpose or conviction, her chutzpa took control and she became difficult or impossible to derail. But she had no fight in her now and acquiesced to their authority.

It seemed the only thing she could do was move. She was walking in circles again near a 20 m.p.h. speed limit sign, which for some reason had become her focus, when a TV reporter armed with a camera approached.

"Can we turn this on and get a statement?"

"Are you serious?" Joan stammered, disgusted at the audacity of the reporter. "Please, leave me alone."

"She's in no condition to give an interview," a paramedic rebuked, shooing the reporter away. Joan didn't realize that this was only the first of many more encounters she would have with the media.

The cold was damp and penetrating. Joan had become numb, not from the cold but also from trying to grasp the incomprehensible. When Witte noticed Robin had exited the ambulance and was wearing only a thin blouse and a light sweater, she gave her a blanket to wrap around her shoulders. She urged the two women to get in the back of the rig to escape the frigid morning air.

"Where is your coat?" Joan asked Robin.

"It's in the house," Robin responded automatically, motioning with her hand toward the burning building.

Witte glimpsed a puzzled look which flashed briefly across Joan's face. When Witte noticed Robin staring through the back windows of the vehicle at the fire, she asked her, "Do you want them covered?"

"No," Robin responded with no emotion.

"He agreed to go to counseling and said, 'I love you.' Those were his last words to me." Robin began to babble about her relationship with her husband, telling Witte that they had separated over the weekend and that she had talked to him on the phone just the night before.

"Why didn't the smoke alarms go off?" Robin asked suddenly.

"We don't know whether they went off or not," Witte answered.

Joan joined the conversation explaining to Witte that this was a double tragedy as Robin had lost another child almost twelve years before. "It's so incredible, so horrible that something like this could happen more than once in her lifetime. I don't know whether Robin can survive this much grief." Joan fretted, too, about the stress Robin had been under recently.

Witte wanted the two women out of there as soon as possible, especially before daylight. Since Joan couldn't drive a stick-shift, she called Bernie again and told him they had arranged for an officer to pick him up and deliver him to Seneca so that he could drive her and Robin back to their apartment. They had been at the scene for about two hours – it seemed to Joan as though it had been two days. Robin's daughter hadn't been found, and Randy had not been taken out of the embers and ashes.

"Can you talk about your first loss?" Witte asked Robin, trying to help initiate the grieving process.

"Not much," she answered, her voice a monotone. "They say what I don't remember is worse than what I do remember. They were able to pull me out of the fire, but not my child," Robin said with a far-away look in her eyes. Then she fell silent, clutching the blanket around her as if it could shroud her emotions. Through the rear window, she continued to watch the fire.

✳ ✳ ✳

At 4:00 that morning, John Healy had pulled himself out of bed. His wife, Cathy, had already left for her early shift at the hospital. The duplex where they lived was enveloped in a damp, misty haze of fog that hung like an omen over the quiet neighborhood.

John walked halfway down the stairs heading to the kitchen. He stopped abruptly, squinting and sniffing the air, concentrating on identifying the faint, peculiar odor. He swiftly climbed back up the stairs to check on his two children, Shane and Kelli. He inspected all the bedrooms; everything appeared fine. He galloped downstairs and noticed that the scent got stronger on the main floor.

Sprinting back upstairs, John woke his children, got them out of the duplex and safely settled in the family car to wait while he checked the main floor again, the kitchen, and the garage. Nothing seemed amiss, but there was definitely a smoky smell. He didn't know if the problem was on his side of the duplex or on the other side of the duplex, which was occupied by Randy and Robin Row and their children Joshua and Tabitha.

He caught sight of it in his peripheral vision first. Smoke billowed from the windows in the other side of the duplex, the side where his son Shane's good friend Josh lived.

He flew next door, pounded on the front door, rang the doorbell, and banged on the windows. Nobody answered. One of the two cars belonging to Robin and Randy was missing. Maybe, he thought, they were all gone and everybody would be safe. He rushed back inside to call the fire department.

Whatever dreams Captain Tom Thacker, veteran firefighter Ed Shannon, and firefighter John Peugh were dreaming that night were shattered at 4:36 a.m. by the shrill peal of the fire alarm. They shook off the remnants of sleep and dressed quickly in the protective clothing that lay deflated over their boots.

Lights flashing, the Whitney Fire District fire trucks screamed out of the station, brazenly splintering the predawn stillness. Hurtling through shopping complexes, intruding on farmland, they sped south on Five Mile Road through empty streets and out beyond the city limits. Their headlights cast ghostly beams through the vaporous darkness.

They were headed for a county subdivision firemen referred to as the "ghetto" because many of the dwellings there were overcrowded and in need of repair. Because of the blend of fog and smoke, pulling up directly in front of their destination, 10489 Seneca Drive, was difficult.

The men's adrenaline kicked in when they saw the inferno. The two-story, two-family dwelling with single-car garages book-ending the structure was being consumed. The south end of the duplex was "fully involved" – heavy black smoke billowed from every door and upper and lower-level windows.

Dispatch had not been able to tell them if there were people inside, but at this time of night there was a strong possibility that there would be "civilians" to be rescued or pulled out for the coroner's bag. But maybe

7

the family was away. There was only one car in the driveway and Mr. Healy had said his neighbors owned two.

While Ed and John masked up, Captain Thacker hauled a 150-foot preconnected line to the front door. It was locked. All the outside doors were locked. He raced back to the engine for an axe. He pried open the front door, splintering the wood frame, and it swung inward. Warily, Captain Thacker peered inside. Seeing nothing but thick smoke, he jerked the door shut to prevent a deadly backdraft, then immediately called Cole-Collister Fire Station for backup.

Encased in protective suits and packing fifty pounds of gear, Ed and John cautiously stepped through the front door of the burning apartment. Like miners entering a pit, their only illumination came from flashlights on their helmets.

With John on the nozzle and Ed backing him up on the line, they crawled on hands and knees, feeling their way around the living room perimeter, searching for any inhabitants and looking for the stairway to the second floor. Ed clutched onto John's boot. Touch along with muffled shouts and body language was the only way to communicate in the thick, dark smoke.

Still on hands and knees, the two men made a beeline toward the popping red glow ahead and sprayed in a circular motion to "fog it out." Directly above their heads the fire was ravaging the ceiling and charging into the master bedroom upstairs; crackling beside them and rolling down in front of them, it consumed everything in its path. They were at its epicenter.

Seeing the deep hole burned in what they supposed was the base of the staircase, the firemen assumed that the access to the second floor had burned away. They were unaware that the entrance to the stairs was actually at the opposite end, where the heavy hoses blocked the front door open against the staircase threshold. They had felt their way past it when they had entered.

When the fire began to vent through the ceiling, enough smoke escaped so the firemen could see a little better. In the living room, there were piles of clothing, small mounds burning and smoldering like tiny bonfires.

Another firefighter, sent in to assist, was in front of John when the floorboards collapsed under his weight, sending him suddenly through the floor. The other two men scrambled.

"Who the hell was that?!" Ed yelled. He was unable to see the person behind the mask.

Fear tightened its grip. They didn't know if there might be a deep crawl space or a basement beneath them. Building a human chain, Ed grabbed John while John frantically groped through the mouth of the hole. He felt arms, clutched and pulled, hauling firefighter Carl Malotte up through the floor.

John and Ed felt the vibrations of their masks warning them they had almost used up the twenty minutes of air in their packs. They had to exit without having found the stairs. They changed air packs, briefed Captain Thacker, then went back in.

Captain Thacker sent two firemen to ladder in through the upstairs master bedroom window. "We found the stairs!" one of them hollered down from above.

Out of control, the fire continued to burn relentlessly through the roof, licking and lapping at the wood, then bursting through the back wall shooting a Fourth-of-July shower of flames into the sky. The upstairs was incredibly hot. Smoke rolled out and it looked as though the fire might flash over. It was a dangerous, potentially deadly situation, so Captain Thacker "blew everybody out" with three blasts of the air horn.

By the time Tracy Geisler and Doug Layne arrived from the Cole-Collister Fire Department to assist, the duplex was safe enough to occupy again. Command ordered them upstairs to search for bodies. Randy Christensen, from the Whitney Fire Department, joined them on the line. The smoke was down low, forcing the three men to crawl cautiously up the dim stairs.

Tracy, at the front of the line, stopped suddenly. He had found a gaping hole in the landing at the top of the stairs. Had Ed and John found the stairs when they first entered the building, they might have fallen through the hole which covered nearly half of the inside of the master bedroom and extended into the hallway.

Looking left, Tracy, Doug, and Randy saw the fire raging in the master bedroom. The door was virtually burned away. The floor was mostly gone except for the joists that supported the legs of the queen-sized bed. At this time they could not enter the room.

9

Even though they assumed there was nobody inside, Doug continued suppressing the fire while Tracy and Randy, starting from the upstairs landing, began a right-hand search for people.

They entered a small bedroom decorated for a child. In one corner of the room, a passel of stuffed animals were held captive in a net hanging from the ceiling. The white, gilded four-poster bed looked rumpled, slept in. After combing the room, the men breathed a sigh of relief at not finding a child's body.

Tracy left his partner and continued the search, out the door and around the edge of the wall. To the right he felt a closed door. Tracy met Doug coming from the opposite direction and, apprehensively, they entered an even smaller, closet-sized bedroom. Doug began to "pull ceiling" to get at the fire when Tracy lost his footing and fell onto a waterbed.

Doug yelled, "Are you all right?"

"No!" The answer was swift and intense. "We've got a body in here!"

The waterbed covered most of the floor space in the bedroom. On the bed was a 10-year-old boy wearing a T-shirt and underwear, lying face down, head toward the foot of the bed. He was outside the covers, lying diagonally with his arms sprawled out, in a position typical of a younger child. Randy hoped the boy had not died trying to escape the smoke.

The boy was heavy for his age and wrestling his body from the waterbed was difficult. Randy and Tracy hustled, thinking only about getting him out, not about the length of time he had inhaled the deadly fumes. Tracy hooked his arms under the boy's arms while Randy carried the feet. They brought him outside and gently laid him on the front lawn.

"Ah, Jesus Christ, look at that," one veteran firefighter said, tears springing from his eyes.

Although Randy Christensen had never performed a resuscitation, his instincts and training were automatic. He began CPR, while Tracy checked for a pulse, blowing breath after breath into the still figure. When the paramedic arrived, he just shook his head and told the firemen that the boy was already gone. Not until after the paramedic had covered the body with a disposable yellow plastic blanket did they walk quietly away. Later they would be able to put a name to the child's body – Joshua Cornellier.

Then the realization struck head-on – the firemen knew from experience you don't usually have a young boy by himself in a house – they knew they had to go back in and continue their search.

Back inside the duplex, Randy and John took the news with dread. Captain Thacker had gotten information from the mother that there were two more people somewhere inside – her husband and her daughter. The firemen redoubled their efforts, tearing through debris, searching under sheetrock, but they could find nothing. Where could the girl have gone? Her bed appeared to have been slept in. A sliver of hope existed that somehow she had gotten out. If not, the firemen were sure no lives would be saved. Captain Thacker was convinced they were now going in after bodies.

Tracy climbed a ladder to the second story and poked through the dormer window of the master bedroom with a pipe pole. Shale-like debris cluttered the queen-sized bed. Underneath, lying on his left side in a comfortable sleeping position, was a large adult male. The covers were crunched in a mound at the foot of the bed. The man wore jeans, no shirt, no shoes. He had third-degree burns from the waist up, and his feet were also badly burned. The only obvious identifying mark was a belt buckle imprinted with the name "Randy."

Daylight had muscled through the mist of fog and smoke by the time conditions were safe enough for a five-man body recovery crew, lead by Captain Robert Saum of the Whitney Fire District, to enter the duplex.

The crew trudged up the stairs carrying the body bags. Much of the master bedroom floor had fallen into the garage. They had to maneuver the man's weighty body over the hole in the floor between the bed and the doorway. Steeling themselves, two on each side of the bed, the men spread the bag, rolled the body onto it, zipped it closed, and rolled the body onto a board. By straddling the hole and handing off the body bag, they managed to get their unwieldy load across the cavity.

Only one person still was unaccounted for – the little girl whose room had been torn apart earlier. Captain Saum assumed that she had gone through to the floor of the garage along with a bookcase. He soon found out she had not.

On the floor near the foot of her parents' bed, exactly where her mother had finally remembered she must be, buried under books and slabs of ceiling, Tabitha was found frozen in a sleeping pose, covered with an afghan and wearing pink underwear and a multi-colored flowered top. She was looking toward the doorway, with her arm outstretched, almost as if she was reaching for her mother. Captain Saum recalled how horrified he felt when he learned he had unknowingly been standing on the broken ceiling that had fallen and concealed the little girl's body.

Tabitha Cornellier was 8 years old. The cherubic girl with light brown hair and peaches and cream complexion was charred with third-degree burns on both her upper and lower body, but was still recognizable.

The coroner would conclude that Randy Row and his stepchildren, Tabitha and Joshua, had all died of asphyxia and had been dead for several hours. The firemen felt a stab of pain for the mother outside who was left alive to suffer the loss of her loved ones.

Ashes and sorrow were the residue left in the wake of the furious fire. The firemen shed tears along with their professional armor. In the days that followed, many had nightmares and difficulty sleeping.

Even those more seasoned would never forget this fire. It was more than tragic; it was strange as well. There were the piles of laundry that had been scattered, apparently randomly, in the living room, some burning, some heaped against a portable electric heater. And no fire alarm was ever heard.

Suspicion of arson raced like an electric current through the emergency personnel at the scene. Even before the firemen left, investigators had been contacted and were on their way.

CHAPTER TWO

Dawn, February 10, 1992

It was still dark when Bernie pulled the car away from the scene. Firefighters continued working and emergency vehicles were still parked in the street.

"The son of a bitch did it!" Bernie growled through gritted teeth during the drive home.

"We'll get through it. We're here for you." Joan repeatedly tried to comfort her silent friend. "If you need your family, we'll find a way to get them here."

Robin shook her head and said no. She hardly spoke during the trip across town.

Joan and Bernie were both convinced that Randy was the culprit. Like a macabre drama, visions of the abuse and torture he had heaped on Robin for the last month filled Joan's mind.

When the shock began to wear off a little, she became angry. Angry at Randy. She kept thinking, he did something. He did something stupid and, my God, what a price to pay. Maybe he decided to burn something else of Robin's. Or maybe he had been fooling around with something electronic and it accidently started the fire. A host of possibilities occurred to Joan.

When they got back to the apartment, Joan called Danny at work and he came right home. He held Robin in his arms while she sobbed, and they all cried together. Robin seemed lost and in shock. Nobody could sit still and each took their turn periodically pacing through the living room and kitchen of the small apartment, then sitting on the couch that had been Robin's bed the night before. Nobody knew what to say to help.

"If you want to talk, we'll talk," Joan said. "If you want to be quiet, that's fine too. Tell us what we can do." When all else fails, Joan thought, make tea.

Absently sipping Joan's brew, Robin was jarred by the phone ringing. It was the coroner. "God, Joan, that was terrible," Robin said quietly when she hung up the phone. "They found Tabitha. He wanted to know about identifying scars or marks because they were all burned beyond recognition. It was difficult," she stammered, staring off into space.

* * *

It was a little before 7 a.m. when Robin called her dear friends, the Woods. When Alyce answered, Robin asked her to put Jack on the phone. Alyce told Robin that her husband wasn't there.

"There's been an accident, let me talk to Steven," Robin said, preferring to break the news to Alyce's son.

"There's been an accident," she repeated to Steven, "and Josh and Tab are gone. The kids are gone and it's all my fault."

"Robin, it's not your fault," Steven reassured her.

Listening to the one-sided conversation, Alyce nearly fell apart. Robin didn't explain what kind of "accident," and she hung up before Alyce had an opportunity to talk to her.

In a near hysterical screech, Alyce implored her son to give her an answer he didn't have. "What gone?! Dead gone?!" Her head was spinning. She felt her sanity drain away along with the color in her face. What did Robin mean by "gone"?

Alyce called 911 in Boise and asked if there had been a car wreck. They checked and told her that there had been no car fatalities that day. "All I know is that it was an accident and I'm just assuming a car accident." The emergency dispatchers hung up and checked again, then called Alyce back.

She felt part of her life was ripped from her when she heard the news. There was a fire in progress and three unidentified fatalities. The phone slipped from her fingers. She couldn't comprehend it. She thought, "Fire in progress?!! And Robin is on the phone calling me?!"

* * *

Robin collapsed on the stairs crying, Joan persuaded her to go up and take a nap in the master bedroom. Everything was quiet for half an hour.

Then a blood-curdling scream echoed down from upstairs. Danny bounded up the steps first, followed by Joan and Bernie. They found Robin crouched in the corner of the bedroom jabbering something about Randy coming at her with a knife. Danny knelt beside her and tried to calm her.

"It's okay," Joan said soothingly, "Randy can never hurt you again." When would it stop? He had abused her mentally and physically, then killed her kids, and even in death his presence lingered to torture Robin. At that moment, Joan knew a depth of hatred she hadn't realized she was capable of feeling.

The rest of the day, Robin was nervous and couldn't seem to sit still. She tore sheets off beds, washed and dried them. Joan took most of the many sympathy calls that poured in and screened calls from reporters looking for a story. She knew she must be strong for Robin, to protect her so that she could attempt to deal with her loss.

Support came from many people. Mary Lou went to the morgue to identify the bodies. Janice Johnson knew that Robin needed money for the memorial service, so when *The Idaho Statesman* daily newspaper called her wanting to know if Robin needed help, Janice told them, "Yes. She lives from paycheck to paycheck." The newspaper promptly set up a bank account for donations.

* * *

By noon the media was announcing the names of the victims. Barbara Fawcett heard about the fire on the radio and immediately called the McHughs' apartment. She learned from Joan about the kidnapping over the weekend and Robin working with the police. When Robin called her back, Barbara asked if there was anything she could do and offered to open her home to any of Robin's out-of-town family who needed a place to stay.

"Oh, dear, thank you for everything, I don't think my family is coming," Robin answered graciously.

Sue Fellen called Robin to express her sorrow. The women who worked with Robin at the YWCA felt a profound sadness at the loss of her children. They had a special attachment to Joshua and Tabitha, especially Tabitha. The two kids had been in and out of the office ever since Robin had started working at the YWCA in 1989. Barbara smiled when she thought of Tabitha and the special pictures that the child had meticulously drawn and placed on each desk. She remembered the little girl's bouncing personality. To Tabitha, life was a bowl of cherries. She was a social creature, a chatterbox who floated through life smiling, wanting others to be happy too. She loved looking pretty and wearing earrings, especially the faux diamond studs Joan had given her recently.

Joan felt she should take the brunt of the worry and help Robin make the tough decisions. They discussed the arrangements and where they would get money for the funeral and burials. Joan asked about insurance. Robin told her that she had a small amount of insurance on the children that was a part of her benefit package at work. She didn't think she had any insurance on Randy because, after his motorcycle accident, she believed that he had been labeled "uninsurable."

As it turned out, the county paid for the cremation, the burial plots were donated, and Joan bought the urns for the remains of Joshua and Tabitha. Because Robin wanted to get the memorial service over with, she moved up her initial plans of a Saturday service to Wednesday, just two days away.

When Robin mentioned cremation to Randy's family, they vehemently rejected the idea. Robin responded, "Well, fine, you take care of Randy and I'll take care of the children."

It was late morning on this seemingly never-ending day when Sheriff's Detective Gary Raney called for Robin. When she got off the phone, Robin told Joan that the investigator wanted to talk with her that afternoon. She appeared distressed. Robin said she didn't like detectives and didn't want to see Detective Gary Raney, but there was no way out of it.

CHAPTER THREE

Fall 1990 (two years earlier)

Joan and Bernie had been together 14 years living in Boston, Massachusetts. Theirs was a relationship that people had said would never last. Bernie's alcoholism was a monkey on his back and an ache in Joan's heart. Bernie didn't like the taste of booze, never had. Nevertheless, he had been chasing the bottle for nearly 38 years. He couldn't remember when it stopped being fun. Bernie was a lovable drunk, never mean or obnoxious. He could be charming and droll and had definitely missed his calling as a stand-up comic.

He had jobs off and on. When he did work, he was industrious until the effects of the alcohol interfered. Occasionally, Bernie had gone on hiatus from his poison, even attending some AA meetings, but he hadn't stuck with it.

To decide where she and Bernie would begin their new life, Joan sat in front of a map with her eyes closed, twirled her finger in the air and planted it directly on Boise, the capital city of Idaho. The wild west! Maybe a drastic change would shake up the pieces in the kaleidoscope of their lives, shifting them into a more positive configuration.

The 1984 Chrysler New Yorker, audibly afflicted, chugged toward Boise on Interstate 84. Sagebrush whizzed by the windows and a cold autumn wind buffeted the car. The McHughs wondered how anything could grow in the frosty desert they were crossing.

As they dropped down into the valley, they saw that the trees stood barely dressed in muted hues of browns and oranges, a watered-down version of the vibrant autumn palette they had just left behind in New

England. They had heard that the winters were less intense in the Boise Valley than in their home state of Massachusetts, but the biting wind and bone-chilling cold belied the rumor.

The McHughs were now seeing the valley that French-Canadian trappers had christened "Boisé" (pronounced "boy-see" by latter-day natives and "boy-zee" by newcomers) from the French term meaning "wooded." As they got closer, Joan and Bernie could see why it was sometimes referred to as "the place where desert meets mountain." Boise, with 150 varieties of trees, had truly earned its nickname "City of Trees."

The big city dwellers weren't used to seeing so much wide-open space, and the sight of the snow-capped mountains was thrilling. They seemed to wrap around the town like a security blanket.

The beauty of the area contradicted the impression the McHughs held before coming to Boise. Like many Easterners, Joan and Bernie imagined the city to be typical of "The West" with bonnet-clad women and swaggering leathery men in spurs walking down dusty planked sidewalks. Although that picture was extreme for the time, it was not completely off base. Driving into the city, Joan exclaimed, "My God, Bernie. Look at that! There's only one tall building!"

Boise rapidly drew residents like the McHughs. By the time Joan and Bernie arrived, the green shoots of culture that had lain relatively dormant, unable to break through the hard crust of the conservative agricultural community, had begun to sprout. Idaho was home to the arts and many thriving industries, including construction, electronics, and mining. However, the state got much of its national acclaim from its prized produce – the famous Idaho potato. Idaho's more positive qualities were often eclipsed by the negative publicity generated when the Aryan Nations white supremacist group planted their headquarters in the midst of the beauty and evergreen seclusion of the northern Idaho panhandle. Their presence was an ugly and embarrassing scar to most Idahoans. But nothing dampened Joan and Bernie's hopes for their new home.

For a city in the midst of rapid growth, jobs in Boise were not that easy to find. While Joan looked for work, Bernie looked for an answer at the bottom of a bottle. If they were going to make it, Bernie had to get help. Even though her decision would leave her with practically nothing to live on, with a kiss and a prayer, Joan put Bernie on a plane to Sacramento, California, where he would enter a detoxification center. He vowed to come back sober and promised from then on he would faithfully attend Alcoholics Anonymous meetings.

While Bernie was drying out, Joan's supply of money was drying up. By Christmastime she was literally out in the cold – jobless, homeless, alone, and on the streets.

The winter of 1990 would prove to be one of the coldest on record in Boise. Being in a protected valley, the city could be considered almost tropical at times compared to many parts of Idaho. But this year the mercury would drop to seventeen degrees below zero before the cold snap ended.

On Christmas Eve day Joan sought help at Saint Michael's Episcopal Church. They helped find her a temporary home. The motel room was a paradise to Joan, a respite from the bitter, relentless cold.

Joan worried about Bernie and couldn't shake the empty and foreboding feeling in the pit of her stomach. How had this happened to them? What would she do? She had never pictured herself homeless. She couldn't stay in the motel forever, and she couldn't go home without Bernie. Joan would not ask her grown children to send her money; they were raising children of their own on limited budgets. She was scared.

Joan spent two nights in the motel. Christmas Day, when most people were enjoying family get-togethers, she sat alone on the thin, garish floral bedspread that covered the hard mattress, staring at a generic print hanging above the bed. No wise men materialized to offer her sage advice.

The day after Christmas, panic overwhelmed Joan. She had never had to depend on others for survival. To accept help, she would have to temporarily discard the image of herself as strong and independent. She had no other choice but to let pride take a back seat.

Sitting behind the only desk in the room at the YWCA's Harambee Center (pronounced Ha-rum-bah, a Swahili word meaning "we do it ourselves"), surrounded by bags of food was Robin Row, the manager. She asked Joan for her name and Social Security number. Formalities out of the way, she asked, "How are you feeling?"

"It's wicked cold out there," Joan shivered, quickly sizing up her surroundings: two couches, newspapers, phone books, toys, and one telephone. Articles of clothing were folded in boxes or hung on racks. Making up the dozen or so displaced people waiting their turns were different types and personalities, mostly women and children, some clean, some dirty and haggard. It surprised Joan that these impoverished people seemed so casual about their circumstances. To Joan, this was the most frightening experience in her life. Hopelessness and an uncharacteristic feeling of quiet humility settled over her. Pinning her purse under her arm and gripping the straps like a lifeline, she shifted into automatic pilot.

"My God!" Robin perked up, "I haven't heard that expression since I left New Hampshire!"

Robin's familiar east coast accent relaxed Joan a bit. They were speaking the same language.

"You can make some coffee if you like," Robin offered, motioning toward the coffee pot. Joan would learn that Robin drank mostly tea and although there was always coffee available, Robin never made it. "Look through the newspaper and find an apartment," she suggested.

"Excuse me?" Joan said, puzzled. "What good does it do me to find an apartment when I don't have any money?"

"You find the apartment. I'll get you the money," Robin assured her.

Robin was good at what she did. She had learned to identify the people who would remain bogged down in the quagmire of homelessness and to distinguish them from the others – those who only needed a temporary hand up. She picked Joan out as one of the latter and efficiently set about getting the 59-year-old Boston transplant back on her feet.

Robin had connections, knew how to get donations, and understood the welfare system inside and out. She ran the shelter well.

As promised, Robin did find the money and put it down on a small, two-room, furnished apartment for Joan. She made sure Joan had household necessities and introduced her to the career center at the YWCA to help her prepare for the job market.

To others who came into the center, Robin was more perfunctory. But Robin took a special interest in Joan, went out of her way to help her, in fact. When she spoke to Joan, her smile was warm and friendly, her manner congenial. She made Joan believe there was a way out of her mess, buttressing the smidgen of confidence that had survived. Besides their common New England accent, Joan and Robin had an additional bond. Joan's kinship with her newest friend and benefactress was strengthened by the similar misfortunes they had suffered. Robin had shared her own bad luck stories. Robin's gifts were more than mere items. It was difficult to attach a monetary value to the most important gift she gave Joan – hope. In Joan's eyes Robin was standing on a pedestal next to Mother Teresa.

Joan assumed, after Robin's initial help, that she would never see her again but Robin pursued the friendship. She made sure Joan always had transportation. On New Year's Day she sent her husband, Randy, to escort Joan to their home for a buffet dinner. Joan met Robin's children, Joshua and Tabitha. By the next Thanksgiving, they would be calling Joan "Grandma."

CHAPTER FOUR

August 1987

Three years before the McHughs relocated to Boise, 30-year-old Robin Lee Cornellier and her two children had arrived there. Robin's move to Boise occurred by chance. Like Joan and Bernie, she hoped to find in this new place the elusive formula for happiness that she had searched for in other parts of the country and never found.

The family of three stepped off the bus in the middle of downtown with two suitcases and two bucks. Robin, her 5-year-old son Joshua, and her 3-year-old daughter Tabitha, were homeless.

Ada County Sheriff's Office dispatchers sent the family to a temporary shelter where they were given dinner, sleeping quarters, and breakfast. For five days, they tramped the city or sat in front of the shelter waiting for it to open since lodging was available only at night. Robin claimed it was useless to apply for work because she didn't have a phone or a permanent address.

After going without lunch for days, Robin discovered a soup kitchen at Saint Michael's Episcopal Cathedral. The coordinator, Mary Lou Beck, met Robin and her children that day and, touched by their plight, took the family under her benevolent wing. She helped get them settled, and enrolled Tabitha in preschool. Mary Lou even took the kids to church with her. Robin wouldn't step inside a church; she said she wasn't comfortable with God.

Robin would later describe Mary Lou as "my salvation, my surrogate mother" and said she had never met anyone like her. By some who had worked with her, Mary Lou was characterized as a "soul-saver" type, a die-hard humanitarian who seemed to derive personal fulfillment from helping people who were down and out.

Mary Lou and others helped Robin get food stamps, welfare benefits, and subsidized housing. Ada County gave her money to stay in a motel for several weeks until she could get a homeless certificate, subsidizing her rent. The fine people of Boise were reaching out to this poor family.

The heart-wrenching ordeal that had caused Robin's plight touched Mary Lou. Robin said she and her children had left the Sacramento Valley in California where her husband was an unemployed mechanic and she had been an advocate for disadvantaged families. Their plan was to go back to New Hampshire, the state where Robin was raised, and look for jobs.

They stopped to rest in Nevada. Robin and her husband argued. "He slapped me," she said. "We stopped at this little rinky-dink town that was a gas station, store, and post office all in one, and I took the kids into the bathroom."

When they came out of the bathroom, Robin and her children were greeted only by their suitcases and oncoming darkness. "I thought he would be back," Robin said forlornly, adding that she couldn't remember the town's name. "I was crying and hysterical. I hitched a ride with this Mexican family to Winnemucca.

"When he left, he took my purse, driver's license…everything," Robin lamented. "Luckily, when we had stopped before, I put a quarter in a slot machine and won fifty dollars and stuck it in my pocket." With the $50 stash, Robin said she bought bus tickets to the closest city. Their money took them only as far as Boise, a place she'd never heard of.

Mary Lou was taken by Robin's tenacity, her strength. She was so impressed, in fact, that she cut a special groove for her on the inside track of a new project. It was a joint effort between Mary Lou's church and the YWCA, a daytime refuge that would help families just like Robin's.

To help publicize the soon-to-open shelter, Robin and her children posed for a picture that would run with an article in the local newspaper reporting the story Robin had told Mary Lou. With their backs to the camera, the three were shot in shadows in a bare room. Robin was seated looking out a window with Joshua standing, leaning heavily on her shoulder; Tabitha was sitting in her mother's lap, her head resting on Robin's bosom. It was a lonely, pitiful portrait. As a result of the coverage, the philanthropic citizens opened their hearts and pocketbooks to help get the shelter running.

Robin was Mary Lou's choice to fill one of two openings in a job-sharing position. She seemed eager to work, competent, articulate, intelligent, and her resumé showed she had the right experience. Without checking Robin's background, Mary Lou wholeheartedly endorsed the woman from California.

With Mary Lou's stamp of approval, Robin submitted her resume and a handwritten letter to the YWCA. The resume began with a brief personal history.

Robin Cornellier was born September 9, 1957. She was a divorced mother of two. It was followed by an educational history that included business courses in high school; two years of business and accounting classes at Hesser College, a junior college in New Hampshire; and a year of business-related courses at Shasta College in Redding, California. Under work history, Robin listed clerk/secretarial positions, a program coordinator position, and experience on a "help-line" for crisis calls. The administration at the YWCA felt confident Robin had the necessary skills to manage the Harambee Center.

Sue Fellen, Director of the Women's and Children's Crisis Center at the YWCA, interviewed several applicants for the position. Initially, Sue was not overly impressed with Robin; she actually favored some of the other contenders. She knew how important it was to Mary Lou that Robin get one of the coordinator positions, and she was well aware the seed money for the center had been donated by Mary Lou's church.

So when the YWCA gave birth to the Harambee Center, February 1, 1988, Robin Cornellier and Fran Matthews, two welfare mothers, were named to share the job of coordinator.

In the beginning, Robin and Fran were tucked away in a dinky office upstairs behind the gymnasium in the YWCA's three-story building. The furnishings were "early garage sale": a desk, a couple of recycled couches, and a coffee pot.

Those around Robin noticed that she was very quiet and projected an aura of responsibility, capability, and honesty. She did her job with

marked detachment, unruffled at having to deal with all types of characters and situations: women with children, male transients, and mentally
ill street people. Working in the drab, cramped room not much bigger
than a walk-in closet, with people who had not bathed, didn't seem to
bother Robin. She understood the public system inside and out and had
answers for people who desperately needed them.

Robin had abandoned her old life in California and was free to start
a new life. She did not remain a struggling single parent for long. In
March 1988, she met 31-year-old Randy Row. At the time, he was dating
Polly Washam, a friend of Robin's. Over drinks, Polly introduced Randy
to Robin. The two hit it off so well that they went home together that
night and were together from then on.

Robin and Randy had a whirlwind courtship, intense from the
beginning – each was a port in a storm for the other. After only two and
a half months, they were married. They didn't want to go to a justice of
the peace. Polly arranged for a Mormon bishop to marry them in her
mother's home. It was a small service, with neither the bride's nor the
groom's family members in attendance.

After moving several times during their four-year marriage, Robin
and Randy's final nest would be one side of a duplex on Seneca Drive
in southwest Boise.

CHAPTER FIVE

Fall, 1989

The Harambee Center quickly outgrew the tiny upstairs office. A larger room in the basement of the YWCA building was renovated to accommodate 15 to 20 people, two desks, and storage. It was exciting. The coordinators' elbows would no longer bump the walls when they tipped their coffee cups to drink.

Above them, in the upper two floors, were the domestic crisis apartments, sometimes occupied by more than 25 people at a time, mostly women and children.

In October, hours after Robin and Fran had locked up and gone home, two mothers residing upstairs heard a strange noise beneath them. It sounded like something being dropped or broken. It struck them as unusual that the sound came from below, where it was always quiet at 1 a.m. Soon after, they smelled a musty, unusual odor but decided it was nothing.

Around 3:30 a.m., the smell could no longer be ignored. It was a heavier, smoky smell. The fire department was called.

By the time the colored lights of the fire trucks splashed over the brick building, the fire was blazing in the crisis center office. The firefighters extinguished the blaze in five minutes, estimating it had been burning about two and a half hours.

It was the day of a big management conference for YWCA Executive Director Barbara Fawcett. The trill of the telephone jolted her awake at 4 a.m.

"You'd better come down here. There's been a fire," Sue Fellen alerted the groggy director.

When Barbara faced the basement office, she stood in stunned silence. It was a black mess, totally destroyed inside. Smoke damage marred even the recently-painted walls upstairs. All the desk and filing cabinet drawers had been opened, and charred, donated clothing was strewn everywhere.

It was clearly an arson fire. Its origin seemed to be a large pile of clothing. Although a small electric heater was on, it was not the cause of the fire. The blaze had been set on the opposite side of the room behind a portable room divider.

As investigators scratched their heads over suspects and motive, they learned that the upstairs occupants had no access to the basement. There were only four people who had a key to the office: the two female employees who occupied it, Robin Row and Fran Matthews; a daytime supervisor; and a cleaning person. When questioned by the investigators, Robin, Fran, and the cleaning person insisted that when they left, the office door was locked and the heater was off. One basement window had a broken crank and was always open a few inches. The investigators were left with only two possibilities: either someone had entered through that broken basement window, ransacked the office and lit the fire, or someone with a key had done it.

Barbara Fawcett and Sue Fellen couldn't understand why anyone would want to break into a shelter for homeless people. Nothing seemed to be missing. The only valuable items were bus tokens, about $15 in petty cash, and a microwave oven. Why would someone break in, open all the drawers, not take anything, then start a fire in a pile of clothing? And why, most peculiarly, would someone turn on an electric heater before starting a fire at the opposite end of the room?

It was a bizarre case. Robin and Fran were unable to think of any clients whom they would consider suspects, although there were many no-name, strange street people who frequented the shelter.

With few clues, no suspects, and little motive, the case would go unsolved and the questions would remain unanswered. The damage totaled $35,000, including Christmas presents of Robin's that she said were destroyed in the fire, and was covered by insurance. The damage was repaired. The incident was forgotten.

That same month, disaster stuck Robin's life again. Riding his motorcycle was a soothing salve for stress in her husband Randy's life.

When he left the house on the morning of October 24 and sped away on his bike, no one could have predicted how Randy's life would change in an instant.

When he crashed into the pickup truck on the corner of Five Mile Road and Hollandale, he wasn't wearing a helmet. He was rushed to Saint Alphonsus Regional Medical Center with a severe head injury which left him in a coma. The doctors didn't know if he would survive.

In November, soon after the YWCA fire and Randy's accident, Fran Matthews moved to Washington, leaving Robin as sole coordinator at the center. As her responsibilities increased, Robin came out of her shell. She began to flourish personally as well as professionally. The recent calamities in her life hadn't seemed to slow her down. According to Sue Fellen, Robin seemed to be adapting to her position of authority well. She had no qualms about Robin's ability to handle the job, nor did anyone else.

By December, Randy was well enough to be moved from Saint Alphonsus to the Veterans Administration Hospital for rehabilitation. Robin didn't visit him as much as her in-laws thought appropriate. After Randy recovered, his father, Charlie, let Robin know he thought she should have spent more time at the hospital.

"Charlie, I had two kids; I had to work. He was in a coma; there wasn't anything I could do," Robin explained. Robin was now the sole supporter and caretaker in her household and soon would be caring for Randy at home. Christmas was coming and the holidays were looking pretty bleak.

It was just a month after the children had gone through a unit on bicycle safety in which they were drilled about helmet use, that Randy had his accident. Robin had dutifully contacted the teachers to make sure they understood her children's emotional needs. She also said that they had bought Randy a helmet and put it away for Christmas and wished now that they had given it to him early.

Regular routine at home had fallen apart. Joshua and Tabitha were teetering on the precipice of losing the man they had come to rely upon as a father.

To alleviate some of the burden on the family, the teachers prepared and delivered food to the Rows. The employees of the YWCA decided to forgo their usual gift exchange. Instead, they took up a collection to help Robin with the expenses.

K-106, a local radio station, accepted pleas for needy families. Those with the greatest need were chosen to receive donations: money, clothes, gift certificates, toys, rent, groceries. This particular year, K-106 received the following heart-wrenching, anonymous letter in the mail:

> I'm writing about my neighbors. There are four in the family, two children ages eight and six; the oldest is a boy, the youngest is a girl. On October 24, 1989, the father was in a motorcycle accident. He's at Saint Al's in a coma. The family is hitting hard times. The mother works a full-time job and is having a rough time making ends meet because they are used to two incomes. They have no medical insurance and the person who hit him has no car insurance. I've talked to my neighbor about what she's going to do with Christmas coming. She told me that she already told her children that they will have a Christmas as they will be together, but not to expect any gifts. These kids are so brave that they said it was OK; they understood. (Also, if you pick her, don't let her know that I told you this.) She took back the gifts that she had already gotten so she could use the money for food and gas for the car...Please help her with gifts, food, or something. The family is Robin Roe [sic], 10489 Seneca. I do not wish to leave my name. Thank you.

That Christmas, Robin Row received a $100 gift certificate for gas, $200 from a grocery/variety store, and toys from Santa.

Randy eventually improved enough to come home in February of 1990 but still had a long way to go before he fully recuperated. He would never recover completely and was left somewhat impaired. He became a house-husband by default, and took care of the children while Robin worked.

Robin let her children's teachers know that she couldn't be available during the day because she worked, and if there was anything the children needed, they were to contact Randy. From what the teachers saw, Robin was a typical caring, working mother. She seemed interested in her children's well-being.

Those close to the family had noticed that Robin had always occupied the top rung on the ladder of their household hierarchy, but now it had become more obvious. Randy's disability and his squabbles with the kids made it harder for Robin to cope. She was often heard screaming at Randy or the kids. Robin complained to people that she had to walk Randy through most tasks, even the simplest, and sometimes over the phone while she was at work.

Robin confided in Sue Fellen that her feelings toward Randy had changed. She said she felt guilty about that and thought she should stay in the marriage even though she was unhappy. When Robin told Sue there was no sex in her marriage anymore, Sue suggested that the problem might be caused by Randy's medication.

Robin candidly admitted that it wasn't the medication, but that she didn't want Randy to touch her. They hadn't even reached the two-year mark of their marriage. The passionate fires in the relationship should still be burning, or at least the embers glowing, but the flame was dangerously near burnout.

CHAPTER SIX

Winter, 1990

Barbara Fawcett had begun working as executive director of the YWCA late in 1988. Her good sense of humor and friendly, smiling face belied her reputation as a tough businesswoman. She was always ready to wholeheartedly dig into the fund-raising trenches of the nonprofit projects she felt were worthwhile.

Fawcett's first occasion to work directly with Robin was late in 1990. Robin had been with the YWCA for over two and a half years and was full-time manager of the Harambee Center. Everyone within the organization liked and respected Robin.

Fawcett was aware that Robin had built a network of contributors whom she called on for donations which included a group of private philanthropists, wives of Albertsons food stores executives informally referred to as the "Albertsons wives."

When Fawcett needed an assistant to find a way to fund a transitional housing project for the homeless, she thought of Robin. She was pleased with Robin's work and impressed with her verbal skills.

The two began their search for funding at a meeting of the Downtown Rotary Club. Robin had spoken to the affluent organization before, working her magic to raise money for smaller projects like Christmas baskets for the homeless. The members didn't have a clue that she had ever been homeless herself.

Robin had given the same speech all over town that she would give this day to the Downtown Rotary Club. Barbara set the bait on the hook with a 10-minute introduction, then proudly introduced

Robin as a flesh-and-blood example of a homeless person's success story:

"And now, ladies and gentlemen," Barbara motioned proudly to her new mouthpiece as Robin rose confidently, "I would like to introduce you to 'the woman who stepped off the bus,' Robin Row."

The audience was riveted. Robin was well-prepared to reel in the catch. Speaking quietly, she told her pitiful, personal story in a natural, casual way. She finished up her speech by redirecting their compassion toward the many other homeless people who find themselves in the same fix she had found herself in three years before. Her sincerity was very convincing. As a speech and drama major, Barbara recognized immediately that Robin spoke effectively and knew how to pull all the right strings. Robin epitomized triumph over adversity, a destitute woman starting with nothing and building a productive life for herself and her children.

The club didn't think twice about raising $50,000 in cash and donating another $25,000 in in-kind services.

Barbara began hearing positive praise for another type of fund-raising project. In the beginning, she was wary of the prospect of raising money from bingo, a game she knew precious little about. The mental picture in her mind's eye as it reached through the cobwebs of her past was of kidney beans on cards. She began investigating the possibilities with cautious optimism.

When Robin caught wind of the new enterprise, she approached her boss with a bold proposition, "I'd like the chance to manage the bingo center."

Barbara didn't have a clue how to run a bingo center, had never even been in one. Now, faced with implementing this sizable undertaking, she felt lucky that working right under her own roof was a trusted employee touted as a bingo expert. Because Robin was doing an excellent job and had said she had experience working at a bingo game in California, she seemed a perfect choice to manage the new establishment. No one knew that bingo was Robin's addiction. To no one's surprise, she was rewarded with another promotion.

Securing the bingo manager position meant Robin's salary jumped from approximately $10,000 to $15,000 a year. Her last day at the Harambee Center was February 15, 1991.

Acting as her mentor, Barbara began to coach Robin. "Okay, Robin, you've been down with the homeless folks until now, and that's fine, but this is a different role. I will extend you some money for a better wardrobe," Barbara offered. "You need to class up your act because you are going to be the manager."

Robin was not put off by the advice. She went on a diet and lost some weight, shopped for new clothes, and had her hair and nails done – a whole new image. She garnished her new wardrobe with accessories: four pairs of shoes, blue, pink, red, and black, and four handbags to match. She could have posed for a before-and-after makeover advertisement, even though the after still left a little to be desired.

The Robin Cornellier who had come to Boise and worked with the homeless had been short, overweight, and dumpy, her hair straight and cut in a chopped-off Dutch-boy style. She had worn old-fashioned glasses and big maternity-type tops over polyester pants. Although her kinky, permed hair and flowered dresses made her look older than she was, the new Robin Row was more professional looking

Barbara gave her new protégé free rein to organize the new nonprofit bingo fund-raising venture. In addition to this green light came a healthy incentive for Robin to create a success. Barbara promised her that if they did well and made money, Robin would receive two percent of the gross take.

Since Randy didn't have a job outside of taking care of Joshua and Tabitha, he spent quite a bit of time helping with the bingo project. Sometimes he would bring the kids with him to the center located in the Hillcrest Shopping Center. When Barbara saw Randy, he was always cheerful, wearing a happy grin and enjoying being useful.

If Randy had one special talent, it would have been his mechanical ability. Robin had a good business head and was good with figures, but Randy was the one who fixed things when they were on the blink. He was useful to Robin in that respect, but because his comprehension was slow, she had to constantly explain things to him. His presence was often exasperating to her.

* * *

Only a rare few got truly close to Joan. Her introversion, she felt, was an asset in certain ways. It went hand in hand with her ability to be a good listener and an observer of life. She absorbed the nuances of each person she met, sizing up and then dismissing from her mind those who didn't measure up. Although she liked Robin, she had not anticipated the friendship that had developed. When Bernie returned to Boise following his stay in rehab, he found that his wife and her new friend had built a strong relationship.

Even though Bernie had quit drinking and smoking and had begun to exercise excessively, Joan thought he looked older, haggard. But she was just glad to have him back with her. They had always been inseparable.

Bernie was vigilant about making up for what Joan had gone through. He secured a night job at a grocery store and cheerfully helped Robin and Joan set up the bingo enterprise.

Robin awarded Joan the job of running the canteen. She would prove a hard, dependable, and honest worker and within a matter of weeks would be working full time five nights a week.

Before long, the bingo center ran smoothly and with the regularity of a casino. Almost immediately it began to make a profit. Barbara kept a close eye on the operation of her brainchild, dropping in three or four nights a week to check.

"I am so pleased, Robin," Barbara would often say, "that I have somebody I can trust in this position because there is so much cash coming through that door."

Because of all the cash, a security guard was hired to accompany older patrons safely to their cars and to escort Robin and the money to her car at the end of the evening. Some nights the games netted $2,000 or more in cash, plus checks. After closing, Robin had been directed to make night deposits at the Key Bank located nearby. Eventually, she fell into the habit of holding the money until the next day or two, a practice that concerned her friend Joan.

"Why don't you just make the deposit in the night depository before you go home, Robin?" Joan asked with motherly concern. "What if one of the players followed you home?"

"I can't deposit at this Key Bank because the account was taken out at the downtown branch. It's too late for me to go clear into town," Robin explained.

Robin was also in charge of hiring and firing. She hired Boise State University students to serve as runners, who would weave in and out among the tables selling additional cards. During job interviews, Robin made very clear the importance of honesty. The policy was cut and dried: if an employee was caught cheating, they were out. And she strictly enforced that rule. When one young man was caught skimming, Robin fired him on the spot and promptly reported him to the police.

There was no denying it, Robin had made a few enemies. Patrons who couldn't afford to pay were allowed to play free, but as punishment, Robin found ways to publicly humiliate them. Rather than giving them a package of games for the evening, like the paying customers received, Robin gave them only one card at a time. This required the nonpaying players to walk up in front of everyone between each game to get a new card.

Most evenings the bingo hall was full, typically 40 to 50 customers; some nights 85 people packed the parlor. In bingo circles, the YWCA's game was known as "a GOOD game."

As one of the regulars, Randy liked to sit at a front table so that he could get a clear view of the numbered balls as they were pulled from the tumbler. Robin was sometimes abrupt with Randy, even cruel at times, for no apparent reason. In a game called "speed bingo" the announcer would call numbers in rapid succession until someone got a bingo. Condescendingly, Robin would grab the "speed bingo" card away from Randy, telling him he wasn't fast enough to play.

Randy rarely talked back to his wife, not even when she sharply told him to "shut up and play the game!" Frustration played across Randy's face like an incoming storm, suddenly replacing his normally sunny expression, but with his head down, childlike, he did as he was told.

When Barbara Fawcett left her position at the YWCA on June 16, the bingo enterprise was healthy and cash flow was steady. With Barbara gone, Robin was the only person at the YWCA with the extensive knowledge and experience of the inner workings of the bingo project. Her superiors had no doubts that she would keep it profitable.

Five nights a week Robin managed bingo solo and Joan ran the canteen. It seemed they spent more time with each other than they did with their own families. They carpooled to work and socialized outside of work. The two women often stopped late at night after bingo for a bite to eat. From their initial friendship, a quasi mother/daughter relationship emerged. Robin talked a lot about her own life's ups and downs while

Joan, lending a sympathetic ear, told Robin very little about herself. Robin sought out mother figures. She had already collected two, Mary Lou Beck and Joan, since she had come to Boise. Maybe it had something to do with a deficiency in her own family or wanting to find the type of relationship she never had with her own mother.

* * *

Following his mother's path, Danny McHugh, Joan's 31-year-old son, moved to Boise from Boston in June with his 5-year-old son, Ryan. The two moved in with Joan and Bernie, occupying one of the two upstairs bedrooms in their apartment. The day Danny and Ryan arrived, Robin and Joan were busy working. To welcome them, Robin had made arrangements for Randy to take Danny, Ryan, Joshua, and Tabitha to the circus. Later, she made sure that they all went to the Boise River Festival, a popular event held in the city parks adjacent to the Boise River.

As Joan had been, Danny and Ryan were quickly embraced by the Rows. The two families began spending even more time together, enjoying backyard barbecues, birthday celebrations, and outings.

With so much contact between the families, Robin noticed immediately that Danny was attractive and intelligent. He had dark, thoughtful eyes and a quiet, gentle demeanor.

When Robin offered Danny a job as a bingo runner one night a week, he accepted. He was grateful for the kindness Robin had shown his family. Besides, they could always use the extra money to add to what he made working at the Idaho State Library. Gradually, Robin added more hours to Danny's work schedule.

Joan and Robin's relationship solidified throughout 1991. By year's end, the McHughs and the Rows had grown very close.

* * *

In December, Robin, Randy, Joshua, and Tabitha flew to New Hampshire for a couple of weeks over Christmas to visit Robin's family. Randy had encouraged Robin to reconcile with her mother and, after many years, this was accomplished to a degree.

Joan and others wondered how Robin, who was living from pay check to pay check, could afford this expensive trip. It was especially puzzling since Robin had just bought a spanking new, white bedroom furniture set for Tabitha, new wedding rings for herself and Randy, and a television set for each of her children. She sent $200 cash and $100 worth of toys to her sister Tammy and her children and gave each relative back east $100 cash, telling them all that she had won a lottery. Robin explained to Joan that she had been saving her money and used coupons when she shopped. Joan took that response to mean "it's none of your business."

A couple of weeks before Robin left for her trip, Joan saw a change in her friend. She became cold and difficult to work with. Something must have set Robin off, but Joan didn't have a clue as to what it was. Then, paradoxically, just before she left, Robin made sure that Joan's family had a Christmas tree, decorations, and gifts. Her Jekyll and Hyde behavior was maddening and confusing. Joan had seen Robin's cold, nasty side with other people, but she had never before been the victim of it.

Joan noticed a drastic transformation in Robin when she returned – she was happy. New Year's Day, 1992, the McHughs and the Rows celebrated. They casually discussed the possibility of both families moving to a different city together. The mood was bright and cheerful. But soon after that day, the relationship between Robin and Randy seemed to abruptly crumble.

The friction was noticeable, even more than the daily irritation Robin had exhibited since Randy's accident. Joan thought the monotonous grind of being nursemaid to her disabled husband for two years had frayed Robin's nerves to their limit.

Robin had begun to spend more and more time at the McHugh home and to find more excuses to be near Danny. By January, she had worked Danny into a four- to five-night work week as a bingo runner. That was when the nature of their friendship began to change – at least as far as Robin was concerned. They would go out together and talk. Danny was a good listener, the perfect choice for someone who needed a solid sounding board. Robin talked about divorcing Randy and moving with the kids to Seattle.

Joan observed the relationship between Robin and her son develop. Since moving to Boise, Danny hadn't met anyone special. But Robin had done the groundwork with Danny. She had put herself out whenever she could where he was concerned. It seemed to Joan that Danny was all Robin could talk about. In the middle of their conversations, with a school-girlish giggle, Robin would often interrupt Joan to ask about him. What was he doing? Where had he been? How was he feeling?

Joan was aware that Danny, on the other hand, viewed his relationship with Robin differently than she did. In his mind, they were good friends. Robin was in the race to win the big prize while Danny was just along for the ride.

CHAPTER SEVEN

January, 1992

During the second week in January, Robin dropped a bomb on Joan's contentment.

As they often did after work, Joan and Robin stopped at JB's, a 24-hour restaurant. The name had been changed from JB's Big Boy and still displayed a gargantuan statue of a chubby boy in a checkered apron menacingly close to the entrance. This was where they usually had their heaviest conversations. On this evening, however, Joan wasn't prepared for this particular conversation.

Leaning over her hash browns and eggs, Robin whispered that Randy had been abusing her, brutally beating her. She had been covering it up, literally and figuratively, wearing slacks instead of skirts so the bruises wouldn't show.

Joan's jaw dropped. She was shocked mute, her eyes fixed on Robin's face as she listened in horror. Joan had never been in an abusive relationship, and she would never have suspected Randy of brutality. She didn't have a classic 1950's TV marriage, but who did?

Robin blamed her nasty behavior before the new year on the abuse she had been suffering. Apologetically, she claimed Randy was at the root of her stress.

Toward the end of this week filled with worry, Joan got an upsetting evening call. Her voice quavering, Robin whispered into the receiver that Randy had just been beating her and had thrown her up against a wall; her ribs were hurting her, she said. A picture flashed through Joan's mind of Randy's bulk hanging over her 5-foot-2-inch friend's soft, plump frame.

Joan's emotions teetered between sympathy for Robin and fury toward Randy. She was a broken record telling Robin she had to call the police and get out immediately. But Robin replied, "You don't understand; I can't do that." She then convinced Joan that Randy had settled down and she knew the best ways to deal with him. Sleep was elusive for Joan that night.

The next day, Robin told Joan her ribs were wrapped up, taped securely to ease the pain of movement. Joan again implored her friend to get help, but to no avail.

Although she had rarely missed a night of bingo, Robin now told Joan she didn't want to go to work because of her ribs. She knew people would ask about her. To save face, she and Joan invented an excuse that she had fallen down the stairs into a curio cabinet.

Later that same week, Robin arrived at the bingo hall with a bandage wrapped around her arm and an adhesive bandage on her face. In hushed tones Robin told Patty Coler, a bingo regular, that she'd like to talk to her – it was important.

"There's more to the story than meets the eye," Robin said cryptically, referring to her fall. She didn't elaborate or explain.

Patty was concerned and agreed to meet her the next morning. Robin again recounted her story of abuse. She told Patty that she had not fallen but had been pushed down the stairs by Randy. He kicked and hit her in places it wouldn't show, she said.

She blamed Randy's medication. When he took it, she explained, he would get very angry – that's when the abuse would start. Patty asked if Robin wasn't concerned that Randy would get abusive toward the children. Robin responded with a definite, no; he was very good with the children.

Patty had seen Randy and Robin together many times, and she thought he seemed so docile and subservient. She, too, felt he was good with the children. Robin told Patty she was going to ask Randy for a divorce.

* * *

During a brainstorming session Joan, Bernie, and Danny let Robin know they felt it was crucial to get her and the kids as far away from Randy as possible, as quickly as possible. They urged Robin to relocate immediately while the divorce was going through. They even discussed the possibility of all of them moving somewhere together. Robin was insistent about moving to a place like Seattle, Washington, which she told the McHughs she believed was not a community property state. She said she didn't want to pay alimony to an abuser.

Bernie was itching to speak to Randy about the abuse, to set him straight. When he brought it up to Robin, she was adamant that Bernie not say anything to Randy. It might topple him over the edge, she said, causing even more violent behavior.

As the stories of abuse intensified, Robin began seeking asylum more often at the McHughs' apartment. They welcomed her into their humble home with open arms, offering her their decrepit "antique tripod" as a bed. The three-legged couch, with its torn upholstery, was propped up on one end by books. It was the couch that Robin, through the Harambee Center, had donated earlier to Joan.

* * *

Robin's coworkers began learning about her predicament. On separate occasions, she had come to work with a bandage on her face, her arm in a sling, her wrists wrapped, and alarming explanations about less visible injuries beneath her clothing.

She was encouraged to talk to Sue Fellen, the YWCA's Crisis Center Director and Robin's former boss. They met in Sue's office. It was a typical story of abuse, one Sue was accustomed to hearing, but it was not one she expected to hear from an employee. Robin seemed composed when she told Sue that Randy had been battering her.

When Sue expressed concern for the children's safety, Robin responded with certainty, "Randy would never hurt the children."

"But what would happen if he was being abusive to you and Josh or Tabby got in the middle of it and got hurt? What would you do about that?"

"I would kill him," Robin said matter-of-factly.

Robin was lukewarm about Sue's recommendation that she stay at the Crisis Center. She didn't file for a protection order or move into the Crisis Center, but she did talk to Janice Johnson, the executive director who had succeeded Barbara Fawcett.

Her description of Randy's abuse was more a statement of fact than a plea for help. She told Janice the reason she had missed so many staff meetings was that Randy wouldn't let her out of the house. He had put special locks on the windows and doors so she couldn't get out. She also said that Randy had hit her on her back and left marks. Like Sue, Janice also recommended the Crisis Center. Robin again demurred.

The day Robin wore Ace bandages on her wrists, Janice became even more concerned. Robin recounted a terrifying scenario in which Randy had tied her wrists together with some kind of rope and dragged her around the house. It had left red marks, she said, and she wore the bandages to protect her wrists.

Janice had also questioned Robin on the day she had worn a bandage on her face. "I wore the bandage because I don't want the staff to see," Robin had explained. "Randy hit me and it's real bad; it's bruised and it's got abrasions."

Each woman Robin spoke to, including Sue Fellen, thought she was the only person privy to Robin's very personal problem, and they all took the confidentiality part of their creed seriously. They did not gossip or compare stories.

✳ ✳ ✳

The third week in January, Joan got another evening call from Robin that turned her stomach inside out.

"He's in the next room," Robin whispered into the receiver, her voice filled with fear. "He's sharpening his hunting knife. I'm afraid he's going to cut me like he's done before."

In the past, Robin said, he had cut her in one of the most private and sensitive places on a woman's body – he had slashed her nipples.

Joan was terrified for Robin but powerless to get her out. Joan insisted that Robin call the police. Robin said she was afraid to call. She couldn't. Randy had something on her, something bad that he would use against her.

"If you won't call the police now, then call me every ten minutes," Joan demanded. "The first ten minutes I don't hear from you, I'm going to assume something terrible has gone wrong and I'll call the police myself."

Just as she was told, Robin called back every ten minutes. The third time she called Joan, she said that Randy had quieted down and was going upstairs to bed. Joan gave a mental sigh of relief. Robin was safe for now, but when would it happen again?

42

Joan remembered many conversations with Robin about a man named Jim Greenwell from the Department of Health and Welfare. Robin and Jim had interfaced many times working with homeless and mentally ill people. She had confided in Jim about her troubles, she said, specifically about Randy's violent outbursts. As a favor, Robin said, Jim offered to come to her home to evaluate Randy's condition. On one occasion, according to Robin, Jim gave Randy a shot to calm him down; another time, he administered Dilantin, an antiseizure medication.

But Joan still didn't understand Robin's fear of calling the police. What would keep her and the children tied to this intolerable situation? What would be a good enough reason for her to risk her own and her children's safety, sanity, and possibly their lives? Joan just could not endure seeing her friend stuck in this brutal vise. She wanted to know the answer and pointedly pressed Robin about it.

Robin finally recounted for Joan an unbelievably shocking story, one from her life before she came to Idaho:

She was living in California with Joshua and Tabitha, separated from her husband, when 2-year-old Tabitha pulled a pan of boiling water off the stove, suffering burns that required hospitalization. While Tabitha was recovering, Robin's estranged husband kidnapped the little girl from her hospital bed and spirited her away. It was several weeks before the police located her in Nevada with her father and returned her to Robin.

A couple of months later, while Tabitha was playing at a neighbor's house, Robin's husband appeared again and demanded to see his daughter. Robin refused him. They fought. He struck Robin with a powerful blow from his fist which caused her to fear for her life. Trying to protect herself, she grabbed a kitchen knife and slashed at her husband, sinking the blade into his flesh. He called the police and Robin was arrested and charged with assault with intent to kill.

This was the shameful story, Robin said. She didn't want anyone to know. Joan now understood what Randy was threatening to do if Robin left him. She would be exposed, then arrested.

On the positive side, Robin told Joan she had written down everything that had been happening in a journal and had begun saving her money in a separate account bearing only her name. She had to start saving all over again, she explained, because Randy had been getting up in the middle of the night, sneaking off to the ATM and withdrawing $100 each time until he had drained their savings account of $1,500.

Robin had news for Joan nearly every day that January. Late one night, Robin showed up on the McHughs' doorstep with her children. She was clad only in a nightie and had red marks resembling a handprint on her neck. She divulged that beneath her clothes, scars marred her back, reminders of Randy's past brutality.

Joan's first instinct was to grab Randy by the throat and throttle him. Joan wanted Robin to get out immediately. But again, Robin went back home the next day. Joan worried and waited, wondering when the other shoe would drop.

Rape. It was another evening call. Robin recounted the horror she felt when Randy tied her to the bed and raped her. She detailed how the next-door neighbors had heard the screaming and called the police. She said it was embarrassing and humiliating for her when Mr. Healy had to break the door down and Mrs. Healy had to untie her.

After the police came, Robin said, the fighting just continued because Randy was "out of his mind." While they were outside with the police, Randy had jumped on Robin, knocked her down, and smashed her head on the concrete. When the officer tried to pull Randy off, he assaulted the policeman and was arrested. Then, Robin said, she had gone with Sue Fellen from the YWCA to the hospital for a rape exam and to press charges.

"You would be very proud of me," Robin told Joan. Robin beamed and trumpeted the fact that Randy had to appear in court February 18 to face charges. She knew Joan would respect her for finally following through and holding Randy accountable. Disdainfully, Robin said that Randy's mother had bailed him out.

"Of course he's in a rage," Joan said to Bernie. "He's losing control of Robin. She's finally calling his bluff and he doesn't like it!" As much as she wanted to blast Randy with a piece of her mind, she knew better. Joan remembered Robin's warning not to confront Randy because it might set him off. Especially now, his fuse was short and he might explode.

The stress and tension couldn't help but spill over onto Joshua and Tabitha, causing them to act out their frustration in the only way they knew. They were driving their mother crazy with their fighting. Robin talked about sending Joshua and Tabitha to California to stay with the people she referred to as the children's godparents, Jack and Alyce Woods.

* * *

"Godparents" was more than just an honorary designation; Jack and Alyce Woods loved Robin's children as much as they did their own. They and their two boys were an extended family to Joshua and Tabitha.

Randy called Alyce Woods. He seemed sad and upset over Robin's talk of divorce, which he said came abruptly. He said he didn't know or understand why and for well over an hour poured out his feelings.

I love the kids, he told her. Robin's always complaining that we argue a lot and that's why she wants a divorce. We do just fine until she walks through the door...she stirs things up.

The next day Robin called Alyce. She was quite angry when she found out that Randy had called her and she told Alyce in no uncertain terms that their marital problems were nobody's business. She confirmed that she was contemplating divorce but didn't mention any physical abuse.

* * *

With all the talk of divorce and Robin's spending so much time at Joan's, Randy's frustration and anger boiled over. He suspected that his wife was having an affair with Danny McHugh. The burn of humiliation left him livid. He left embittered, profane messages on Joan's answering service, his only connection to Robin at this point. He wanted Robin home. One message contained a threat that she had better get home or something bad would happen.

Joan asked Robin about the "bad thing" Randy had referred to. Robin said Randy knew about the outstanding warrant in California, the "assault with intent to kill," and his insinuation meant that he would call the police if she didn't come home.

Two days later Robin placed a brief call to Alyce. She let her know that she and Randy had talked things over and they were both willing to go to counseling. Then she went to work.

Bingo began normally enough. The game was now being held at the YWCA in order to cut overhead. Before starting the climb to the stage to call bingo numbers, Robin unexpectedly, slowly, melted first onto one knee, then crumpled to the floor. Joan McHugh called 911.

When the paramedics came, Joan warned them to be careful because Robin's ribs were taped. As the paramedics began to probe, Robin became belligerent and refused to lift her sweater for them to examine her.

After the paramedics left, Robin returned to the bingo game. Just prior to closing, she told Dave Coler, a friend and bingo regular, that she had no feeling in her arm. Dave insisted on driving her to St. Luke's Regional Medical Center where Robin underwent a CT scan on her brain.

Joan followed Robin to the hospital. She was concerned and wanted to know all the details. Robin explained that the hospital had found that the lining of her brain had been bruised and she might have a slight concussion. It had been caused by Randy, she said, when he hit her head on the concrete.

CHAPTER EIGHT

February, 1992

Paralleling the disintegration in the Rows' relationship, the YWCA's bingo game was falling apart financially. The last day of January the bad news came from upper management that bingo would be shut down Saturday, February 8. Robin and Joan would both be out of a job. However, the main worry on Joan's mind was her friend's unstable home life. Joan thought, at least I have my family's support. Who did Robin have to lean on? With an abusive husband and her immediate family scattered across the country, Robin really had only Joan. Joan vowed to herself to stay by Robin's side through whatever lay ahead.

The first week in February, Robin told Joan that Jim Greenwell, from the Health and Welfare Department, had a court order committing Randy to a mental hospital. Robin acted relieved that he would be committed February 6. Joan felt a weight had been lifted from her chest; it was only a few days away.

Once Randy was committed, Robin told Joan, she could take the children and their property and move to Washington. Joan thought the idea of Robin moving with the children was sound. Robin was finally making a sensible decision.

During the break from Randy, Robin said she was going to have the children stay with their godparents in California for a while to shield them from the upsetting events. Robin seemed to be putting calculated thought into her future without Randy.

When February 6 arrived and Randy had not been picked up by the health and welfare people, Joan wondered why. Robin told her that when they had come to get him, he wasn't home.

Robin called Alyce Woods that Thursday morning, crying and angry. The YWCA had laid her off with only one week's notice. She had been a good employee and felt that this was unfair. She told Alyce that she would be facing some financial hardships and that she would have to move her family into a smaller place. Alyce and Jack generally kept the kids during the summer, and Robin asked if they would consider also taking the children for the remainder of the current school year while she and Randy regrouped.

"Well, let me just run it by 'Papa,'" Alyce replied, using the children's pet name for Jack, "and we'll get back to you later."

Before Alyce had a chance to "run it by Papa," Robin called back that evening and told her that they'd changed their minds; she was going to get paid through the end of the month and somehow she and Randy were going to try to work things out. Separating the family shouldn't be the answer, Robin had said.

✳ ✳ ✳

Friday, February 7, Robin and Joan drove to Amity Elementary to pick up Joshua and Tabitha. Her plan, Robin told Joan, was to take the kids to California to stay with Jack and Alyce before Randy knew they were gone. But they were too late; Randy had already picked up the children.

Without knocking, Randy had stuck his head in the door of Shirley Jackson's fourth grade class and he called hurriedly to his stepson. Josh looked up in surprise. A strange look of fear and disappointment crossed his face.

"Oh, it's okay, Josh," Shirley reassured him, glancing up at the clock. "Just put your things away; your dad's here a little early. You can go on home."

Josh walked over to the wall and unhooked his backpack. Shirley watched him get his things. "We'll see you Monday, okay?" Shirley smiled. Josh's face relaxed a bit and he smiled back. Randy picked up Tabitha next and the three drove away.

Robin and Joan drove to Seneca Drive. As they pulled up to Robin's house, Randy approached with the children in the Row's other car. Robin stopped and got out to talk to him.

Back in the Mazda, Robin told Joan that Randy wouldn't let her take the kids. He was going to take them away and she didn't know where.

Joan knew the way he had been treating Robin and was beside herself about the children. Randy had appeared angry. She didn't know what he was capable of doing if provoked. As far as she was concerned, it was kidnapping, and she badgered Robin until she convinced her to call the sheriff's department. They drove to a convenience store where Robin made a call on a pay phone while Joan waited in the car.

She told Joan she had called mental health, then the sheriff's department and had spoken to a detective about the kidnapping. They had advised her that they couldn't act for 48 hours.

Joan and Robin squawked about the ridiculous policy. What in the world was wrong with these police that they wouldn't help keep the children safely away from Randy?

The only thing the police could do, Robin said, was to pick Randy up Monday morning when he took the kids to school. Once Randy was arrested, Robin foretold, Jim Greenwell would make it known that there were commitment papers and Randy would be committed.

That night Robin and Joan went to work as usual. When Robin told Joan that Randy was bringing cabinet keys by, Joan's logical mind began clicking. "Perfect! Call the police; tell them Randy is coming and they can pick him up. You'll have the kids!"

Robin went into her private office to make the call. Joan tried to cover her jitters and keep her mind on her work, frequently glancing up at the door.

Several minutes later, Robin reappeared. "It didn't work," she said. "Randy had Josh drop the keys at the desk."

Damn it! Another opportunity botched, Joan thought.

That night, Robin slept downstairs on the couch near the front door; Joan slept upstairs with the rest of her family.

Saturday morning when Joan got up, Robin was gone. She didn't see her again until late afternoon. When Robin returned, she was clearly upset; as a matter of fact, she had worked herself into a rage. Her husband, she said, had not only kidnapped her children but had wreaked havoc in her home.

Mr. Washam, her friend Polly's father, was a former sheriff, Robin explained, and had offered to go with her to get some clothes at her duplex to provide protection in case Randy was there. The house was a mess, Robin told Joan. She was trembling with rage, venom dripping from her voice. Randy and the kids were gone. Her clothes had been destroyed, cut up; her side of the mattress had been slashed; her knick-knacks had been broken.

"Randy did it," Robin spat. She didn't hide her repugnance when she reported that there was slashed clothing in the living room and in her closet, and her diary was found burnt on the living room floor. Mr. Washam had told her that she needed pictures of the vandalism, Robin said, so he called a police photographer and told Robin to call her attorney, Ellison Matthews. "Ellie" agreed to meet the police photographer there, Robin added.

Joan shuddered to think what Randy would have done if Robin had been at home. Again, they decided it would be best for her to stay at Joan's that night and not go to work. Joan left for work with Robin's warning ringing in her ears, "Don't upset him," she said. "If he calls, don't ask him where he is or anything because he might hang up."

Later that evening Joan did get a call from Randy looking for Robin. She told him Robin couldn't come to the phone just then, she was upstairs helping Sue Fellen and that he should call back in half an hour. She hung up and immediately called Robin. "You'd better get down here NOW so you're here when he calls back. I'm going to call the sheriff's department."

"No," Robin said. "I've already called them."

Robin was at the bingo hall within minutes to get Randy's call. After she hung up, she told Joan that Randy wouldn't disclose his location and wouldn't let Tabitha talk to her.

After work, Robin and Joan drove by Randy's sister Janet's house. Seeing lights on inside, Joan insisted they look through the front window.

"No, Joan," Robin protested. "Someone will see you and call the police."

"Good!" Joan shot back. "Then they can do their job and help get the children back!"

Over Robin's objections, Joan jumped out of the car and sidled up to Janet's living room window to see if Joshua and Tabitha were inside. If she could see them, she thought, she could get them to come out.

The only movements inside were the spectral images cast on the wall from the flickering of a TV set. Joan got back in the car, and she and Robin drove around the neighborhood looking for Randy's car. When they ran out of places to look, they went back to Joan's apartment and went to bed.

✳ ✳ ✳

Just as on the previous morning, Joan awoke that Sunday to an empty couch. She didn't know when Robin had left. With the couch being right next to the front door, she could have easily slipped out anytime without being heard. She had strange sleeping habits; Joan knew that nocturnal activity was not unusual for Robin.

Robin reappeared at Joan's again around lunchtime, explaining that she had spent the morning being counseled by Sue Fellen at the Crisis Center because she was so distraught about Randy kidnapping the children.

That afternoon Danny and Robin cruised to Ontario, Oregon, about an hour's drive from Boise, to buy lottery tickets and the Sunday New York Times. As they drove, Robin talked about Randy kidnapping the children. She seemed excited and relieved about his impending mental commitment.

When the phone rang about 8 p.m., Joan was surprised it was Tabitha calling for her mother and even more surprised that Randy and the kids were at home. Robin told Joan that Randy wanted to know when they could sit down and talk out their problems. To pacify him, she agreed to meet with him the next day after he took the kids to school.

It seemed bizarre to Joan that things appeared to be business as usual: Randy calling for Robin to come home, the kids asking to stay up past bedtime. But it made more sense to her when Robin explained that her main concern was to keep Randy calm until the next morning when the police would pick him up.

Later that evening, Bernie borrowed Robin's car to drive to his AA meeting. As was their habit, Danny and Ryan went upstairs to their shared bedroom. At 9 p.m., Danny shut off the TV, tucked Ryan into bed, closed the bedroom door, and fell asleep listening to the radio. Downstairs, Joan and Robin watched some TV and did some laundry while they visited. It seemed to Joan that Robin was unsettled. At one point, Robin took a shower and washed her hair.

When Bernie got back from his meeting, Robin asked him to go fill up her car with gas. She requested that he park it in the small lot behind the apartment building instead of the usual spot in the front.

When the phone rang about 10:30 p.m., Joan almost jumped out of her skin.

"Hello?" she said, trying to swallow the racing heartbeats in her throat. Her insides turned to jelly when she heard the voice. It was Randy again, and he was definitely angry.

"Tell Robin she'd better get home or she doesn't need to bother coming home because she'll be locked out!" he roared.

"You really should talk to your wife about this," Joan said, trying to sound reasonable. She suggested that he call back and she would let Robin answer downstairs.

"Will she pick up the phone?" Randy asked.

"Yes."

"Fine." He hung up abruptly.

Robin picked up the next call. Joan sat on the edge of her bed kneading her hands. After a few minutes, she went downstairs to find out if everything was okay.

"Did you hear the call?" Robin asked. Joan thought she must be imagining that Robin's tone suggested there was something said that Robin didn't want her to hear.

"Of course I didn't listen to the call," Joan responded.

"He locked me out," Robin said simply. She assured Joan that she had calmed him down and he would be okay for tonight, and tomorrow it would all be over.

Emotionally exhausted, Joan trudged upstairs to bed a second time. Robin again settled herself on the couch by the front door.

Worrying about the next morning and the possibility of a confrontation with Randy, Joan slept fitfully. As she tossed and turned and floated in a nebulous state of half-sleep, the sound of the washing machine swished in and out of her dreams, the dryer droned, and she heard the spray of the shower.

She never did fall into a sound sleep. At 5:30 a.m. Joan awoke, sitting upright as if connected to a spring, almost simultaneously with the sound of Robin's voice. Fully clothed, Robin stood in her bedroom doorway.

"Joan, I have to go out to the house. I just have this terrible feeling that something is wrong," Robin was shaking. "Will you come with me? I need to see if they are there."

She told Joan and Bernie that she had experienced a premonition – a bad feeling when she awoke at 3 a.m., a feeling something wasn't right at home. She said that she tried to ignore the feeling by keeping busy, doing a load of laundry and taking a shower. But the feeling didn't go away. It made sense to Joan that her friend would be anxious about the kids; she herself was as edgy as an alley cat.

"Of course," Joan said groggily. She tried to reassure Robin that everything was fine and dressed immediately. They hurried out into the pitch black, frigid morning, stepped into Robin's cold Mazda, and drove quickly through the quiet, foggy streets to Seneca Drive – to be greeted by an inferno.

CHAPTER NINE

9 a.m., February 10, 1992

Sheriff's Detective Gary Raney settled into his chair as he'd done a thousand times before. He had no reason to believe this wouldn't be just another day at the office – black coffee, phone calls and reports, many involving the ever present petty theft crimes perpetrated by punks.

He quickly scanned a new report written earlier by a patrol deputy: "A house fire at 10489 Seneca...dense smoke coming from the upstairs windows. Front and rear doors were locked...a white female, Robin Row, arrived and said she and her husband were having family problems so she stayed with a friend and came over to pick up the children...Possible victims are Randy Row, Joshua Row, and Tabitha Row."

When he first read the report, Detective Gary Raney took it at face value: a typical fatal house fire. Then the calls began to trickle in. First, acquaintances of Randy's family called saying, in essence, that they thought there was more to this fire than met the eye.

At 8:24 a.m., dispatch got a call from an agitated woman. June Row, Randy Row's mother, wanted to talk to someone about the call she had just gotten from Randy's wife telling her that he and the kids had been killed last night in a fire. Shortly after the call from Randy's mother, one of Randy's older sisters called the sheriff's office.

"Is it true?" she asked. "I can't believe it. Because if it's true, my sister-in-law killed them all!"

Most members of the Row family believed that Randy was domineered by Robin, and June had never gotten along with her daughter-in-law. So, when the family began to talk, it wasn't a giant leap for them to arrive at their conclusion – their conviction – that Robin was responsible for the fire.

It wasn't unusual for the sheriff's office to receive unsubstantiated accusations when there was a tragedy. At this juncture, Detective Raney was not all that concerned about the calls. But something tickled his instincts; maybe the calls, or the wife of the deceased showing up at the scene when she did. It was enough to pique his interest.

Around 9 a.m. Raney went to the scene to meet with Whitney Fire Department's arson investigator, Assistant Chief Doug McGrew, and Chief Deputy State Fire Marshal Don Dillard. The investigators brought him up to speed on what had transpired during the early morning hours. It was obvious from the first examination that the main intensity of the fire originated inside a closet near the exit from the house into the garage. They had also discovered a second area of concentration – a heavily burned spot where some clothing had been piled in front of a large television set.

The physical evidence, even at this early stage, strongly indicated arson. The fire investigators spent the day sifting through the ruins, working backwards through a process of elimination. Raney approached his investigation from a different angle. A pile of clothing lying on a living room carpet doesn't spontaneously burn, he thought. Beginning with an educated theory, Raney would gather evidence and either disprove his initial theory or solidify it.

In the process of clearing away the rubble a "pour pattern" had emerged, snaking across the living room carpet from the stairway by the front door to the interior of the closet near the door to the garage. It was obvious that someone had intentionally laced the carpet with an accelerant and touched a match to it. What they hadn't found was any singular evidence pointing to a specific person.

They had uncovered a triple homicide. The home at 10489 Seneca was declared a crime scene, roped off with evidence tape, and secured with a guard.

Raney learned that the children who had died in the fire were Robin's natural children and Randy's step-children. Also, it appeared to be common knowledge that Robin was going to divorce Randy. Raney also learned that Randy had been in a motorcycle accident that had caused some permanent mental disability and that he had been rehabilitated to the point where he could perform normal daily functions.

Raney went to Saint Alphonsus Regional Medical Center to meet with the coroner who confirmed that the three victims of the house fire had died from breathing lethal levels of carbon monoxide. When Raney saw the corpse of Randy Row, he noted that the body was charred, especially on the face, trunk, and abdomen and his extremities showed extensive peeling of the skin. It was obvious from the marked post-mortem lividity that had settled in Randy's body that he had been lying on his side at the time of death, apparently in a sleeping position. His tongue protruded from his mouth and the fingers of both his hands showed clawing caused from postmortem rigidity.

Next was Tabitha's body. She was the most severely burned of the three. Joshua was not burned but had the highest level of carbon monoxide in his system. This indicated he had breathed the poisonous gas the longest.

Despite the charring, blackening, puffiness, and extensive peeling of the skin, all three cadavers were recognizable. All three had soot accumulated in the "nares," nasal passages. All three had died of smoke inhalation and probably without regaining consciousness. What bothered Raney the most was the probability that three innocent people were dead because of the callous act of another.

But Raney thrived on the pursuit, the gamesmanship of tracking, interrogating, and outsmarting an adversary. Bringing perpetrators to justice was what motivated him to get up in the middle of the night for stakeouts or to follow leads. Attention to the details made the difference between a good detective and a mediocre one. These qualities had earned Detective Raney a reputation for being one of the best. It was late morning on this seemingly never-ending day when he called for Robin. Raney hadn't yet realized he was working on what would become one of the most challenging cases of his career.

CHAPTER TEN

Afternoon, February 10, 1992

At 2 p.m., Bernie McHugh drove Robin Row to the Ada County Sheriff's Office. Detective Gary Raney wanted to talk to Robin, not as a suspect, but as a witness. This was a "lock-in" interview, a nonaccusatory, detailed exploration that might shed some light on the cause of the fire.

Robin walked tentatively into the interrogation room. The room was small and unadorned. A hidden camera captured every gesture of the interviewee and an audiotape recorder whirled out of sight. Over her black polyester slacks, Robin wore a colorful floral blouse and a roomy sweater. Stiffly perched on a chair, Robin's 5-foot-2-inch frame conjured up an image: part Buddha, part Whistler's Mother.

Detective Raney draped his 6-foot-3-inch form casually over a chair directly across from Robin.

Raney's personality and interrogation style were easygoing, friendly. Always immaculately groomed, his customary uniform was a suit or sport coat accessorized with a trendy tie. His easy, winning smile and youthful charm was antithetic to the job he did every day. It effectively hid his tenacity which, if anyone paid close attention, was signaled by the glint in his eyes.

He introduced Detective Ken Smith, who would assist him with the interview. They were both seasoned detectives who were willing to dig for the less than obvious evidence. Each man had a distinct style. Having worked together on many cases, the two had become a well-oiled machine, a marriage made in heaven – or hell – depending on an individual's perspective. The detectives were sometimes accused of playing the "good cop/bad cop" routine.

In a soft, compassionate voice and a we-need-your-help tone, Raney explained the process they used to understand how the fire started.

"We first look at the physical evidence, then we talk to the people who were there last. Which I assume's gonna be you," Raney said.

Robin nodded her head, clutching her purse in her lap for security.

"I guess one of the most obvious questions I could start with is, do you have any idea what may have caused it? And when were you there last?"

"Today's Monday?" Robin asked in a small voice.

"Yeah."

"Yesterday morning."

"Sunday morning?"

Robin nodded in the affirmative.

"And who was there then?"

"Randy and the children," she answered, barely audible.

"What's the house normally like as far as how things are laid out? Obviously, there's quite a bit of damage to it now."

To get a handle on Robin's level of truthfulness, Raney deliberately led her to believe there was extensive damage when, in fact, there were many clues found in the rubble.

"Do you want me to, like, draw you a diagram?" Robin asked.

Using the pen and legal pad on the desk, Robin began drawing and describing her apartment room by room, the furniture stick by stick. She was very cooperative.

"Any problems with anything electrical?" Raney asked.

"Not that I'm aware of."

"Ever have any problems with circuit breakers tripping or anything like that?"

"No, my husband, um, it doesn't trip, he goes out and turns – we gave the kids TVs for Christmas, and Tabitha gets up in the middle of the night and watches hers. So when she does that, he'll turn off the breaker to her room so she can't watch the TV." Robin began to speak up.

"Why doesn't he just take the TV?" Raney didn't have children, but it seemed like a strange way to discipline since the breaker switch would turn off much of the electricity upstairs.

"It was a constant argument between us." Robin let out an exasperated sigh.

"How about electrical cords and overload?"

Robin explained about a two-plug outlet that she said her husband had converted to a multiple with five electrical appliances attached. The arson investigators had made note of that multiple connection, thinking it strange because there were enough standard wall outlets to accommodate all the appliances.

Raney asked whether she or Randy kept any solvents such as engine degreaser, kerosene, diesel, or gasoline.

"I'm not sure there's kerosene, but we have a bottle…and it's got red stuff in it…I assume it's kerosene."

Raney wondered if Robin was playing up her ignorance about the kerosene; but, then, he was trained to be suspicious. She said Randy might have had a small gas can for the lawn mower. She also explained that her husband used a plug-in heater every once in a while for his arm. Last year he'd had a seizure and got burnt with hot water, she said. "His arm turns purple, and he uses the heater in the living room to heat his arm."

"Had he done that recently?"

"Well, I know it wasn't in the living room when I left yesterday. He puts it back out in the garage when he's done."

During the investigation, the heater had been found in the living room with clothes in front of it. If the heater was normally stored in the garage and was not out when Robin was there last, Raney wondered why she brought it up at all; but he didn't pursue the issue. She was not really a suspect. On the other hand, everyone was a suspect at this stage of the investigation.

"Was there anything that was piled up anywhere?"

"Well, Tabitha decided to do laundry. There was a big pile right in front of the doors to the washer and dryer. Sometimes my daughter will do it." Robin choked back some emotion, regaining her composure quickly. "When I left Sunday, Tabitha said she was going to clean. She's my Susie Homemaker." A fleeting grin passed over Robin's face when she spoke about her dead daughter, but she immediately regained her stolid manner.

"Why weren't you there last night?" Raney asked.

"I haven't been there since Thursday...we've been having problems for a long time. He was in a serious motorcycle accident a couple of years ago and has not been right mentally. I just told him I had to work Friday and Saturday night, and I just said that I was gonna stay over at Joan's and think. And we were supposed to, umm, meet today after he took the kids to school and talk about getting counseling and stuff. And that's why I wasn't there. And I don't know what you call it, but when I was at Joan's house today, I went upstairs and got her and I said, 'something's not right,' and we went home...and I knew right then that something was wrong. But we thought it was fog. And apparently it was smoke." Robin was warmed up now, chatty and using her hands to augment her words.

"What made you...?"

"I don't know, it...just a feeling I got in my stomach that something wasn't right."

"Now, were you up or did it wake you up?"

"It woke me up."

"If we could back up a little." Raney was buying time. Robin's reference to a premonition that woke her up in the middle of the night caught him off guard. Not sure what direction to take, he decided to back up before getting too far along on the wrong track. He was also confused about the days she was telling him that she was at her home. "You were there Thursday and then you weren't there until Sunday morning?"

"Uh, no, I went back and changed and took a shower. Like, I was there, umm, Saturday afternoon to see the kids and do things with them. I just didn't sleep there."

"Let's start with Friday. Were you there Friday morning?"

"Yeah, I guess I didn't leave until Friday night, so I must've stayed there Thursday. I remember Randy wanted to take the kids for the weekend. They were gonna go camping but they never did. He picked them up after school on Friday. I work nights. I think he took 'em to McDonald's. When I left for work, I didn't go back home until the next day. I went home Saturday, slept until noon; Joshua came and got me. We went out for lunch. And then I went to work. I was home Sunday morning. Read the paper, picked out a movie for the kids to go see."

She told Raney that her children called her at 8:30 Sunday night to ask if they could stay up past bedtime and to tell her they needed milk.

"I told Randy to go get some. Randy has to be told what to do since his accident. Then he called a couple of times, and the last time he called me was at 11 o'clock telling me that he was locking me outta the house, which he does very often. He was just talking about, when are we gonna sit down and talk this out, and we agreed to do it today after he took the kids to school. I was gonna meet him at the house."

Robin said that during their last conversation Sunday night, Randy told her he loved her.

Then she said that in the last call he had said, "Well, I'm going to bed and you're locked outta the house."

"What did he mean by that?" Raney's tone was still casual and pleasant.

"He locks me out all the time. He was mad because I wouldn't go home then," Robin said, exasperation coating each word.

"So did he ask you to come back? To come home?"

"Oh, yes, every time I talked to him."

"I'm trying to think if there could be another clue in that conversation as to what may have happened later. Could you remember any other details of the conversation?" Raney probed.

"He got angry at one point, but I don't remember which phone call because he called three or four times. But he says this all the time, he said, 'Oh, you're never gonna see me and the kids again.' And a couple of weeks ago he took an overdose of Dilantin – so he says. I seriously doubt he did."

"You don't think it's important that he said, 'You won't see me and the kids'?" Raney tried to hide his surprise. Why this far into the interview did she suddenly remember Randy's suicide threat?

"He says it all the time. He's been saying it for two years. You know, I used to panic. I don't anymore. And he called me several times at work over the weekend and told me that they weren't at home, that they were somewhere else, but I think they were really at home. And Joan wanted me to report it to the sheriff's department, that he took the kids and all this. And I just told her, sure."

"Were the kids with him...?"

"All weekend."

61

"And Randy was violent, too," Robin interjected. And when he got real violent, I would leave…if I could."

"What do you mean by violent?"

"Oh, he'd slap me around," Robin said casually.

"Was he ever violent with the kids?"

"No, never," Robin said emphatically.

Both children preferred to stay home with their father when she was gone, Robin explained. "Tabitha is real fond of Dad."

"Did he treat them well?"

"Yes. They had their share of arguments, but he would never, never strike them because he knows I'd throw him out."

"What was going to happen with the kids if you were getting divorced?"

"He could have 'em on the weekends."

Raney asked Robin if she had a key to the house. She didn't answer directly but instead explained that the security latches, sometimes referred to as swing or hinge locks and typically found on the inside of a motel room door, would be locked from the inside. Those locks were what Randy referred to when he said he was going to lock her out.

"You can't open it with a key," Robin explained, still talking with her hands. "In one of the conversations, he did ask me to come home and I said, no, that I would be there today. See, I didn't know what I'd be walking home to. I don't go home when he's like that.

"I…I…I do have one question," Robin changed the subject. "Umm, the paramedics – we have a smoke alarm upstairs. I can't understand why that didn't wake them up. It's very loud."

"I don't know." Raney was noncommittal. His gut told him that for some reason she was on a fishing expedition.

"But that's the only question I have. And I'm sure you can't answer it. Randy's a heavy sleeper but the children usually aren't…I mean, it's LOUD. The only thing we come up with is – I sleep with a fan on, and he had said Saturday night that he was running the fan because it made him feel like I was there."

"Those things like the smoke detector – that's what the fire department's doing, tracking down wiring and checking all that kind of stuff, so hopefully we can answer this."

Raney steered the questioning back to Robin's waking up with a premonition that something was wrong.

"I woke up at 3 o'clock and just felt uneasy," Robin began. "So I did some laundry – folded some laundry – did my bingo paperwork, and I took a shower. And when I got out, I still felt uncomfortable and I just – I don't know how to explain it. I just didn't feel right. And I asked Joan to drive out there with me."

"If it's any consolation, it's a peaceful process [carbon monoxide poisoning]. It's good that nobody suffered," said Raney.

"Yeah, they told me that," Robin spoke quietly, bowing her head. She seemed to have quite a strong rein on her emotions. She had been speaking to Raney for over an hour and had not shed a single tear.

"It's obviously quite a tragedy – everybody involved, but especially you."

Mute, Robin just bobbed her head up and down and crawled back into herself, fidgeting with her fingers.

"Somebody mentioned that you had said that this had happened to you before?"

"Well, I had a son who died in a fire in Pine Creek, California. It was electrical. It was almost 12 years ago. I was in the hospital for smoke inhalation for about three weeks or so. I remember very little. A counselor said that the part that I blocked out was worse than what I remember," Robin described the tragedy in hushed tones, occasionally glancing at her busy fingers.

"How old was he?" Raney asked.

"Just turned 6."

"I'd heard you'd lost two. But it was just a boy there, huh?"

"I lost a little girl to crib death. In 1977."

"In the same place?"

"Huh-uh. Nashua, New Hampshire. That's where I was born and raised. It's the second largest city."

"Well, you've definitely had your share of tragedy."

Raney excused himself and Detective Smith. He needed to give the fire department a call, he said, to see if there was anything they would like him to ask her. That would give him time to talk to Smith and decide on his next line of inquiry.

Raney knew Robin could get up and leave any time she chose. Later, he watched a tape taken from a hidden camera in the interrogation room. The tape showed that after the detectives had left the room, Robin did get up and step gingerly over to the door and press a cupped ear to the surface to listen. Presumably not hearing anything, she sat back down and remained as still as a figurine until the detectives returned.

✳   ✳   ✳

"There's some evidence that something was set on fire out there," Raney said bluntly. "One of the things we'll do is take a laser out there." This was a "bullshit" technique that often worked to flush out a perpetrator. "Smoke works real well setting in things like footprints and fingerprints and the timing of things. I think we're gonna have some pretty good evidence coming out of there of exactly what happened." Raney leaned forward, practically in Robin's face, with confident, intense body language. If Robin had anything to do with the fire, this would hopefully plant nervous tension.

"Okay," Robin nodded, expressionless. The information seemed to wash over her causing little effect.

Raney asked if there was anyone else Robin could think of that may have been in the house over the weekend. Randy didn't say, she replied; she didn't know of anyone.

"Do you have insurance?" Raney casually inquired, spinning the questioning 180 degrees.

"Pardon me?"

"Do you have insurance for them?"

"My children – I have a dental plan through the YWCA and it's also a life insurance. My boss is checking into that."

"At least that will help."

Changing the subject abruptly, Robin declared that none of her family lived in Boise. They were in Massachusetts and New Hampshire.

Raney gave the laser technique another try. "Okay. Like I say, we'll take the laser out there."

He took a sip of coffee. Leaning forward, his body posture intense again, Raney's large fawn-like eyes fixed on Robin. "And by the end of it, I'm confident we'll know two things: We'll know how the fire was set, whether it was accidental or whether it was some type of arson, and who did it if it was arson."

"Joan said that five different people called and said they thought Randy set it himself," Robin spoke up.

"Do you know who said that?"

"No."

"Do you know why somebody would say that?"

"Ahh, a lotta people knew what was going on and, like, yesterday he told me that he set my diary on fire."

Again, why so late in the interview did Robin bring out the fact that Randy had set her diary on fire?

"Anything else like that? Those kinds of things are important," Raney reprimanded.

"Not that I can recall. But if you locked the door, nobody could get in," Robin offered, again referring to the swing lock.

"I guess there's always the possibility of somebody who was sleeping there or a back door that might have been unlocked."

"But they're all – " Robin began then interrupted herself. "Well, I don't know, I'm assuming they're all [locked] – so there's no way someone could get in...or out."

"Okay. Those are the kinds of things that we'll probably be able to prove out. Whatta you think happened?" Raney probed.

"Honestly? I'd like to think it was an accident."

I'll bet you would, Raney thought to himself, getting more suspicious with each disclosure. "That wasn't the question, though," he chuckled.

"I think he did it, too – " Robin's voice broke. Her head dropped; her eyes fixed on her hands in her lap, "'cause that's his way of getting back at me."

"Was he seeing a psychologist or – "

"We went to marriage counseling for a while, and he saw Dr. Read not too long ago to see if he was still eligible for Social Security. I never took him seriously, but Joan's got messages on her machine of his rage. A couple of weeks ago he says, 'Well, by tomorrow it won't matter anymore.' But I never took him seriously, 'cause he's not the type to take his own life. He said it so often it didn't matter..."

Changing the subject suddenly, her hands moving like hummingbird wings, Robin shot rapid-fire words at Raney. "And then I fainted at work, oh, a week ago Tuesday I think it was. And they took me to the hospital, and I had to have a CT scan, and they said my wall of my brain was bruised from being slapped. And he's locked me outta the house, like, times that he would be in a rage and I would get outta the house in my nightgown, but I'd get out and I'd go to Joan's until he calmed down. Or I'd just stay overnight. You know, when she said that, it had gone through my mind, but I cannot actually see anybody starting a fire and going upstairs and laying down. I mean, that is – "

"It's kinda hard [to imagine]," Raney said, concentrating on Robin's every move and expression, listening intently for clues, while outwardly appearing to be politely attentive, as if participating in a casual tête-`a-tête.

"That's the only thing that I can't imagine," Robin interrupted, speaking rapidly. " Umm, Joan's thought or her son's thought was maybe he's – because he said he burnt my diary – they were thinking maybe he thought it was out and it wasn't…but you'll be able to tell that."

"Yeah. Yeah. I'm sure we'll be able to tell things like that. Technology has come a long way. If he was gonna do something, what do you think he would do?"

"I don't know. Because I can't see him hurting the children. I mean, he's – like last year, umm, he attacked Joshua outside and hurt him, I think he kicked him and – but he was going to counseling at that time. You know, so we'd try and work it out. But to actually just do something to them, I honestly don't think he would." Robin seemed to jump aimlessly through her thoughts, sometimes contradicting herself.

"I mean, he has problems but he's not crazy; he's not sick. He's not gonna start a fire, go upstairs, and lay down. You know. Nobody's gonna do that," Robin acted puzzled.

"Uh-huh," Raney let her ramble on.

Barely stopping for breath, she continued, "But the idea of if it had smoldered and he thought it was out, that maybe…but if you can't find something that caused it when the doors are latched, nobody could get in, that would leave just him."

Raney posed a hypothetical. "If, say, the investigation out there says that the back door's unlatched, or the front door's unlatched, something where somebody else could get in. And then if we said this was an arson…what would your thoughts be?"

"I wouldn't believe it. Who would wanna come in?"

"Well, that's what I'm trying to get you to think about. Anybody else…at all?"

"I couldn't think of anybody that…no. No. I couldn't think of one person."

No one else has a key to the apartment, is that correct?"

"I don't remember; I think he took his sister's key…yeah, so no one else does."

"Okay. If somebody was going to be spreading some type of rumor that they suspected foul play in this, who would it be?"

"My mother-in-law. June. She's a doll." Robin's eyes rolled upward, her voice dripped sarcasm.

"What would she say? Would she say that you did it?"

"Probably. I wouldn't doubt it. Because Randy got in an accident. I wasn't even on the bike with him, and it's all my fault. And then, a couple of months ago, June had said some nasty rumors – she does 'em all the time – about my sister-in-law and I. So I just stopped talking to them. My father-in-law came over one day and attacked me because I wasn't at Randy's side 24 hours a day when he was in the hospital…they certainly weren't gonna offer financial help."

Robin went on, "She [June] spreads rumors all the time. She's not worth wasting my time on. She's just a vindictive, nasty old lady. The first thing everybody said this morning when she turned around and said, 'Well, how come Robin didn't turn up in the fire?' is, 'Well, there goes June again…she's off.' She's a wonderful woman, bless her soul – I can't stand her."

"One of the things that I can anticipate coming out is just that it's so unusual for somebody to lose four children in three different accidents. That's going to seem suspicious in itself."

"Why?" Robin asked contentiously.

"Just because it's so unusual. People are going to interpret that as she must have gotten away with something."

"That doesn't bother me." Robin shrugged. "Let 'em."

"Were any of these investigated or – do you know by who?"

"Oh, no, I don't remember."

"Was it the place in New Hampshire…did the police come out?"

"Oh, yeah, they did. Nashua police, I assume."

"And what was her name?"

"Kristina…Cornellier," timidity quickly replaced the aggressive color in Robin's tone.

"This is really none of my business, but were you married before or –"

"I got married after she died."

"And she was how old?"

"Oh, 15 months," Robin's hands were back in her lap gripping her purse.

"Do you remember what her date of birth was?"

"Uh-huh. October 14th of '75."

"And you said she died of crib death?"

"Crib death. Sudden Infant Death Syndrome. SIDS. And it happened at my mom's," Robin clipped her words.

"And in California? Who did anything on that? Was it the police department, the fire department –"

"Umm, I don't remember," a loud sigh deflated Robin's chest, her posture collapsed.

"And when was that?"

"June 19, 1980."

"Who died in the fire? Just your son?"

"Keith – Cornellier – Hamilton."

"And do you remember his date of birth?"

"June 6, 1974. He had just turned 6."

Raney and Smith stepped outside again. Shaking their heads, they gave each other a where-do-we-go-from-here look. Raney knew they weren't ready to go back in and accuse her of setting the fire – they could be wrong – but they knew something wasn't right.

Other detectives and office personnel who had observed the interview in progress on the remote monitor agreed that Robin's behavior was way off, not even close to being appropriate.

Stepping back into the interview room, Raney took Robin's statistical information then posed a "bait" question.

"The reason for the delay is that the fire department called in. They've been checking with some of the neighbors and somebody said that they thought they saw your car there early this morning. Would there be any reason –"

"Huh-uh," Robin said with certainty. "Not until 5 o'clock or so."

"Would there be any reason anybody would have seen the car there before?"

"No, because I had it at Joan's."

"None at all? You didn't loan it out to anybody?"

"No. Bernie used it last night and put gas in it."

She wasn't taking the bait. She didn't appear the least bit bothered that someone said they might have seen her car.

"One of the options we have is to give you a polygraph test. That helps clear the air and take some of the suspicion off you.

"I know. I took one with the other fire," Robin volunteered.

Raney took a big mental gulp which he expertly concealed.

"Would you want to take one again? Or would you be willing to if it came to that?" he said casually.

"I don't have a problem with that," Robin said confidently.

"How did you do on that?"

"I passed it."

In Raney's experience, most people will agree to take a polygraph but when asked how they think they would do, invariably, the guilty will rattle off explanations of why they won't pass the test.

"How would you do on this one?"

"I'd pass it," Robin replied confidently.

Raney took a final stab at breaking down her confidence.

"Well, I thank you for coming down today. And we're gonna see if we can get an answer to this and, hopefully, put your mind at ease. Technology's come a long way...and there's no doubt in my mind that we'll be able to tell who did it. Okay?"

Robin nodded. "Thank you."

Raney had begun the interview with what he thought was probably a grieving widow and had come away with what he now thought might be a possible suspect. Even though he had wielded his best techniques and she had survived them, something still didn't feel right to him. Robin Row might have easily walked out with him thinking she was blameless, but instead, his detective's radar was registering a blip.

✳ ✳ ✳

When Robin returned to the McHugh apartment, she and Joan had an intense police-bashing session. Joan already harbored a distrust for the police. So when Detective Raney had called to ask Joan to come to the sheriff's office later that evening to answer some questions, a part of her was glad for the opportunity to say what was on her mind.

Before Joan left for the sheriff's office, Robin perched on a chair in the living room and confessed her fear. She told Joan she was afraid she was going to be blamed for the fire. Evidently, she had sensed that Raney was zeroing in on her as a suspect.

"Don't tell them anything about the abuse or the kidnapping. It's none of their business. Don't tell them ANYTHING," Robin coached Joan.

"I'll just tell them the truth. They have to know that to see that you're innocent," Joan reasoned.

"You can't tell them. They'll use the 'burning bed syndrome' against me." Robin referred to a movie about an abused wife who set her husband's bed on fire while he slept.

"Robin, I'm just going to tell the truth," Joan reiterated.

Robin was adept at persuasion, and it seemed to upset her that she couldn't convince her friend to keep her mouth shut.

"If you tell the truth, you'll kill me," Robin said bluntly.

The remark chilled and confused Joan; she was taken totally off balance. "I have to tell them the truth, Robin."

"The truth will KILL me!" Robin wailed.

She was just overwrought, Joan thought. Under the circumstances it was understandable. When the police heard the facts – the truth – they would have to understand. On the other hand, maybe Robin did sense the direction the investigation was taking. Maybe they would frame her. Joan knew the police always suspected the spouse when something like this happened. It was so unfair. All they cared about was a quick-solve to the case. Even though Robin was very stoic in public, Joan knew she let her emotions out when she was with those who cared about her. She had seen Robin break down in her home that very day, had even had to get medication to help calm her down. Joan was convinced who was responsible for the fire – and it wasn't Robin.

On the way to the sheriff's office, Joan worried. The police could twist her words and use them to frame Robin. But if she said nothing, they might suspect she was covering for Robin.

* * *

Raney opened with what he thought was an easy question. He could tell by Joan's stiff posture and slightly raised shoulder that he would have to use his most cordial manner. "Could you tell me who lives in your home?"

"Why would I do that?" Joan answered icily, posturing herself for combat.

"It would make it easier in our conversation."

"This isn't a conversation," Joan spat out the words in her most urbane Bostonian accent. It's an interrogation, she thought.

"If it weren't for all you people in the sheriff's office, those children would be alive."

Joan unleashed her pent-up hostility. By her own admission she had somewhat of an arrogant, eastern liberal attitude and wasn't known for mincing her words. But, even when angry, she always retained her dignity. She would not leave that interview without letting these stupid, hick cops know what a grave mistake they were making. She'd never forget the day Robin had to call their office in an effort to protect her children and had gotten no help.

"Who do you think did it?" Raney asked politely, in keeping with his good cop image.

"Randy did it. Of course." Joan hadn't a shred of doubt in her mind that he had set the fire, whether on purpose or by accident. She knew from Robin that he had burnt her journal, slashed her clothes, and broken her knickknacks – not to mention the escalating abuse over the last couple of months. These cops should have it figured out by now – SHE shouldn't have to explain it to them.

Raney sustained his pleasant demeanor. He was so congenial, Joan wanted to punch him. "Why don't you let me call my answering service so you can listen to the abusive calls Randy made – then you'll know who did it!"

Joan did simmer down long enough to tell Raney about how she had met Robin; the abuse Robin had suffered recently; the fact that Robin had said that Randy would be involuntarily committed to a mental hospital; and that Randy had kidnapped Joshua and Tabitha on Friday. Talking about the kids transmuted Joan's anger to tears.

After talking to Joan, the possibility of Randy as a suspect fleetingly crossed Raney's mind. How stable was he? Would he have set a fire then gone up to his bed to sleep? Or maybe he did leave something smoldering. His dominant thought, however, was that Joan was a victim too – big time.

CHAPTER ELEVEN

February 11, 1992

"BOISE FIRE KILLS MAN, TWO CHILDREN," was the headline in the local newspaper. Janice Johnson, YWCA Director, was quoted as saying that Robin had no savings and lived paycheck to paycheck. The article included a plea for donations.

Detective Raney didn't have much time to read the newspaper. One of the first rules a cop learns is that the first 48 hours after a crime has been committed are the most crucial to the solution of that crime. After that, the chances of finding out "whodunit" become progressively slimmer.

Detectives Raney and Smith began working diligently contacting and interviewing friends, neighbors, and family members. He also called Chuck Sanborn, a detective with the county sheriff's department in Pine Creek, California, where Robin's son Keith had died.

Raney found out about a storage unit registered to Robin and Randy Row in the nearby town of Meridian, Idaho. This could turn out to be a gold mine of evidence or a dead end. They would have to get a search warrant to find out.

Wednesday, two days after the fire, the arson investigators finished with their cause and origin investigation. The carpet in the duplex had been cleared, revealing obvious pour patterns burned into the fibers, a fingerprint of sorts. There was now no question they had an arson and triple homicide.

The detectives learned from Assistant Chief Doug McGrew that the fire began around 3:30 in the morning, no accidental cause was found, and the circuit breaker that controlled the smoke detector had been manually shut off. Learning about the breaker switch was a major suspicion jump for Raney.

With the assistance of Deputy Ada County Prosecutor Roger Bourne, Raney secured four search warrants: One for 10489 Seneca, the second for the McHughs' apartment, the third for Robin's Mazda, and the last for the storage unit in Meridian.

The 10-by-15-foot unit #827, rented by the Rows in November of 1991, was filled with items that were in new or excellent condition: furniture, a hutch, end tables, holiday decorations, bingo supplies, a TV set, home interior decorations, kitchen utensils, boxes, family pictures, dishes, and women's clothing. There were also collector-quality Barbie dolls in original, mint condition boxes. A red flag shot up when detectives saw the newspaper used to wrap breakables. It was dated Friday, February 7, 1992.

✳ ✳ ✳

The day that the memorial service was scheduled for Randy and the children took everyone by surprise. It was supposed to take place Saturday, five days after the tragedy, to accommodate the godparents who were coming from California. Instead, by Tuesday, Robin changed the memorial service to Wednesday afternoon, February 12, at Saint Michael's Episcopal Church.

Alyce Woods, who had planned to fly to Boise on Saturday, was stunned. Robin told her not to come, that the service was being postponed because Randy's parents were asking for an investigation.

Forty-five minutes before the service was to begin, Robin and Joan stopped at the YWCA across the street from the church. Robin had some business to take care of at their old place of employment. Robin chatted and laughed with the receptionist while waiting for her boss, Janice Johnson. Robin told Janice, she had come for her payroll check and life insurance forms.

"I'm sorry to have to tell you this at a time like this, Robin," Janice said, "but I can't give you your check until I get the keys and bingo money from you."

Robin told Janice that she had left the money in her house and it had burned in the fire. She turned on her heel and walked across the street to attend the memorial service for her family.

The service was held in the chapel. Everything had been organized in just one day and from all accounts this was obvious to those entering the foyer. Mourners were greeted with the framed smiling faces of Randy, Joshua, and Tabitha posed happily together in an 8-by-10 color portrait set on a small table decorated with one potted plant. The same picture had been flashed on TV and would be worn as a badge by Randy's parents who had it adhered to the back window of their van. No other flowers adorned the church. It was "cold", many would say later of the church and the service.

Some 75 people filed into the chapel. Robin walked in from the front flanked by her friends Joan, Bernie, and Danny. Composed, Robin displayed a shy, perfunctory smile as she scanned the people in attendance: bingo players, YWCA employees, the "Albertsons wives" founders, teachers from Amity Elementary, and even some of the homeless she had helped.

Although Robin hadn't seen much of her throughout the past year or two, Mary Lou Beck Weiner, now married and an ordained deacon, officiated. The service was described as unemotional and impersonal. It was a one-size-fits-all memorial service that lasted barely fifteen minutes. Robin seemed composed throughout the service. Although sometimes tearful, it seemed that for the most part she had blocked off her emotions. Many thought she must be in shock.

Afterward, with the McHughs at her side, Robin walked sedately to the foyer to form the reception line with Randy's parents at the opposite end. Standing next to the picture of her late family, Robin greeted and shook hands with people as they filed out. She made polite dialogue with most.

Robin's emotions went from one end of the spectrum to the other in a matter of moments. With some who offered their condolences she chatted, with others she gushed, and at times she cried. Shirley Jackson remembered thinking how amazed she was at Robin's composure and the way she talked about her tragedies as if they had been visited upon someone else.

Those Robin knew better she clutched, sobbing. When Barbara Fawcett came through the line, she held Robin as the grieving mother sobbed, "How will I ever live without my children?"

"Robin, we'll do everything we can to help you," Barbara said with sincerity, handing Joan the $1,000 she had raised, checks and $150 in cash, with $100 of the cash coming from Barbara.

The rumors had begun quietly, directly on the heels of Amity's spaghetti supper for an emergency fund to help defray funeral costs for Robin. Close to $1,000 had been raised.

After the service, all the way back to school, Shirley Jackson contemplated the tragedy and pondered the strange vibes that she had felt during the memorial. Rumors about the fire that had taken two well-liked students had begun to spread like chicken pox at Amity Elementary. Shirley hadn't believed the stories that had sprung up overnight about Robin Row. This bereaved mother couldn't possibly have had anything to do with the death of her family, she had thought, outraged. Now, Shirley wasn't sure. That evening she said to her husband, "This lady is either the strongest person I know, or she's in shock, or she is simply wicked."

✳ ✳ ✳

Two days after the memorial service was Saint Valentine's Day. Before school began, Shirley Jackson remembered being at her desk working when she looked up to see a friend of Josh's standing in her classroom, gazing uneasily at the floor. "Did you lose something?" Shirley inquired of the boy.

"No, no." He said self-consciously. "Can I just put something in Josh's desk?"

"Sure," Shirley said.

The boy walked over to his friend's desk, hesitated a minute, then looked inside. He pushed Josh's things out of the way to make an empty spot right in front, carefully laid his valentine down, then walked out.

Shirley looked to see what he had put inside the desk. She knew the sensitive little boy had done some deep thinking after his friend had died. Through the thin white envelope she could make out enough to tell that it was a good-bye note. For grief therapy the children wrote "memory" letters to Tabitha and Joshua.

CHAPTER TWELVE

Robin was hungry for Chinese food after the memorial service, so the McHughs indulged her even though they didn't feel like eating. If Joan and Bernie had known what was going on back at their apartment, they would have come straight home.

While they were squirting soy sauce, Chief Deputy Fire Marshal Don Dillard was wriggling through the unlocked kitchen window at the back of the McHughs' apartment. Stepping over dirty dishes on the counter, he jumped to the floor and let Detective Gary Raney inside.

The investigators were carefully combing the McHughs' home for specific items of Robin's when her Mazda pulled up in front. Raney met her and the McHughs at the door, search warrant in hand.

Robin was holding an insurance claim form in her hands. Her attitude was casual, but Joan was horrified and thought it disgraceful that the investigators were stampeding through her house unannounced. Seething, she tried to keep her temper in check and almost succeeded, but one comment slipped through her teeth. Her eyes narrowed and she cut her words sharply.

"You could have picked a better time. Why don't you go find the REAL killer and leave this woman alone!" Joan raised her right shoulder and gave the detectives a dismissive toss of her head as she walked through the front door. She was certain she would find her couch slashed, drawers overturned, and books pulled from shelves. Surprisingly, everything was intact.

The detectives had confiscated some clothing, personal papers, life insurance papers showing ongoing correspondence, and a check register. The air was thick with feigned cooperation.

"I knew you were coming," Robin said, smirking.

"What makes you say you knew we were coming?" Raney asked.

"Paranoia, I guess." Robin answered.

"Okay, let me tell you why we're here. People are making accusations against you; Randy's family is saying that you're responsible for this," Raney explained.

"Somebody kissed and hugged me today and said how sorry they were for me," Robin said out of the blue.

"What was today?" Raney asked quizzically.

"The memorial service we just returned from."

"I didn't realize that was today. I'm sorry for the timing. We have some other simple questions. Where are your shoes?"

"On my feet," Robin quipped.

"Your other shoes."

"These are the ones I was wearing the night the fire was discovered." Robin pointed to a pair of white tennis shoes.

"What really bothers me about this," Robin continued, "is you talked about fingerprints the other day, now you're talking about shoes. I lived there for three years; my fingerprints are going to be all over that place! My shoes are going to be all over!"

"I understand that," Raney answered.

"And the door was locked," Robin suddenly switched gears.

"Which door?"

"The front door. Randy called and said he was going to lock me out. There's no way I can get in. You turn that top latch over and you can't get in."

"What about the back door?"

"Okay. The sliding glass door should have a stick in it."

Robin went on to explain in detail how all the doors in the house were secured that night to prevent even a person with a key from entering.

"Do any insurance policies exist?" Raney asked.

"I told you about the one at the YWCA."

"That's on Joshua and Tabitha, right?"

"It's my dental plan and it carries life with it. As a matter of fact, I don't even know how much it's for."

"How about on Randy?"

"I'm not sure, to be honest with you. We had one through our bank that we got about three years ago, and I don't recall if he is still on it or not. You'd have to check with the bank."

"Do you know if any premiums are still being paid?"

"Yes, they come out every three months, $45."

"And it's in your name?"

"It's a joint checking account…I believe I'm the principal holder and he's the secondary. We talked about getting life insurance, but we knew the premiums would be too high.

"If you'd like me to get my clothes, I'd be more than happy to," Robin volunteered, veering away from the insurance issue. "Well, to be honest with you, Detective Raney, everything I have here has been washed since Monday."

"Answer this for me," Raney ventured. "If you're gonna say I want to do everything I can to figure out what caused this fire, then I'd like to go where I've got all my notes and sit down with you again and talk."

"I'm afraid to go down there, to be honest with ya, because –"

"We can go to a different room." Raney was not going to give her more line until she was in his net, then she could have all the line she wanted. Given enough, he surmised, she would hang herself with it.

"Well, you know, you lock me in that room and I have this fear of being arrested, and to be honest with you, I don't trust policemen. You've already talked to Chuck Sanborn. I can't stand the ground he walks on. He doesn't like me either." Robin's reference was to the California detective whose name she hadn't been able to remember during her first interview with Raney.

"Like I told you, I'm going to talk to everybody I can."

"Oh, I understand that. And this other thing that bothers me is you're saying that a neighbor saw my car out there. That really bothers me."

"It bothers me too," Raney said.

"Because it never left that driveway, and I don't know how to convince you. And like I told my lawyer, what I fear is my prints are going to be all over that house."

This was the first time Robin had mentioned her newly-retained attorney to Raney. The detective noticed Robin's bravado weakening.

"Sure."

"And next you're going to come back and say it's arson. I knew that yesterday. That's what they told my lawyer. And you're going to come back and say, 'We found your fingerprint on the space heater, so you must have started it.'"

"I can understand that concern, but give us some credit. I know your fingerprints are going to be all over the house."

"I'm sitting here finding I have to prove that I wasn't there. And how do I go about doing that?"

"I'm not asking you to do that. All I'm asking you to do is help us figure out what started the fire."

Robin could not leave it at that. She agreed to go to the sheriff's office again to convince Raney of her innocence.

* * *

Joan lent moral support to Robin by accompanying her to Raney's office, but she was not allowed into the interrogation room. Another officer kept Joan occupied elsewhere in the building while Raney concentrated on Robin.

Back in the same small interview room, Raney told Robin he wanted to talk about suspicions that had arisen since they had last spoken. Robin had some questions too, she said, and Raney promised to try to answer them.

"The stuff with the bank accounts. Why would people bring that up?" He scrutinized Robin's face.

"I beg your pardon?" Robin stiffened. "What do they bring up?"

"That there's three bank accounts and that you've been shifting 'em into your name or moving money toward you."

Her explanation seemed to go on forever, and she stressed that she had to take care of Randy's money. Raney's eyes began to glaze over. With Robin there was seldom a simple, abbreviated answer for a simple question. She seemed to enjoy weaving her explanations into long narratives stitched together with anecdotes.

"Oh, so you like have to control –"

"I hafta control his money…a whole $365," Robin sneered, then did an about-face and said, "He's better at money than I am. I spend it, he doesn't." Robin spoke in the present tense as if Randy were still alive.

"Anything moved into, like, your name that had been in his name or something…like the Mazda?"

"Right. That was in both our names...we both signed off on it."

"Another thing along this line. Somebody brought up that he [Randy] had changed his Social Security check somehow."

"Okay," Robin took a breath and launched into another long recital. "His mother – September of '90, I believe it was – his mother's a bitch," Robin interrupted herself. "She had my brother-in-law take Randy to Social Security to have me taken off. She felt that I didn't control his money well enough. And I said, 'June, you can have this $365 and manage it yourself.' We were not getting along, mind you."

"And this is January '90?" Raney asked.

"No, last month. Or this last week. I got this letter from Social Security addressed to him. Well, I just open all the mail, and I read it, and I confronted him with it."

"Uh-huh."

"And he said, 'Well, my mother says since we're separating that you shouldn't control my money.' And I said, 'Fine.' We got into an argument over it. I said, 'Sign the damn paper, send it in, and then you get outta my house because I'm not gonna support you.' Because he'll take that money and blow it," she said.

Raney was again surprised at the contradiction in Robin's statement.

"What else do you think they're going to say?"

"Lemme tell ya a little bitta background. I met Randy in March of '88. When I met him, he had absolutely no contact with anyone in his family. We got married in June of that year. I had a hysterectomy in August of that year. When I was in the hospital, she called me and said, 'Robin, this is Mom Row.' Never talked to her in my life. She was trying to find Randy. There's two brothers and a sister that don't even talk to him but they were at the memorial service today. I would have liked to have thrown 'em out."

"Who are they? If you don't mind."

Robin went down the list of brothers, sisters, and in-laws. "His other sister, the only good one in the family, is Janet. Her and I are very close. She told me that she doesn't associate with her family at all. Randy's the only one she associates with."

"Okay."

"[June] just came entwined in our lives. She's the typical mother-in-law, has always meddled. Randy got in his motorcycle accident in

81

October of '89, and that started the big battle because they didn't want him to go to the VA [Veteran's Hospital]. He had to go to the VA because we had no insurance. At that time we had that policy that I told you about, through West One. And that's why we never closed that account because the premiums went through there. I'm not gonna hide anything from ya," Robin assured Raney.

"I appreciate that."

"And she made the comment, 'Well, if he dies, you'll have $100,000.' He's only in there two hours fighting for his life, and she's saying crap like this?"

"Uh-huh." Raney let her ramble.

"That wasn't enough. In July or August, she went over and saw Randy and told him – 'cause she's trying to isolate him – she's telling him Janet, his sister, and I are having an affair."

"Uh-huh."

"When he burnt himself – I was never told that head injuries sometimes have seizures – it was February 6 of last year, of '91. Tabitha was sitting against the wall, Joshua's back was to the kitchen. Randy was making me a cup of tea; he does every morning. He picked up the pot of hot water to pour it and had a seizure. My daughter started screaming, and I turned around, and he was jerking on the floor. The paramedics came; they put him on Dilantin. His brother made the comment to my children, 'Did your mother pour that hot water on Dad?' To my kids!"

"Just by telling me the story, you're giving me a good understanding…just keep going."

She did. Robin went on about her history with her mother-in-law. It was tedious and time-consuming but Raney was sifting out a lot of background as she prattled on.

"We got to the point where I said, 'I can't put up with your family anymore. I want a divorce.'"

"If my timing's about right from what I've heard, throw in the deal when Joan comes into the picture here."

"I met Joan through my job. I really like her. My kids are real fond of her. Randy didn't start disliking her, though, until that summer because after bingo we would go out and have tea, coffee until 1 o'clock, and he

82

started to get angry about that. The violence started getting real bad in December. Joan said she suspected something was wrong 'cause of my mood swings, but, see, I didn't talk about it because I was ashamed."

"You should probably be more specific about the violence."

"Well, he would get mad if Joan and I were together. He would just slap me or keep me locked in the house so I couldn't leave. It escalated in January. He bruised my ribs; I had to have a CT scan at St. Luke's, and I have a bruise on my brain wall because he was hitting me in the ear. He would yell a lot. His personality changed after his accident. When I told him I was getting a divorce, it escalated. The kids and I left several times and would go over and stay with Joan. I think Danny noticed that I was favoring an arm."

"What had he done?"

"Twisted it. He would twist it behind my back if I tried to leave the house when he didn't want me to go, and he'd lock me in and took the phone away."

"What did he do to your face?"

"He had hit me and I had a bruise. I had a Band-Aid on it so nobody [at the YWCA] would notice. I told 'em I'd cut myself shaving and every-body laughed. It was that same week that he hurt my wrist. And, like I said, this weekend he asked me if he could have the kids. I let him."

"Uh-huh."

"I talked to him Sunday night and said, 'Take the kids to school; we'll sit down and talk about this.' I think he thought I meant coming back. But then he called back and said, 'I'm locking you outta the house.' And that was the last time I talked to him."

"Go ahead."

"Randy decided that he wanted the kids all weekend. And he kinda wasn't gonna let me see 'em type thing. And Joan said, 'Call the sheriff's department.' So I finally told her, 'Okay, I'll call.' And I never did. She thinks I did, and don't tell her I didn't call, she'll be so disappointed.

"When the abuse started happening, I lied to him to get outta the house. I'd say I'm going to work...most of the time I went over to Danny's. I'll tell ya some rumors I've heard this week. I heard Danny and I – I fell in love with Danny so I killed my family to be with him. That one pissed me off," Robin said without much rancor. She was becoming

83

quite comfortable with Raney. They were gabbing like old friends now, Robin doing most of the talking, Raney listening and encouraging.

"Were you and Danny – exactly what was your relationship?"

"Best friends. We did not sleep together. I was married. He is involved with somebody back in Boston, the mother of his children."

"One of the things I heard is that somebody has seen you two kissing. Could that be?"

Robin let out an air-filled snort, accompanied by a "how absurd" expression. "On my birthday…and it was on the cheek." Robin nearly blushed and began to describe Danny with the pride of a new mother.

"He's a financial person. He's very boring too. He's my best friend. He's probably a little bit more intelligent than I am. And when he starts talking about mutual funds, he just loses me."

"Umm, I guess that's my other question. If there's anything more," Raney nudged.

"He rented a room for me one night in his name because I couldn't get out of the house.

"Well, you can hear this one on the other side, can't ya?" The two shared a conspiratorial giggle.

"Yeah, I know. I know. But he did not stay with me." Robin was becoming even more relaxed and loquacious.

"Make it simple on me. What motel?" Raney asked, his smile lingering on his face and in his voice.

"Red Lion."

"And when was that?"

"I think it was a Saturday, January 18th or the 25th. We didn't do anything, but nobody's gonna know that. He's my best friend. He's just a nice guy." Wearing a shy smile Robin leaned closer, purposefully laying her hand on Raney's thigh. Looking unabashedly into his eyes, she commented, "He's handsome and charming, like you."

Her come-on came from left field – from out of the ballpark, in fact. Raney had run into eyelash-batting suspects before, and he knew he had to shut it down right away to retain his authoritative posture.

"Uh, any other motels?" Raney laughed.

"No. I stayed at the Red Lion another time, too. I don't like sleazy places."

84

Raney went over the weekend prior to the fire, clarifying Robin's whereabouts each day. She told him that she had left Joan's at 8:30 or 9 a.m. on Saturday morning.

"I didn't tell her I was going home, though. Didn't tell her Sunday either. 'Cause she would've lectured me…because she didn't want me to be alone with him," Robin laughed. Her voice suggested that she was pleased and even a little giddy that she had circumvented Joan, put one over on her persistent, protective friend. "She's my surrogate mother."

"What did she think you were doing?"

"I don't know," Robin threw up her hands, her inflection suggesting, it doesn't matter. "I probably told her I went to a friend's or something. I don't know."

Raney was getting tired. Getting to the bare bones of Robin's activities that weekend was difficult. Drinking coffee helped as he concentrated to keep from getting lost in the maze of details. To make it even more difficult, Joan had given him an almost entirely different version of the same weekend.

Talking about Sunday, Robin rattled on, "He [Randy] was real agitated, antsy, and at the time I didn't know what was going on."

Robin's chronology was jumbled and sometimes the actions she described didn't fit with the circumstances she outlined. But Raney couldn't complain that she wasn't talking.

"We picked out a movie. Okay, I think I made a mistake. I think it was Sunday that they got the videos and stuff at Video Excitement, not Saturday.

"Anyways, they were gonna go to that double feature and then go out and get something to eat. We hardly ever eat at home. I didn't have any time to cook," Robin jabbered on merrily. "Didn't have the time to clean my house either. My daughter did it. Which I noticed on the news that night, too. Something she had done that was unusual. I'm assuming she did it. Well, I had these…plastic tablecloths that you use on picnic tables."

"Uh-huh," Robin hadn't noticed that Raney was no longer joining her in the animated jollity of the conversation. He was serious, intent on observing Robin's baffling behavior – her blithe indifference. He kept expecting tears.

"I recognized the plastic tablecloth because I remember looking at it and saying, 'Why didn't that melt?' Then she had my gingerbread doll sitting on the wood stove. So she was playing house again. Which – she made it worse, but that's okay," Robin laughed.

"Lemme back up for a little bit." Robin's dialogue was now like a runaway train, and Raney needed to take a mental pause before going on. He bought time by trying to clarify details.

"I don't mean to be rude, but what does this all hafta do with anything?" Robin said with a slight edge to her voice.

"Just trying to figure out what happened."

"But it wasn't the same time. I mean, I could understand if you were saying, 'Well let's talk about what you did during 4:00, 4:30 when the fire started.'"

"Well, at this point, I'm just looking for anything that they might have done."

"Okay. Yeah, 'cause I remember seeing on the TV [news broadcast showing the gut of Robin's home] the heater, which should explain why you asked me about it. 'Cause when you asked me about it, I'm saying, 'Whatta you care about the stupid heater for?' Well, I didn't know it was in the house. I assumed it was in the garage. And that's what kind of started me off that Randy was doing something. And I told Joan about it. So we're thinking, well, maybe 'cause he ripped some of my clothes up and smashed some knickknacks, and he was in a rage."

"Recently?"

"Oh, yeah. It was Friday or Saturday."

"Just out of anger?"

"Yeah, it's not the first time. I used to say, 'Why when you get mad is it always my stuff you break?' Stupid question," Robin laughed. "He's not gonna break his own."

"What'd he do with your clothes?"

"He just ripped 'em up. It looked like he probably used a razor blade or a hunting knife. Then I took the ones that he slashed and threw 'em away. Lemme take that back. I threw 'em on the floor in the living room 'cause I was angry. I yanked 'em offa the hangers and screamed and hollered at him whiles I was doing it. Went downstairs, threw 'em in a pile on the floor and said, 'Now, look…you see what your father did?' My poor children. They didn't need to live that way," Robin said. Her voice was flat, dispassionate.

Robin didn't mention the Sunday afternoon trip to Ontario with Danny. She said that Tabitha had called to say good night. She chattered about her children with a casual lilt to her voice that Raney found very disturbing.

"Joshua got on, and this is sad, he started to give me a lecture on my life. My last conversation with him was not pleasant. And I said, 'Joshua, just get off my back.'"

"What'd he say?" Raney asked.

"'Oh, Mom, you're hurting Dad' and 'You can't get a divorce' and 'Why aren't you home?' And finally I said, 'Joshua, get off my back. It's time for bed.' But I did, you know, when we hung up [say], 'Good night, I love you. See ya in the morning.' And that was the last time I talked to them. Ever. And Randy called a couple of times after that and just argued with me." Still with no tears in her eyes or in her voice, the sigh that escaped Robin's lips sounded like she was perturbed with her family for pestering her rather than sad that they were gone.

Robin told Raney that Randy was angry over hearing the rumor that she was filing for divorce and another rumor that Danny and Robin were hanging all over each other.

"Lemme give you a little history here. Danny is attractive. Randy suspected way back then that we were fooling around. We weren't even friends then...yet. I used to tell Randy all the time, and I still do, 'Randy, I told you if I ever have an affair, I will tell you before I do it.' I am basically not a dishonest person as far as things like that."

"He called a couple of times, and then he called probably around 11:00 or so...I remembered – and I don't even know if I'm gonna tell ya this yet because I remembered part of the conversation after I talked to ya the other night, and if I say it, it's gonna look bad – so I won't."

"I don't –" Raney started.

Robin launched into her account without any encouragement. "Well, I told him, 'Randy, don't call me again.' And he turned around and said, 'I won't call you again unless the house burns down.' And I said, 'Don't say that,' because he knows how I feel about that 'cause of Keith."

"Let's start –"

"I'm tired."

"This can be a real important conversation. Let's start with, you answer the phone."

"Okay. The call came around 11:00, a little after. I said, 'What are you calling me for now?' And I don't remember what he said. Oh, yeah, uh, locking me outta the house. And I said I wasn't coming home anyways. [Randy said] 'Well, just in case you think about it.' And then I said, 'Randy, don't call me again.' I was really, really agitated. And he said, 'Oh, don't worry, I won't call unless the house burns down.' And I said, 'Don't say that, you know how I feel about that.'" Robin spoke as if she were gossiping with a neighbor about an acquaintance. She glanced at her watch.

"He always says these little things like, 'You won't see me again' or 'Don't worry about the divorce; I got it taken care of.' In other words, hinting that he's gonna kill himself. And I don't fall for it. I remember one time I went home the next day and I said, 'Oh, you're here.' I'm real cold," Robin laughed. "I know it sounds cold, but you gotta – this marriage was a mess. He said, 'Well, you know, sometimes it doesn't always work out.' And I said, 'Oh, you're telling me you took an OD and puked it up?'" Robin sounded exasperated with her late husband.

"Lemme back up here –"

"Okay. I said, 'Just take the children to school in the morning, and I will be over and we will discuss this.' I think he thought I meant our marriage, getting back together, but…I wanted to discuss finding him a place to live. 'Cause I knew if I didn't, he'd call me a hundred more times. It was in that conversation that he said…'I found your journal; pretty nice stuff.' He said, 'I destroyed it.' I said, 'How?' He said he burnt it," Robin sighed, as if even thinking about Randy irked her. "It was one of those conversations, too, that he couldn't live without me and the kids, that we had to work it out."

"So you go to sleep after this?"

"I think so."

"Was anybody else up? Danny or anybody?"

"Oh, no, Danny goes to bed at 2:00 in the afternoon it seems. He goes to bed when Ryan does," Robin chuckled.

"Did you go to sleep?"

"Yeah, I went to sleep. And then I told ya how I woke up at 3:00 not feeling quite right."

"Okay. Just out of curiosity, what was the feeling that you had?"

"My stomach was in knots and...I don't know. I couldn't explain it. I just felt uncomfortable. Did a load of laundry."

"Why did you do laundry at 3:00 in the morning?"

"Something to do."

"Well, didn't it wake other people up?"

"No. Joan told me later she heard it."

Raney had to prod Robin as they wandered through a labyrinth of confusing and sometimes contradictory explanations about laundry, bingo books she had worked on, and her shower.

"Let me back up just a little. What was the feeling like? What were you worried about?"

"I just felt something wasn't right when I was in the shower."

"Do you remember what time you woke up Joan?"

"No. Joan remembers looking at her clock, but we found out later that her clock was set an hour ahead," Robin snickered. "When we got to Overland and Five Mile, I told her, 'Oh, forget it; nothing's wrong.' My feeling had gone away."

"What was your first thought when you saw what was going on? Were the flames still going?"

"Yes, yes," Robin said. "I looked up and saw the flames coming outta Joshua's room and realized." Robin's retelling was detached as if it were someone else's story – no catches in her voice, no emotion.

"Paramedics came over, and I started running towards the house, 'cause he said something like, 'Boy, you run fast in heels.'"

Raney remembered her pointing out a pair of tennis shoes that she said she had worn that night.

As if she had told the story a thousand times and was tired of it, Robin continued in a singsong rhythm. "They kept asking me the names. They were asking me where they were sleeping. They'd already found Joshua...but they couldn't find Tabitha.

"And Joshua was in a van, and I was babbling about putting a blanket on him 'cause he gets cold. And then the lady, Barbara, kept saying,

'It's okay to cry.' And I said, 'No, it's not. I don't cry in public.' And I said, 'I can't because I always tell Joshua not to cry, be a big boy.'"

"Tough," Raney sympathized.

"The coroner came in and told me that he was gonna take 'em down for autopsies…Why didn't they do the kids?"

"Yet."

"Oh, they haven't done 'em yet. Are they going to?"

"Yeah."

"Well, he called me and told me that they died of a lethal dose of carbon monoxide. He told me what Tabitha was wearing. He said she had on shorts, pink shorts, which I found amazing that they could tell me that. And a flowered top. And I said, 'Yeah, she never wears PJs.' He told me that Joshua was burnt on his legs and his back, but he didn't tell me what he was wearing. But Joshua always wore pajamas."

Raney noticed there were still no breaks in Robin's voice.

"Well, let me give you a minute to pull together here," Raney made the considerate comment given the subject matter, even though Robin didn't seem to have anything to pull together.

"Thank you."

"Can I get you anything – coffee?"

"No, I'm fine. I don't drink it. Do you know all cops smoke and drink coffee on TV?" Robin quipped.

Robin asked Raney to not close the door all the way. Then she got up, stretched, adjusted her clothing, and sat still as a portrait model.

Her behavior was so bizarre, like nobody the detective had ever seen. Even the hard-core cons – murderers, thieves, rapists – displayed more emotion. He had to break through Robin's barrier to her feelings. The detective planned to aim his next arrow at Robin's past.

CHAPTER THIRTEEN

Detective Raney resumed the interview, treading lightly to see if Robin would volunteer any critical information about her past.

"Is there anything you think somebody's gonna throw up? I mean, not throw up like vomit, but bring up, you know?" Raney asked.

"For instance? Who? My family? Their family?"

"I don't know."

"I told Randy all about it, but, see, when I came to Idaho, that closed a whole chapter in my life, and I've been a good girl."

Robin wasn't enthusiastic about opening that book, especially to a detective. Raney wasn't getting anywhere using subtlety, but he had an advantage – he had already researched her past.

"You know you've got a warrant in New Hampshire?" Raney cut to the chase.

"Do I?" Robin said, with a steady gaze and a giggle.

"Yeah."

"Oh, no, I didn't. I haven't been in New Hampshire except to visit my mom in over ten years." Robin refused to acknowledge a warrant could still be valid from that long ago.

"Is it North Carolina you did some prison time?" Raney moved on to the next chapter.

"Uh-huh. Uh-huh."

"That was for what?"

"Fraud."

"And what was that about?"

"Checks, fraud – checks."

"How much time did you do? Four-year sentence, right?"

"Yeah. Ten months, eleven months. Something like that." She was beginning to realize Raney had done his homework. "I'm not proud of my past. I'm just trying to rebuild."

"No problem. It's just so I understand it."

"I knew you'd go down and check. I've just been waiting for you," Robin said with false savvy and a smug smile.

"Have you done any other prison time except North Carolina?"

"No. No."

"Any extended jail time?"

"Yeah. In California. Good ol' Chuck." Robin remembered the detective that had hounded her years before.

"And what was that for? Like did you ever get, like, a 36-month suspended sentence, some probation, or –"

"I've been on probation before, but I was really young."

"What's your main – problem?"

"Checks. Everything was to do with things like that." Elbow on desk, Robin propped her head with her chin in her hand.

"Forgery-type checks?"

"Yeah, uh-huh."

"Or for writing checks on closed accounts?"

"Both. Both," Robin responded.

"Have you ever had anything that wasn't check related? Let's start with that."

"Don't think so."

"Okay. Because as I remember, they were all like checks or fraud…or embezzlement."

"Yeah."

"Just briefly, what was the embezzlement?"

"Umm, I did nine months county time, I think it was in Pine Creek. I worked for this lady –"

"Scam the books?" Raney cut to the chase again.

"Yeah, that's exactly what it was. 'Cause you can find that out real easy. I'm sure it's on its way now with Chuck." Robin's smile was artificial.

"Has anybody ever accused you of arson?"

"Well, when my house burned down...it came up."

"In Pine Creek?"

"Yeah."

"Let's leave Pine Creek alone for a minute. Nowhere else?"

"No."

"Ever associated with anybody?"

"I was gonna say my first husband, but I didn't know that he did. I knew he got picked up for it after we got together."

"For arson?"

"Yeah, him and a friend – his car."

"Insurance fraud thing?"

"Yeah, that's what it was."

"And where was that?"

"New Hampshire."

"Okay. Let's talk about the fire [in California]."

"Let's not," Robin shook her head. Just ask me questions."

"As I understand it, there was a cabin kind of a house that's out in a remote area."

"Summerville. Oh, yes. And the town was maybe two miles long. You blink, and you passed it."

"Okay. You and Keith are home and you wake up at night?"

"Yeah, it was about 1:30 in the morning, I guess. My cat woke me up...jumped on me."

"Okay. This is like a small place, right?"

"Yes, umm, four rooms, a little lean-to type thing. The living room was completely on fire and his room was off the living room. I remember running to the neighbor's, and I don't remember anything else. I can tell you what they TOLD me. But I do not remember."

"And what was that?"

"They said that I ran back in, and Doug Trowbridge, who was an EMT plus works for the Forest Service, pulled me out; and just as he pulled me out, they said it collapsed. They said it probably took five minutes to consume because it was made of pecky cedar."

"I don't have a clue what that is," Raney said.

"It's a fast-burning wood, from what they tell me."

"And...you were injured?"

"Yeah. Just burnt a little and a lotta smoke inhalation. And I was hospitalized."

"For three weeks?"

"It seems like three weeks. It could have been three months or three days. I honestly don't remember."

"Why were you suspected of arson?"

"I don't know. I don't remember. I have blocked that incident completely, as much as I can."

"Umm." Raney let silence build tension.

"I remember taking a polygraph test. I thought I passed until I found out I didn't. But Ellison was telling me," Robin went on quickly, "that he's had innocent people take it and not pass and guilty people take it and pass. So he told me I wasn't taking one." Robin referred again to her lawyer, Ellison Matthews.

Talking about law enforcement in the Pine Creek/Summerville area, Robin spouted, "I don't like any of 'em. They're just jerks there. I swear to God they're all crooked. I don't trust the cops there. Everybody sleeps with everybody, and everybody knows it."

"Oh, I think that's small town anywhere. The reason you were suspected of arson?" Raney said, getting back on track.

Robin stared straight ahead for several seconds before responding. "You'll have to read it in the report."

"Insurance?"

"No."

"Didn't have any insurance?"

"No. They said I did. I remember – well, either that or they were bluffing."

"But you never got any insurance money?" Raney persisted.

"No."

"'Cause I –"

"That's easy to check," Robin finished his sentence for him.

"Yeah," Raney agreed.

"That's not true," Robin said, as if suddenly struck by a memory. "Yes. My husband had a policy that we collected on while we were still married."

"Who was your husband?"

"Wayne – Hamilton."

"Did he get money?"

"I got it. I got it."

"Is that the $25,000?" Detective Ken Smith interjected. He had been quietly observing the interrogation until now.

"Something like that, yeah. 'Cause I sent most of it to my mother. See, he knows." Robin tossed an accusing look at Detective Smith. "You guys can check this. Whatta you asking me for?"

"It's that line between honesty and dishonesty," Smith said.

"So you knew, and I didn't remember so you thought I was lying. That's not fair," Robin sniveled with a crooked smirk.

"Twenty-five-thousand dollars is an amount that most people don't forget about." Smith was tired of playing softball.

"I – believe me, I've forgotten that whole thing. But, yeah, I remembered it after. I'm not intentionally hiding it."

"Okay. You said the fire – I think you said the other night that it was electrical," Raney stated.

"Uh-huh. That's what they told me."

"Who told you that?"

"Probably Chuck."

"Just outta general information, why is it that you dislike Chuck so much?"

Robin paused before answering. "I caught him doing something that I didn't approve of, and I'll just leave it at that. Everybody sleeps with everybody in small towns…and he's married and she was only 16, and I didn't approve."

"So, it didn't have anything to do with the fire?"

"Oh, no. I disliked him before then. That town is so small everybody knows everybody. I'm really surprised he's still there. I was hoping he wasn't. Because I – I know what he's gonna fill your head with when – you're both cops…I don't trust him."

"Do you distrust the California Fire Marshal's Office?"

"No."

"Well, I'm getting their report, too. So I'll read theirs, and I figure that as far as the arson that they probably –"

"Well," Robin said haughtily, "if it was arson, they never arrested me for it…and they would have if they thought they had a case."

Raney had taken this line of questioning far enough for now. Robin's slander against Detective Chuck Sanborn looked like a vendetta, a technique to shift the attention away from herself. Based on information he had collected and his gut instinct, Raney was beginning to realize that, at the very least, his suspect was an accomplished liar and a fraud; at most, she was a serial murderer, but he needed more information to show the prosecutor.

Raney now changed the focus of his interview to Robin's daughter, Kristina, born October 14, 1975, in Nashua, New Hampshire. Robin had just turned 18 when the baby girl was born. Her older son Keith, born to the 16-year-old mother, was a toddler.

"When did she die?" Raney asked.

Robin answered, "one, thirty-one, seventy-seven," propping her head up with her hand as if it were a burdensome weight.

"Can you tell me a little about that?"

Speaking quietly, Robin said, "It was SIDS. They did an autopsy, couldn't find a cause, so that's what they labeled it as. Crib death."

Robin continued, "At first they thought the dog did it. I mean, my mother had a very large dog, and they thought maybe he had, you know, laid on her. But there was no, umm, they can tell if there's hairs…and choking or suffocating, and they said there wasn't anything like that."

"Do YOU think it was SIDS?"

"That's what they told me."

"Do you have any reason [to think] otherwise?"

"Not at all."

"Did she have any other medical problems?"

"Oh, yeah, she was sick. She was real sick."

"Whatta ya mean by that?"

"She had bronchial pneumonia, like, she died in the winter, but the months before, like, six times. And she had a skin disease that she would be raw from. We used to hafta tie her in her crib to keep her arms straight 'cause of her elbows, they were so raw."

"The reason I asked you is that it's almost unheard of for a 15-month-old to die of SIDS." Raney jumped in with both feet. It was time to take off the toeshoes and start treading a little heavier.

"And it's also unheard of for a 33-year-old, but I know someone that was 33, and now they say it was probably AIDS. Back then they didn't know about AIDS so – but, yeah, they umm – and, as a matter of fact, I can save ya a lotta time on that. They investigated that –"

"Whatta you mean investigated?"

"Child Protection. You know, out there when Joshua was born. And he went to a foster home 'cause I went to jail. Well, the lady that was handling it sent for copies of the death certificate and everything. In California."

"Do you know what her death certificate said?"

"I have no idea, I've never seen it – and there was no insurance on her at all."

"The reason I ask, obviously…it's unusually tragic for somebody to lose four kids."

"You told me that already. I'm not meant to have children; I'm meant to work with 'em."

Raney felt he had exhausted that route and moved on to questions about the storage unit. Robin admitted that she and Randy had rented a storage unit in Meridian. "Randy always goes out there. I don't even know the code."

"What's in the storage unit?"

"Umm, YWCA bingo chairs…umm, summer fans, Christmas decorations, Halloween decorations, bean bag –"

"Any personal –"

"Personal, like my dolls, music boxes, things like that. We were planning on moving at one point, and that's why we got it. Most of it's our couch and seasonal stuff."

Detective Smith now took the reins, moving into a different area.

"Someone told us that you told them about Randy getting arrested for beating you up. And you told 'em when he was gonna get arraigned. In fact, there actually were two or three people that you told that to." Smith waited for her reaction.

"I know. Joan thinks he was arrested. 'Cause she kept pressuring me, so I just said sure."

"So you just were telling people that he got arrested for beating ya up." Ken kept the heat on.

"I remember I was going to press charges against him."

97

"But you…never, ever, ever, never called the police."

"No, I did not," Robin said flatly. "You guys would know that."

"So, I mean, why would you say something like that?" Smith wasn't going to let her slip out of this one, no matter how hard she wriggled and squirmed.

"To get 'em off my back."

"No, these people actually liked Randy more than you," Smith said bluntly.

"Randy more than me?" Robin's eyes grew incredulous. "I have no idea who you're talking about then. Because if they were Randy's friends, I wouldn't talk to 'em."

"In fact, you told them that Randy got arrested for beatin' ya up and that he was gonna get arraigned, like, Thursday at 1:30. Pretty specific kinda information."

"No, I never did."

Ken wasn't wearing her down much, maybe frustrating her somewhat. Raney took over again.

"This is backing up a little bit. You said that Randy would sometimes flip the power off to Tabitha's room so she couldn't watch TV."

"We used to get into a fight about that all the time."

"That's been going on for quite a while?"

"Since we bought the TVs in November."

"I'm still a little confused over why you just wouldn't take the TV away or –"

"Ask Randy…that's what he did," Robin snorted. "He does lotsa things that I cannot explain to you that would make me angry."

"Wouldn't that affect other things?"

"No, he said it was only her room. I know it couldn't have affected the bathroom light because the night-light was still on. Because the kids hafta have a night-light."

"Yeah. Which makes sense. When he'd get up or you'd get up before him, did you notice that it affected anything else? Lights or plug-ins or anything else?" Raney asked.

"I didn't notice, no. Why?" Robin's answers were becoming frosty.

"Well, it just seems strange that you would mention that," Smith said. "So, on nights when he would have turned out the power, obviously, you –"

"Tell me what the heck the TV being off has got to do with the fire." Sparks began to flash from Robin's flinty eyes.

"Well, quite obviously, it turned off more than the TV," Raney chimed in.

"Well, it would turn off the…electricity in her room."

"It's unusual for anybody on the outside looking in that you'd turn off all the power to this section of the house to turn off the TV. I mean, there's a thousand easier ways to do it."

"Not to him. He wouldn't disconnect the TV. We fought over this, Gary."

"You don't use the upstairs at all?" Raney asked.

"What does this hafta do with the fire? It is a TV!"

"Well, it's also a smoke detector." Raney remarked.

"So it looks like I turned off the smoke detector so they wouldn't wake up." Now Robin was getting the idea, and she wasn't happy.

"Well, naw, it's not even that simple – " Smith said.

"Come on, guys. I have a right to know."

"It also turns off all the power in the bathroom, so the night-light can't be on." Smith didn't realize the can of worms he had just opened.

"No, it does not. That night-light is ON. I KNOW it's on," Robin stubbornly brayed. "I'll go back there and show you!"

"It turns off the smoke detector and the power to the plug-ins to the bathroom." Raney challenged.

By focusing so intently on the night-light issue, Robin was circumventing the main point of the accusation.

"The night-light is on in that bathroom!" Robin insisted.

"Okay. Okay." Raney pleaded. "I mean, we can check that out and –"

"Fine! But the night-light is on! I swear to you it is on!" Robin showed more emotion over the night-light issue than either detective had seen from her so far.

"Okay. I believe ya," Raney said, changing the subject. "Couple of people overheard Joshua recently saying that he told you that if you got a divorce, he and Tabitha were going with Randy."

"Uh-huh."

"How'd that strike ya?"

"Made me angry."

99

"Why would he go with Randy rather than you?"

"Probably because Randy spends more time with him. They would've never went with him, though. I wouldn't have let 'em."

Raney's next line of questioning was about Randy's physical therapy after his release from the hospital after his accident.

"Somebody said that you supposedly kept him from – he was supposed to, like, walk or ride a bike or do something like that for therapy at home and that you discouraged that."

"They're lying...I KNOW what you're thinking...Like my bingo players were telling me, 'Well, Robin, you're a battered wife and just couldn't take it anymore and you killed him.' There – and I know that's what you think too. That's why I don't wanna even be here talking to you. Because now I'm getting mad because you're saying things – I'm being honest with you."

"I –"

"I'm being fair. And you come out with playing games about a circuit breaker for a damn TV. Why didn't you just tell me it puts out everything else? Why play games with me, Gary?"

"If I told you the answer and then asked you the questions, it wouldn't do any good. Right?"

"Right. I'm sorry. I'm just getting irritable. People don't know how to shut up. What I do in my life is nobody's business. That's what makes me angry. If I wanna have 14 checking accounts, if I'm not doing anything illegal, nobody should care. You guys are taking my whole life and exposing it."

"No, we're not."

"The media is having a field day 'cause I wasn't home. I didn't know I had to announce to the world that I was getting a divorce and that's why I wasn't there. I think if one more person asks me why I wasn't in that house, I'm gonna scream."

"Bear with me and get mad at them later."

"We were getting divorced. Whether he liked it or not. People get divorced every day. Go on with your next question, please," Robin snapped.

Raney asked Robin if Randy was taking any medication for his violence. "He was given medication by a doctor over a year ago," she replied, "but didn't take it." This contradicted what she had told Joan and others about his medication making him violent.

Determined to pin her down, Smith tried to get Robin to explain the inconsistencies about Randy kidnapping the children.

"You made this kind of show...Randy's beating you; you're calling the police and that now he's kidnapped your kids."

"I never said that." Robin jumped on Smith with claws extended. Suddenly calm, she sat back in her chair, replacing her angry countenance with an insipid expression.

"Did you tell anybody that the police were gonna arrest him Monday morning when he dropped off the kids?"

"No."

"You never told anybody that?"

"I do not recall that."

Smith was like a bulldog with his teeth in the cat, and he wouldn't let go even when she began to scratch and hiss.

"You don't re – "

"That does it! Wait a minute! What does this all matter? It has nothing to do with the fire!" Robin screeched, leaning forward. "Nothing at all! Not a damn thing!"

"Well, now, if I'm going to kill somebody, and I'm gonna –"

"I'm leaving."

"Well, I guess my theory here is...you're painting a picture of a guy that's off the deep end."

"Uh-huh." Robin grunted sarcastically.

"And then the next thing you know, gosh, he burns down his house and kills the kids because he's so distraught about all these things that have been going on."

"I never said that. I never said he was distraught and was gonna burn down the house."

"No, but...people put two and two together and say, 'Well, gosh, here's a seemingly pretty nice guy that everybody kinda liked. And, the next thing you know...the police are arresting him for beating his wife. So, if the police arrested him, then it musta happened."

"It's none of their business. Plain and simple.'"

"But you're telling people that."

"I'm done. I'm leaving. If you wanna arrest me, arrest me. But I think I have done enough."

Raney jumped in, "Well, Robin –"

"I'm really getting angry. First, you don't tell me the truth about the circuit breaker, and then, you know, you made a big thing outta the –"

"Okay," Raney said.

"Her TV's off. You didn't know Randy!" Robin exclaimed.

"What Ken's trying to tell ya is that the overall picture here is that there are people who think you built up to this. That you've been thinking about it a while and that you built up to this, using these beating stories and moving out."

"Then let 'em think it. That's how I feel. Let 'em think it."

"But none of that happened. So then it starts to be a matter of credibility. Those are the two things right now that we know that you told a large number of people that weren't honest. It's all boiling down to your credibility," Smith added.

"But, wait a minute. I wasn't there, first of all." Robin ignored the inference to her lies about the abuse and kidnapping.

"Well, but how do we –" Smith began.

"So I couldn't have done it."

"– know that? Because you told us?"

"Nobody could get in the house. It was locked."

"How do you know that?" Smith asked.

"He told me he locked me out! He does it all the time!"

"What if we told you that he didn't lock ya out?" Smith posed.

"Well, I didn't know that. 'Cause he told me he did."

"Well, but how do we know that he told ya he did?"

"I guess you don't. He told Joan."

"The ultimate point is that you had keys to the house," Raney pointed out.

"Yes, I did have a key to the house. But the key does not unlock the top lock."

"But the top lock wasn't locked."

"But I didn't know that," Robin would not back down.

"Well, how do we know that?" Smith matched his suspect's mulish insistence.

"You don't," Robin pouted.

"Okay. You could have gotten in then."

"Yeah, I guess I could've. Do you want me to tell ya how I did it now?" Robin mocked.

"Yeah," Smith challenged her, enjoying the sparring, using his "bad cop" style to paint her into a corner.

"I didn't. Are we done?…I wanna go home."

Using their best strategies, the detectives had been questioning Robin, who was rapidly becoming their number one suspect, for over two hours. They had uncovered inconsistencies and definite lies, but they weren't breaking her down to the point of getting a confession.

"I spend every day here, and I know exactly how you feel, but I'm trying to get this resolved. I think you would want to, too," Raney said.

"Okay. What else do you have?" Robin relaxed a little, allowing herself to be charmed.

Trying another tactic, Raney attempted to pry a confession from this stolid woman by using a well-worn technique.

"Is there any reason why somebody would see you stepping outside Joan's house Sunday morning when you were doing the washing? Did you step outside for fresh air…or did you go out for a walk or anything?"

"I don't recall. I don't remember. And it wasn't important."

"It's important," Raney said.

"Oh…I don't believe so. Well, when Joan and I left, but I don't believe so other than that."

"You're absolutely sure?"

"Yeah."

Dead end. Raney moved on.

"Randy ever ask you to go to marriage counseling?"

"Yes."

"And what was your response?"

"We went to one. And she was, 'You need to do this for Randy 'cause he's been in an accident. You need to do that.' And I finally told her, 'You can take Randy and shove him,' and I never went back."

"A week before this past Sunday…apparently the whole family was in the car; you were driving, and you and Randy got into an argument, and you smacked him in the face. The kids were in the back seat, and you got mad at Tabitha and told her that you didn't want her. Called her a silly bitch," Smith said.

"I have a question for you. If I was in the car with Randy and the two children, obviously, they couldn't have told YOU."

"But they told somebody else," Raney interjected.

"Oh, I...I never...I don't swear at my children."

"Did you hit Randy?" Smith asked.

"I hit him in the arm. He hit me in the face. I do not talk to my children that way. And I resent the implication."

"Would you have told her that you didn't want her?"

"Never."

"Would that have been around the time that they would've said that they wanted to go with him?"

"Yes. 'Cause I – Joshua said I was ruining his life because I was leaving him – leaving Randy."

"[Do you remember] saying something to the effect of Randy and the kids are driving you crazy and you need a new life?" Raney asked.

"Oh, yeah. Uh-huh. All the time," Robin responded with sarcasm. "Randy was driving me crazy."

"How about the kids?"

"Kids get on your nerves. Do you have children?"

"No."

"Okay. Kids get on your nerves sometimes. But you don't go kill 'em if they get on your nerves."

The natural current of the conversation flowed conveniently toward an eddy that Detective Smith hoped would pull Robin under, and he went with it. He wanted to create a scenario in which Robin could gracefully back away from her denials and confess.

"I don't know that anyone assumes, at this point, that you probably planned on killing them. My sense about what happened is you were angry about the kids not wanting to be with you, and you figured if Randy didn't have a home, then they'd have to come live with you."

"You're entitled to your opinion."

"Obviously, you realize, that at some point in time we're certainly looking at this in a light that would seem to implicate you as –"

"Oh, I knew that Monday night when you called me down here," Robin claimed.

"The question that we're looking at, at this point in time is, was this something that was premeditated – which is first degree murder – or was there something else going on here and things just went bad and you didn't really plan on killing 'em. It was more an accident that happened – which kind of explains why you'd show up back out there. And it certainly appears to me that we're gonna be able to make a case on ya. If it's something less than first degree murder, now'd be a real good time to start talking about it."

"They did not want to go live with him."

"They told a number of different people, school friends –"

"I find that real hard to believe."

"Be that as it may, it's the truth. Randy's talked to people that he was concerned because he knew that that was really, really upsetting you, and he flat told somebody, 'I don't know what she's gonna do because I know that really, really hurt her.' And two days later they all end up dead."

"I'm not gonna sit here and give you a confession for anything. I told you before that I felt that you would railroad me in here."

"I've been pretty damned objective through this whole thing because most people right off the bat say four kids, three accidents, she's guilty. She killed all four kids. And that's the consensus of most people. Where was she that night? Everybody asks me that question…She did it. She killed 'em," Raney stated pointedly.

"I'm just telling you what kind of impressions we're dealing with. There's the prior property crimes. And arson with your husband or whatever it was…Yep, she did it before; she's doing it now. We won't talk about Chuck. I'm not gonna argue with you. Maybe you do hate each other; maybe he's got a vendetta out for ya. But I'll get everything from the different agencies involved in it. According to him, he says it's all gonna say the same thing. That you set the fire, you caused Keith's death, and they just couldn't prove it. But I don't think you meant to kill anybody…Maybe I'm wrong…maybe you're some psychotic serial killer. Do you understand where I'm coming from?"

"I think I'm done. I think I've answered all the questions. The only thing I can say, if you gentlemen would be kind enough, if you are going to arrest me, wait until I bury my children," Robin spat.

"I'm not gonna arrest ya tonight," Raney said.

"I'm not going anywhere," Robin answered.

"What the difference is, is whether you're guilty of a fire that got outta control or whether you're guilty of three counts of first degree murder."

They'd been politely jousting for almost three hours, and Detective Raney was vexed with Robin's avoidance of the main issue. Her concentration on minor details, such as the night-light that meant very little in the scope of the bigger picture, was maddening.

✳ ✳ ✳

While Robin was being questioned, her friend Joan McHugh was embroiled in a mental arm-wrestling match with Detective Denise Webb.

"Did you know she's done it before?" Detective Webb asked.

"She didn't DO anything!" Joan was furious.

"Do you know you're in danger and that your family would have been next?"

"But you don't understand; Randy started the fire! I can't be in danger if she didn't do it. She couldn't get in the house."

"What if he didn't?"

"But he did! You go check on that damn lock! Because you're going to find that he locked her out, and he DID it."

CHAPTER FOURTEEN

On Wednesday, after the memorial service, Barbara Fawcett and Linda Kerr, the YWCA bookkeeper, had gone out for coffee. Linda voiced doubts about Robin, the implications of which neither woman wanted to believe.

When, in an effort to save money, the bingo operation had been moved to the YWCA, some of the accounting records had turned up missing. Robin claimed that all the paperwork had been lost in the move and that the bingo money from the previous Saturday night had burned in the fire. An audit was performed shortly after, and the auditors were not happy.

Linda's insinuation that one of the YWCA's most trusted employees had embezzled money was a preposterous notion to Barbara Fawcett.

"No," Barbara said to Linda, "if Robin Row would take one nickel, I don't know her at all." Barbara would have trusted Robin with her own money, her own household – even her own family.

As the two women sat mulling over the dreadful possibilities, they couldn't believe – wouldn't believe – that, even if Robin had embezzled money, she hadn't had anything to do with the tragic fire that had killed her family. How could they even think about it, Barbara thought, let alone talk about it?

Back at the YWCA after the memorial service, three employees had gone separately to the director's office to express feelings that something was amiss where Robin Row was concerned.

Janice Johnson called her staff together to discuss their concerns about Robin. Each person was surprised to learn that others had the same qualms. How could this woman who was so caring and worked so hard to help people in need take money from the YWCA and the very same people she helped?

Janice knew what she had to do. She picked up the phone and dialed the prosecutor's office.

* * *

When Detective Gary Raney heard that Robin had reported to the YWCA that the bingo files were lost and the money had been destroyed in the fire, a freeze-frame image of the files and cash box he had seen while searching the McHugh apartment flashed through his mind. This was a major inconsistency in Robin's story, one that he could present to a judge.

The embezzlement investigation was assigned to Detective Linda Scown. Her initial inquiries led her to Lynette Porter, a fraud investigator for the Department of Health and Welfare. Ultimately, the two women would spend months "exhuming the dirt" on one of the YWCA's most trusted employees, Robin Row. It soon became clear why the bingo operation had gone under, had, in fact, sunk to the bottom of its fiscal sea. Robin had done more "creative accounting" coupled with out-and-out fraud than they would probably ever be able to track.

* * *

Thursday morning, February 13, Joan and Robin went to Relyea Funeral Home to pick up Randy's effects, which included his wedding ring and belt buckle. Afterward they went shopping so Robin could buy herself some clothes with the cash donations Barbara Fawcett had given to her the day before.

When they returned to the McHughs' apartment, Robin was confronted by Detective Ken Smith and served with a warrant to seize her Mazda. She was militant in her dislike for Smith. Accompanied by expletives, she ripped the warrant in two and told him he had no right to take her car.

Robin turned on Joan after the police left, "See Joan, I let you smoke in my car; now they're going to find smoke in my car!"

Joan advised Robin to call her lawyer because it was clear that they definitely considered her a suspect now. It was ludicrous, Joan thought. Robin may have some skeletons in her closet, like everyone, but Joan would never believe she would hurt her children. Robin was a good mother.

Joan knew the day was not going to get any better when she, Bernie, and Danny were served with summonses to appear at the courthouse for a magistrate's hearing late that afternoon.

During the hearing, Deputy Ada County Prosecutor Roger Bourne questioned the McHughs under oath, trying to prove probable cause that would allow their murder case to be bound over to district court.

Bourne asked Joan several questions about the weekend before the fire and details that Robin had shared with her about the abuse. He questioned her about Robin's insurance, making the most absurd insinuations and allegations, Joan thought. Bourne also elicited from her the fact that Robin took care of all the bingo cash.

"Do you know if she had life insurance on Randy and the kids?" Bourne asked gently.

"I believe that through her job at the YWCA she had a family plan and she was the primary person who was insured."

"You kind of expect under a family plan, wouldn't you, that there'd be a certain amount of insurance on the breadwinner, the person who's making the money, and less on the kids, for instance?"

"Oh, yeah, I'm sure there was," Joan responded.

"And some on Randy? What would you expect that life insurance to be on the kids, in a dollar amount?"

"Probably not a lot. I think the one I had was $500 for each child. They figured there was enough to –"

"Cover funeral expenses?"

"Maybe partly bury them. Not a lot of money."

"Well, what would you think if you knew that she had upwards of $150,000 worth of insurance on those three people?" asked Bourne.

"I beg your pardon?" Joan said, frost coating each syllable.

"Would that be a surprise to you?"

"I would have to see it," she said shortly.

"Okay. But if you did see it, would that be a surprise to you, to think that there was that much?"

"Yes, it would." Joan didn't believe what the prosecutor was telling her. It was a prosecutor's job to persecute, she thought, and it seemed as if he were pulling rabbits out of his briefcase.

"Would it be a surprise to you if you knew that some of that insurance had been purchased on January 24, 1992, just about three weeks ago? Would that be a surprise to you?"

"I don't believe that. I'm sorry. I don't mean you're a liar."

"No, I understand."

"I can't believe that," Joan stated firmly.

"Okay. Would it be a surprise to you, then, if you found out that no call was ever made to the sheriff's office on Friday by her?"

"Then where did she call?" Joan was not going to let these accusations pass without challenge.

"Well, see, I don't know who she was talking to."

One of the final insults to Joan's friend was the questioning that now followed about the early morning hours of the fire.

"Could it have happened that during the night, that Sunday night before the fire occurred, could she have gotten out of the house – could Robin have – and left the house and come back without you knowing it?" Bourne asked.

"I would be a fool if I said to you, 'No, there is no way.' I was not sitting on the couch with her. I was not downstairs with her. I wouldn't insult your intelligence by saying, 'No, there's no way.'"

Joan was furious. When she got off the stand she pointed a finger at Detective Raney and said, "You. I want to talk to you. Where are all these policies you're talking about?"

"I've got them," Raney said confidently.

"I want to see them," Joan hissed. "When did it become illegal to possess insurance policies?"

The policies were discovered by officers during the search of the Row storage unit, buried in a cardboard box. This was the evidence that was the cornerstone of their case.

Immediately after the Magistrate's Inquiry, the prosecutor submitted to Judge Schmidt probable cause for a grand theft charge against Robin Row based on the evidence of embezzlement from the YWCA. It was the warrant Raney needed to detain his suspect and buy him time to work on building a murder case against her.

Raney stepped out of the courtroom and, conveniently, Robin Row was sitting on a bench just outside. When the door swung open, instead of being greeted by her friends as she had expected, Robin met the steady stare of the dogged detective who was followed by the prosecutor. She would get to know both of them much better in the months to come.

"We have a warrant for your arrest. Put your purse down and put your hands behind your back," Raney commanded.

Robin sighed heavily and rolled her eyes. She didn't show shock or surprise and cooperatively offered her wrists, performing her part as if she were an accomplished actress confidently on her mark.

Even though he had just arrested her, Raney, the "good cop" wanted to maintain rapport and immediately started a conversation. He wanted to get Robin into his office for another taped interview.

"Oh, Robin, you know while we were serving that search warrant the other night, we noticed the money in there from the YWCA. The YWCA told us you reported that it had burned in the fire. Detective Scown put this stuff together, and the judge just read it over and issued a warrant for your arrest. So, I've got to arrest you and take you up there," Raney said.

When they got to the detectives' section, Raney read Robin her Miranda rights and the arrest warrant, then let her read it to herself. She asked for permission to call her attorney Ellison Matthews. Raney listened to the one-sided conversation.

"Hi, Ellison; it's Robin. I'm in jail. I just got here. They said I'm charged right now with grand theft...Well, they said it's from the YWCA. $100,000. But I'm sure if I bailed out, they'd have the other one right after it...They say they have witnesses...Okay...Promise...Thank you." Robin hung up the phone.

As expected, Ellison Matthews told her not to talk. But Robin couldn't resist asking questions, which opened the lines of communication.

"What's the charge?"

"As it stands right now? Probably three counts of first degree murder and three counts of aggravated arson. Well, I'm sorry, let me close this door here." Raney sealed them off inside the vault-like room. He had her on the run now and recorded the interplay.

"It would be one count of aggravated arson for the house and three counts of first degree murder," Raney corrected himself.

There was a pause while Robin digested this information. The three charges of murder carried a much higher penalty than the grand theft charge.

"It's a bad situation," Raney said.

"Uh-huh."

"Nothing I do is really gonna make the difference of the whys. I can't show that. You're the only one that can ever do that. That's why you have to feel that it's important to sit here and talk to us. I mean, we can speculate forever. You know, there are insinuations now that you killed your kids for $150-$200,000, whatever the life insurance policies come out to be."

"There wasn't that much insurance on 'em."

"I got a $149,000 sitting on my desk. And that's not all of it. I know that. That accident policy, you know what I'm talking about?"

"Huh-uh."

"You just signed an accident policy. Accident insurance. I think it was through Mutual of Omaha. Twenty-four –"

"Oh, the one I told you about just the other day."

"No, you never told me about that one."

"Yes, I did," Robin insisted.

"The 24th of January, right?"

"I don't recall."

"Somewhere around there. You signed an accident insurance policy that's got if somebody dies in an accident, you get paid a buncha money. And you sign up for that. You already got $149,000 worth of life insurance that you tell people you don't have. And you sign up for that 16 days before your children are killed. How's it look? And that's where it's looking ugly."

"Uh-huh," Robin replied.

Raney was getting little more than grunt-like answers, so he moved on.

"Danny seems like a pretty decent guy. There's getting to be a lot of people who think that maybe you did this out of love for him. The stuff that probably really hurt, too, was all the stuff with the wrapping up your arm, telling people that Randy twisted your arm, when actually nothing happened. The bandages over the bruises that weren't there and stuff like that."

"How do you know they weren't there?"

"Well, that's what my job is. Go around and talk to enough people and you find the answer to your question."

There was no answer, only an empty silence before Raney launched into another area.

"Anyone in your family ever been in really serious trouble before?"

"Huh-uh."

"'Cause, obviously, this is real serious trouble."

"Other than my father."

"What'd he get in trouble for?"

"Uh, murder," Robin responded, her voice lifeless.

"Oh, yeah? And what was that?"

"Him and this other guy, it was during an armed robbery, and they were drunk; he's an alcoholic. And there was a struggle and the gun went off, and they're not sure who did it so they convicted 'em both...or at least, that's my understanding. I was 18."

"Do you think you have any psychological problems?"

"I don't know. I've seen a psychiatrist before."

"For what?"

"Not getting along with my mother."

"Ever for anything real violent or anything to do with fire?"

Robin shook her head no.

"When was the last time you saw one?" Raney asked.

"Quite a while ago."

"Maybe it shoulda been sooner."

Robin didn't seem amused.

"Well, you wanna go down to the jail?" Raney asked.

"I don't have a choice, do I?"

"We can just sit here and talk if you want."

"I wanna know how the thing with the YWCA all came about," Robin asked.

"Everybody thought you'd been scamming money off the bingo game, all your bingo players...I'll be honest with ya, it was first raised because of your record."

"But I didn't handle the money; Joan did," Robin said.

"Anyway." Raney ignored her blame-shifting. "We got to checking, and you just said that all this stuff was burnt up in the fire and, lo and behold, we were there last night and there it was," Raney said with a twinkle in his eye. "So that's the bottom line. Fair enough?"

"Uh-huh."

"This embezzlement isn't my case. Understand that. I didn't get this warrant for you."

"But you said you were gonna arrest me tonight on the other charges."

"On the murder charges? No, I haven't decided on that...But, I won't lie to ya. There's a lot of people that are scared of you 'cause they think you're psychotic. They don't understand how somebody could kill their own kids. And –"

"WHO thinks I'm psychotic?"

"Well, I'm not gonna tell ya."

"Joan?"

"Joan's not...not the one that got you here. I just ran into a whole bunch of people who said, I'm scared of what's gonna happen. Because they think that you're gonna – I'm just being honest – they think you're gonna come burn their house down or kill their kids."

"Oh, gimme a break," Robin said.

Robin asked about attending the upcoming burial for her children, scheduled for February 27. Raney said, "That would be a little bit ironic if somebody's charged with three counts of first-degree murder and they attended the service of their victims."

Robin also asked Raney if he would charge her with murder to keep her from "bonding out." He made it clear to her that he would speed up the process, getting the warrant "tonight," if necessary, to keep her in jail.

"What would be the reason to hurry?" Robin asked.

"Because I think you're a flight risk now."

"You have my car. And I do not have any money on me."

"You've told me about three bank accounts and we found seven."

"No, sir! I'm sorry, that's not true. You wanna tell me where they are? Because I don't believe you."

Raney refreshed her memory about two savings accounts in the children's names. They played cat and mouse; he asserted, she denied and justified.

"You probably have money stashed," Raney dangled the cheese. "You were living above your means...you're spending more money than you're making. And that means you're scamming money off the bingo game or something. That's not what we're here to talk about. I'll stay here and talk to you for as long as you want, or I'll go about my business."

"You can talk all you want. I'll listen to ya," Robin avoided the accusations. "So what did you say to Joan?"

"We asked her if she knew about the life insurance policies, and that caught her quite off guard. We asked her what she thought about your lie about Randy getting arrested and the February 18 court date and all that. That surprised her. I mean, just kind of a series of things like that, that you lied to her about. And we've disproved those things, and we just asked her, 'Do you have any explanation for this?' And by the time we were done, she's feeling real bad."

Robin was silent, motionless, staring at Raney through slitted eyes.

"Well, I assume you're tired of me flapping my gums in here. I don't wanna sit here and worry you all night. I'll answer your questions if I can. But other than that, I think the only significant thing is sometime I would like to hear why. Even if it's when it's all over."

"Be back in a minute," Raney said.

"Okay. Please don't close the door all the way," Robin said like a sullen child forced to sit in the corner. Minutes passed. Robin didn't move a muscle.

"Well, I guess you're officially a celebrity," Raney quipped cheerily when he returned. "The media, the wonderful media. I knew it was coming. I think you kinda did too."

"What, they're here?"

"No, no, they've just got the story out –"

"Which story?"

"Earlier today they got [from the Sheriff's Office] the, 'It's arson, we have a suspect, and we're not gonna say any more' kind of thing. Then, apparently, they found out about this court thing today, and as the media goes, I suspect you are labeled the mass murderer or the child killer or whatever wonderful labels they're gonna put on ya. But I can tell ya whatever it is, it's gonna be ugly."

"I won't ever see 'em."

"Oh, we've got TV in the jail. Heck, we're uptown here." Raney swigged his coffee. "Just to be honest with ya…I've seen these kinds of things before. You can expect the media to be pretty much merciless, and I expect this is going to be pretty darned famous around here because the last triple murder we had – the guy that shotgunned his two kids and his wife – I imagine there's gonna be a lotta comparisons to that just because of the two kids and the wife, and then in this case it's the two kids and the husband. It's gonna be big news. You should just be psychologically prepared to be called the child murderer, the baby killer, and Lizzie Borden, and whatever else they're gonna come up with. None of it's gonna be nice."

Raney looked through Robin's receipts and unpaid bills from the file that had been confiscated from Joan's house.

"Four-hundred-dollar attorney fee. Kinda livin' above your means, Robin."

While looking at unpaid bills and a $390 car repair receipt paid for in cash, Raney said, "Pardon my bluntness, but you're kinda in deep shit financially, aren't ya?"

He handed the receipt to Robin. She looked at it then threw it back at him.

"You know how it's gonna look. Whatever I think doesn't make any difference. But you know how it's gonna look," Raney scolded.

"That I got the car fixed?"

"No. It's gonna look like you killed your husband and your kids for the insurance money."

"What's that got to do with the car getting fixed," Robin leaned forward slightly and whispered.

"'Cause you're in such debt," Raney whispered back. "Now we know why bingo didn't make it."

"What are you takin' these for?" Robin asked when Raney took the tax return.

"Let me ask," Raney said as if it pained him to inquire. "What's your refund?"

"I don't remember. Almost a $1,000, I think. I really don't think that's any of your concern," Robin said testily.

"I'll tell you where this would get ugly. I'm being honest again. Bear with me, okay? On here, you say you made $15,000 last year?"

"Whatever the W-2 form says. I don't remember."

"Say $15,000. Whatta you get paid? If you don't mind me asking."

"$23,000."

"A year?"

"Uh-huh."

"From bingo?"

"And the YWCA."

"Whew – $23,000 a year, throw in Randy's check, you make $30,000 a year." Raney mentally calculated in Randy's Social Security income. "Where's the other $10,000 come from? Bingo! That's why we'd be interested in it.

"You had some cards in your bag, some Valentine's Day cards. I didn't see 'em but I was told that they were, like, for everybody but Randy and the kids."

"Probably 'cause I hadn't bought those yet."

"But, again, it looks bad. I'm serious, this is gonna –"

"There's a Christmas card in there that said, 'To my husband,'" Robin cocked her head and smirked.

Raney continued to look, going through credit cards, a check register, and cash. "It's all gonna look bad," he said becoming somewhat impatient and harsh.

Raney mumbled as he booked Robin's things, "$34 [in bills], $4.70 [in coin], white purse, seized your checkbook, seized your keys, earring, watch, ring, two library cards, your copy as a receipt. I've got your drugs. Okay?"

"Um-hmm."

Raney whistled as he gave Robin a booking form to fill out. Under next of kin Robin wrote "None."

"It's picture time!" Raney said gaily. "Now, I've gotta use up 12 pictures here. And you can just sit there, if you want. 'Cause I'm pretty much just gonna hit the button 12 times. Why don't you look at me for a couple of these?"

"No, you'll blind me."

"Oh, come on, come on," Raney asked playfully.

"Alls I can see is a red flash now."

Raney whistled and flashed.

"All right. Smile for me once. This is the last one."

"Huh-uh." Robin sat motionless and without expression. "I hate pictures."

Raney was still whistling as he scanned Robin's income tax return from the previous year. Listed on the form, claimed as a dependant, was an infant child under 1 year of age.

"Ah, no," he said with mock sadness. "You're not doing, like, tax fraud, are ya? Who's Tara?"

"Maybe it's tax fraud," Robin said defiantly. "Whatever you want to believe."

Raney made a clucking sound. "Less than 1 year old. Looks like tax fraud to me," he said in a singsong voice.

"Just add it to the list," Robin muttered.

"Yeah. All of it gets kind of insignificant after a while. I expect with three capital crimes, they won't give you too much more for cheating on your taxes."

Raney brought out the cuffs.

CHAPTER FIFTEEN

February 13, 1992

In only three days an arson had occurred; investigations, searches, and hearings had begun; a memorial service had taken place, and an arrest had been made. In only three days Robin had gone from grieving widow to prime suspect. In only three days Robin's world changed from the free world, a kaleidoscope of color, to incarceration, a monochromatic world of cold concrete and metal. In the booking room, Robin was strip-searched and relieved of everything but her personality. In exchange for her jewelry, underwear, even fingernail polish, she got state-issued underwear, an orange jumpsuit, handcuffs, and chains. She was given some bare essentials to carry to her cell: a towel, bedding, toothpaste and toothbrush, a comb, and a bar of soap. Her statistics were recorded: height – 5-feet-2-inches tall, weight – 175 pounds, hair – brown, eyes – blue, age – 34, D.O.B. – September 12, 1957.

Cell FB was no-frills. The color scheme was a dirty beige. Three double bunk beds lined the walls. Everything in Robin's new environment was hard. The pillows were flat and the mattresses were like lawn furniture padding left over from last summer's garage sale. In the center of the cell, sprouting like a mushroom from the cement floor, was a metal picnic-like table with attached seats. The toilet and shower facilities were not private. The only amenities were a hot water pot, a TV, and a phone.

A strict schedule had the inmates up at 5 a.m. doing chores. It was a tossup whether to go back to bed afterward or stay up until 7 a.m. for the meal cart that brought cold oatmeal and wheat toast. Lunch was bologna between two pieces of bread. Dinner was a grab bag ranging from weiner tots to dry hamburgers. The only relief from the lousy food was the extra snacks the inmates could buy from the commissary through an account with a ceiling of $15 that, each hoped, a friend or relative would keep in the black.

From all accounts, Robin always had more money than most for extras such as hot chocolate, writing paper, and toiletries. Someone made sure there was always money in Robin's account. She would often loan items to fellow prisoners but expected repayment in a timely manner. Those who failed to do so received a quiet reminder accompanied by a threatening look, which was all that was usually needed.

Robin didn't seem the least concerned about breaking unwritten jailhouse codes. Whereas most inmates earned points with fellow prisoners for "putting one over" on authorities, Robin would snitch to the jailers about drug talk or behavior she didn't like. Because most of the female inmates stayed only two or three days and 80 percent served a month's time or less, Robin moved quickly into a seniority position within the mini-hierarchy of her cellblock.

Seniority brought with it certain perks. Robin attained the status that brought first choice of everything, including the best bunk near the toilet area and furthest from the drafty window. She kept her standing intact mainly through the intimidation her reputation garnered. Many inmates were unnerved by the crimes she was accused of committing.

Robin, however, didn't fit the image of a cold-blooded murderer. She was quiet and kept to herself. She always seemed to be preoccupied – thinking. She played solitaire, wrote and read letters, watched soap operas, and like most inmates, slept a lot.

And while she didn't go out of her way to be friendly, she had a way of winning over the other prisoners by using cryptic references to how she had been wronged by "the system." Many of her cellmates admitted they pitied the soft-spoken woman and believed she couldn't have done what she was accused of doing.

At first, Robin rarely proclaimed her innocence to her cellmates or discussed the facts of her case. She would sometimes allude to her situation and shush everyone when a story about her aired on news broadcasts.

When one inmate, Josie, asked who she was, Robin replied with a hint of pride, "You probably read about me in the newspaper."

She went on to explain that she was being framed. "They" were accusing her, but she was not the one who had done it. "But I know who did," she said.

* * *

Leslie, one of Robin's jailers, came to know and like her. When Robin would go stir-crazy and plead with Leslie to let her out, Leslie would take her to the library or the booking room where they would talk or Robin would write. Once Robin told Leslie that she had overheard a derogatory comment.

"Why can't they believe I'm not guilty?" Robin complained.

Of one thing Leslie felt certain, Robin Row was innocent of murdering her family. She described Robin as a model inmate who never caused any trouble, seemed courteous, gentle, and compassionate. Robin went out of her way to help new inmates adapt.

* * *

Although she didn't get too close to any of the women and was nasty to those she didn't like, Robin did warm up to some. She had "mom-talk" with an inmate named Paige. She spoke of her children in the present tense, mostly talking about Tabitha. It was obvious to Paige there was something troubling Robin where Tabitha was concerned, but for now that mystery would be locked up as securely as the women in Cell FB.

Paige shared pictures of her children, who were close in age to Joshua and Tabitha, but Robin would not share hers. It seemed to Paige that she avoided the pictures of her children because looking at them would force her to face the fact they were dead. She talked often of going home. 'I have to go home and clean up the mess that was made,' she would say with a far-off stare.

"She was like a vulture when she saw my kids," Paige remembered one visiting day when Robin had stared intently at her children.

"Always be good to your kids and hug them," Robin told her. Then she asked, "Do you tuck your kids in bed at night?"

After that, Paige claimed she felt almost irrationally uneasy around Robin. She couldn't quite put her finger on the feeling, an eerie aura, maybe, or a hunch that she should watch her back. Sleeping in a bunk next to this strange mother made Paige feel anxious.

Robin acted as a "cell mom." She was picky about the cleanliness of her "home," governing the TV and making sure the beds were made. When cleaning jobs didn't meet her specifications or something wasn't done right, she would erupt with a high-pitched screech that would echo down the hall. "God damn it!" she would shriek, then do the job herself.

* * *

A few inmates were curious about Robin Row but, at the same time, outraged by her crime. One or two didn't hesitate to voice their opinions. Etta, a large, jovial woman rebelled against Robin's quiet domination of the cell. She made her feelings known one day by performing a little routine for "the girls."

They were all sitting on their bunks when Etta began her performance, center cell. She pranced, "Now, let me see here. I've got to figure out who did what." Going from person to person she pointed, "Did you kill your children?...Nope. Did you kill your children?...Nope." When she got to Robin she said with mock contrition, "Oh, I don't need to ask you."

CHAPTER SIXTEEN

Joan began receiving phone calls from Robin the first day, almost the first moment that her friend stepped into her cell. At first, Joan was a little uncomfortable talking to her. Joan felt sorry for Robin because she was having a difficult time adjusting to life on the inside. Joan realized she was the only constant in Robin's life. As a true friend she should be available whenever Robin needed to talk. Joan was always there for her, despite some of the questions she was beginning to have.

Joan knew Robin had lied about the bingo money, and a lot of people had lost their jobs because of her. Their first few conversations were about finances, the children's and Randy's upcoming burial, the arraignment, and the preposterous bail – which had been set at $100,000. Joan wanted to help, but she didn't have that kind of money.

Before long they were talking about how to get Joan into the jail to visit Robin. The detective was saying things, making accusations that Joan knew Robin could explain. And it hadn't taken the media long to latch onto the story. On Friday morning, the day following Robin's arrest, a story appeared in *The Idaho Statesman* that insinuated that Robin was connected to the fire. Joan knew that eventually she needed to find a way to see her friend face to face.

✳ ✳ ✳

Saturday, February 15 at 11:30 p.m., Detective Raney got a call at home from the jail. Robin had sent out a "kite," a slang term for a slip of paper requesting to see "her" detective (as she referred to him). He quickly pulled on sweats and a baseball cap and hustled to work, hopeful that Robin was ready to spill her guts, or at least reveal something that might help his investigation. At this point, everything he had was circumstantial. He needed some solid evidence soon.

It was after midnight when Robin, Raney, and his partner Detective Ken Smith were reunited, this time at Robin's behest.

"We meet again," Raney quipped.

"Uh-huh. I only have some questions." Robin leaned on the desk next to her chair and stared at Raney who sat two feet across from her. Her manner had swung 180 degrees from what it had been at their first interview the day of the fire. She was more aggressive this time, in speech and body language. Her orange, numbered jumpsuit didn't put a damper on her assertive attitude.

With elbows on knees and hands hanging limply between his long legs, as if talking to a buddy over a beer, Raney leaned closer to Robin. "I'll have some answers."

"Will ya?" Robin said, taking a sip of cola.

"Sure. Although, it's probably about the case." Raney smiled, beginning his command performance in a light-hearted manner.

"Well, I have a list," Robin said, pulling out a sheet of paper. "When are the bodies gonna be released?"

"Saying that the autopsy goes as expected and, that is, if they don't find something that's out of the ordinary, I would say probably late next week," Raney explained.

"Okay. Have you contacted my mother?"

"No."

"Have you called my family at all?"

"No. Although…why do you ask?"

"I was just curious if you were gonna call her."

"Have you talked to her?"

"No, I have not. I don't think she needs to know about this. You can tell her about the other one."

"Whatta you mean?"

"You can tell her about the, what is it," Robin said casually, rubbing her forehead, "aggravated arson and three counts of first degree murder."

"But not the embezzlement?!" Raney was incredulous and shared a look and a laugh with Detective Smith.

"No."

"Why's that?" Raney said, still smiling.

"'Cause it'll just hurt her feelings."

"I'm really confused."

"It's just that, you know, when I left California, I came here and started a whole new life and had been a good girl…well, it's gonna hit national headlines, I'm sure."

"I expect it to."

"You hafta know my mother to understand. My mother and I don't get along very well."

"I remember you were saying that you had kind of a rough childhood."

"Yeah. Something like that." Robin shivered. "It's cold in here, guys."

"Only 'cause you're in a pumpkin suit. I'm comfortable. Where do they all live? New Hampshire?"

"New Hampshire. Yeah."

"How many brothers and sisters do you have?"

"I have two of each."

"And are you the –"

"Oldest."

What are the rest of 'em like? Or what are your folks like?"

"Hmm, well, my dad's in prison. I told you that."

"Still?"

"Will be forever. He's institutionalized."

"Oh, like fixed life?"

"Like, every time he comes up for parole, he does something stupid. He could never live on the streets, basically."

"What was he in for? Was he in there for something before the murder?"

"A long time ago when I was a kid he went in for armed robbery. I was about 14, 11, something like that. I don't remember. And then other things that I never knew."

"Uh-huh."

"My mother…took me years to get over hating her. But she's probably a nice lady. I don't hate her now. She doesn't hate me now either. She will, though. My sister Terry…she's hardworking, had a similar life like I did. She's dying of MS. I have two brothers that live in Florida: one's a jerk who will never straighten out, will be a drunk and a drug addict all his life; the other one's recovering. And then I have a sister who lives in California, and I have no idea where she is. Nobody does. And then I have a half sister."

"And it's okay to say murder and arson, but it's not okay to say embezzlement?" Still floored at the idea that Robin didn't mind her mother knowing about arson and murder charges but was adamant about her not knowing about the embezzlement, Raney laughed at the absurdity. It defied logic.

Robin nodded her head in agreement. "Why are you gonna contact 'em?"

"Well, I get ahold of anybody I can...unless you would prefer that I held off...What's your preference?"

"I suppose you better tell 'em before it hits TV," Robin said with an exasperated sigh. "That's how we found out about my father, and it about killed her."

"Okay. It probably won't, I suspect, be a national story until at least after you're arrested."

"Okay," Robin checked her list, "one thing that concerns me is Joan brought the paper in today and held it up to the glass so I could read it, and they said other people are involved. What's that all about?"

"In this case, of course, we're still looking at Danny and Joan and Bernard, especially Danny."

"Why especially Danny?"

"Well, I don't know enough about what happened behind the scenes to know that he's not involved."

"Why would he be involved?" Now Robin was incredulous.

"Love and money."

"No, no, no, no." Robin shook her head emphatically. "You mean Danny and I, like, somebody accused...oh, that's – I'll tell ya right now that's – Danny and I are just friends."

"I still can't rule it out, even if it's just for the money factor."

"Okay. Fair enough, I guess. What's the New Hampshire warrant? I mean, it's gotta be at least 12 years old," Robin said.

"I think it's out in my car –"

"Fraudulent checks," Robin stated simply.

126

"But they're not wanting you back," Smith added.

The authorities in New Hampshire wanted Robin Cornellier Row to stay as far away from New Hampshire as she could get, so they wouldn't have to deal with her again.

"When I'm done, it won't matter anyways," Robin returned with a dry laugh. What's North Carolina got to do with this? I never told anyone here."

"Now, where we came up with North Carolina was from – "

"A crystal ball," Raney teased.

" – running your record," Smith finished.

"So whatta you do, check every state I lived in?"

"No," Smith answered. "When you run a national check, if you did time, it comes back off a national register."

"Uh-huh. I was a kid. So," Robin sighed, "I take it you ruled out that this could have been accidental."

"Uh-huh," Raney readied himself.

"By Randy?"

"Uh-huh."

"And why?" A distinct edge tinted her voice and made Robin sound as if she were reprimanding a troubled teenager.

"I guess the answer to that is you know that Randy wasn't involved," Smith put it on the line. "And we have enough evidence saying that you're involved, you know?"

"Such as?"

"The guy that follows your vehicle around in the subdivision."

"How does he know it was me?"

"Well, but we have a neighbor lady that sees a car –"

"She didn't see me, though."

"Well, but it's the car that you're driving," Smith insisted.

"When the tests come back," Raney pulled out his favorite technique again, "you could say we're 95 percent there now...when all the lab stuff's done and –"

"You mean like my clothes and my car."

"And the stuff from the scene...they'll go through it piece by piece." Raney remained intentionally vague.

"Here you go again," Robin complained, shaking her head and displaying her palms. "What kinda stuff?"

"Okay. Lemme simplify this," Raney began. "Umm, I know you set the fire, and if —"

"How do you know that?" Robin kept her emotions fairly well under control for someone just accused of a triple homicide.

"Just…bear with me for a minute."

"Okay."

"I know you set the fire. If you were to be open about that, then I would be happy to lay out everything we've got."

A breathy sigh escaped Robin's lips as she looked again at her list. "Can you release the insurance papers from the YWCA to Joan?"

Raney shook his head no.

"Why not?"

"That's the prime motive right now."

"They're not going to pay nothing!" Smith reiterated.

"Okay. That answers that question. You gonna let me do my taxes?" Robin asked insolently.

"You gonna cheat on 'em?" Raney fired back, laughing. Turning to Smith, he explained, "There was a mysterious third child on last year's tax [return]."

"Something else you should consider is using the donation to pay for the funeral expenses," Raney suggested.

"We sent it back," Robin responded.

"You can't send the cash back."

"Well, I'm not aware of any cash," Robin said.

"Joan is handling that. We sent all the checks back…I told her to," Robin said.

In truth, it had been Joan's idea to send the checks back to their owners, and Robin had spent the cash on clothes for herself.

"I think that's good. That's a good idea," said Raney

"Oh, I might have one parta my soul that isn't black," Robin said flippantly.

"I don't know, you tell me."

"No, there's not. I am not a good person," Robin sighed.

"Well, it's like I was saying the other night, whatever happens, I'll remember this case for the rest of my life."

Detective Raney and his suspect were developing a curious relationship. As they both took pains not to let their guards down, they were engaged in a strange mental tango, a matching of wits where the stakes were high for Raney and even higher for Robin. At this point, both players felt lucky.

"We could sit here and talk forever. And there's just a whole lotta questions that I'm dying to know the answers to…what's in your background? 'Cause something tells me it's pretty darned interesting.

"My background?"

"Something happens…" Balancing his weight on his forearms, Raney leaned toward Robin, his coffee mug dangling between his knees. "I've been in this business long enough to know that."

"Whatta you mean something happens?"

"I mean, something usually causes it – way back. The kinda 'what makes people tick' stuff."

"Uh-huh."

"Of course, for other people, it's fascinating what makes cops tick 'cause they can't figure out who the hell wants to do our job." Raney and Smith chuckled heartily.

"So what happens way back when…sexual abuse?"

"I was abused. I mean, well…I'm not sure. Well, yeah, I am sure. I had a stepgrandfather that molested both my sister and I. And I guess we kinda just looked out for my younger sister, Tammy."

Robin continued, "Some physical abuse. Defiance. Did whatever I could to make my mother hate me 'cause I hated her, type stuff. I always had a problem with checks and fraud, which you knew. I think I did that to, umm, call out for help. But she wasn't there helpin'. That type thing. And it just went into my adult life. And I think it did until two years ago when she finally acknowledged that I was somebody in her life. After not talking to me for ten years."

"Too late?"

"No. She went to all the Al-Anon meetings with my sister and realized that we were an extremely dysfunctional family. She just wants to hide her head in the sand because she doesn't want her part played out for her like the rest of us have already done."

"Something tells me I'm starting to play psychologist here," Raney said.

"Oh, my God, I'm in trouble. I don't like psychologists; I don't like cops."

"Well, fine. Fine. I'm hurt," Raney said with mock despair.

"Well, you don't like me either, so we're even," Robin said like a child looking for approval.

"Well, I don't dislike ya; I dislike what you did."

"You don't know me. I have some good qualities."

Raney switched gears suddenly. He was determined to get some questions answered or at least to dig far enough to hit an emotional chord. "So…am I right that Kristina's some kinda turning point?"

"You know, you're wrong about her. Real wrong."

"About what?"

"Thinking that she died from other than crib death."

"Actually, I don't," Raney said to keep Robin talking.

"Kristina was the baby I didn't want. That I resented. And I think it made it worse 'cause she was sick. I was only 18. Real hard to deal with."

"And we see it all the time. That's tough. Especially if you don't have a family support system."

"My mother was wonderful – that's not true. But I don't wanna speak ill of her. She is a nice woman, I just couldn't get along with her. But she is a nice lady." Pushing up her glasses, Robin rubbed her tired eyes with both palms.

"So what happened?" Raney turned the discussion back to Kristina.

"One day she just stopped breathing. And then I realized that I really did love her, but it was too late. She really did die the way I said she did, which was hard for me to accept because she was so sick. I couldn't have handled it…"

"Hmm. Actually, umm, I had pretty well decided, just looking into my crystal ball, that I didn't think you killed her."

If Robin could lie, Raney could stretch the truth to keep her talking. Although there was no hard evidence to support his theory, his gut told him she had killed her second-born child.

"No, I didn't."

"I just think you felt an awful lotta guilt about her death."

"Still do. Tremendous amount."

"So that makes things worse on the rebellion theft. Because it was shortly after that that you went to prison, right?"

"Yep, that same year." Robin was getting more comfortable talking with Raney. The line between cop and counselor blurred, and at times she seemed to forget she hated both.

"I don't know who I was getting back at that time," Robin continued. "What I didn't realize is all these people I was getting back at, I wasn't; I was hurting myself. But, see, I didn't realize that until three or four years ago."

"Well, you don't have anybody to strike out at," Raney sympathized.

"I was striking out at my mother 'cause of some of the awful things she said when it happened."

"What'd she say?"

"Oh, I wanted to put flowers on her grave one time; my mother just smacked me and said, 'She's dead, just leave it alone, forget it, get on with your life,' type thing."

"A real caring grandmother."

"She…in her own way," Robin softened for a moment, then abruptly bristled. "I'm waiting for her to tell me she loves me…and she tells me this crap? See, I don't remember her ever telling me she loved me until…this last year."

Robin seemed to suddenly remember who she was talking to.

"You don't need to hear all this."

"It's interesting…Maybe I flatter myself by saying you'll remember me for a long time to come."

"I'll remember you for a long time…"

"So, how do you live with something like this?…How do you deal with it?" Raney swung the conversation back to the ultimate question.

"I don't think I've dealt with it yet…"

"Well, this'll be the third time. At some point you're gonna hafta start."

"I will."

"So when does that come?"

"I don't know. I'm not a psychologist. Though people say I should be; I'd make a good counselor."

"It's the tough parts that I have a hard time guessing. Like what were your real intentions?"

A heavy silence permeated the room. Possibly the subject was too grave for Robin to deal with. She avoided it by asking another question.

"So, when are you calling my mother?" she said quietly. "So I can be prepared."

"You tell me and that's when I'll call her."

"Before you charge me, I guess. When am I gonna be charged?"

"I don't know."

"I'm sitting in jail...it doesn't really matter, except I wanna get it started and over with."

Robin's confident air was somewhat cavalier considering her life was the poker chip in the center of the table. But, then, she thought she had a good hand. An entirely circumstantial case was all they had.

"Where we're at right now," Raney explained, "is to probably wait for everything to get back. You just don't jump into these things until you're absolutely sure."

Tiring of the banter, Raney felt ready to try a strategically risky new tack.

CHAPTER SEVENTEEN

"So, did you mean to kill the kids?" Detective Raney said gravely, quietly, looking intensely into Robin's face.

Not moving, not incensed or showing any anger, Robin answered evenly, without skipping a beat, "I'm not gonna answer any of those kinds of questions."

"I answered yours."

"I know. But I'm not gonna answer yours."

"That's not fair. Just sitting here and talking to ya, you just don't seem like the kinda woman who would burn up her own kids for insurance," Raney pressed.

"Especially when the insurance was taken out a while ago," Robin encouraged the theory of her innocence.

"Ten days," Raney reminded her.

"No –"

"Like I said the other night, you know how it looks."

"Uh-huh. I do."

"Are you ever gonna answer my questions?"

"Probably not."

"Not even after it's all done?"

"You mean, when I'm sitting on death row, if you have your way?"

"I don't know if I want ya on death row."

"Well, that's what's gonna happen."

"Think you're crazy?"

"Does a crazy person think he's crazy?" Robin responded.

"Good question."

"No, I don't think I'm crazy."

"Without incriminating yourself, do you think a sane person can kill their family?"

"No," Robin answered tersely.

"Then we got a problem…the way I see it. I can tell you it's gonna be a long road between here and there, whatever there is," Raney said.

"Uh-huh. So do you get to testify against me too?" Robin asked. "I don't have anyone in my favor, so I was just curious how many are against me."

"Well, I testify as to what the investigation is. In some respects it's gonna be against ya. It'd just save me so much trouble if I knew what was evidence and what wasn't. Like the heater."

"What about the heater?" Robin's eyes flashed.

"Why it was where it was."

"I don't know where it was."

"Yeah, you do. You told me where it was. You saw it on TV."

"Oh, when we saw it on TV, it was in the middle of the floor. It shouldn't of been in the middle of the floor. I'm sure there are a lotta things that got kicked around and hoses dragged through and water and –"

"Huh-uh. No, that's the magic of arson investigations. Putting everything back where it was."

"Well, the heater shouldn't have been in the middle of the floor. It was never in the middle of the floor," Robin said stubbornly.

"And the circuit breaker. I know about it."

"I already told you about that."

"Well, I think the lab – they're gonna do their little thing,…" Raney paused, letting the full impact sink in.

"Uh-huh."

"Because you said you never touched it," Raney pointed out.

"No, that's not true. I told 'em one time I turned it on so she could watch Turtles," Robin whined.

"The key is recently."

"How recent is recent?" Robin was making an effort to remain nonchalant.

"The last person to touch it…It will show who the last one is," Smith explained.

"Even if it did, you wouldn't tell me," Robin surveyed the detectives' faces for clues.

"That's true," Smith answered.

"So I won't ask."

"The black of this case doesn't portray you very well."

"The serial killer for insurance," Raney added.

"We both feel there's another side to all that happened, and you're gonna hafta be the one that makes the decision in the end. You know, unfortunately, if you save it till the end, no one's gonna listen to it," Smith continued.

"Everybody will decide by then," Raney seconded. "Death row certainly is not out of the realm of possibility."

"I'm not gonna lie about things that you know about," Robin said smirking.

"So, why aren't you ever gonna tell me about it?"

"I don't know," Robin sighed. "Maybe there's nothing to tell."

"No, there is…I feel like I've gotten to know your kids."

"They were good kids," Robin said, her head resting on her hand as if it were weighted.

"They were good kids," Raney affirmed.

"Uh-huh. They were. Very good," Robin said combing the back of her hair with her fingers. "The hardest time I have is the stuff that they supposedly said…about how I didn't want them. I don't believe either one of 'em would say that."

"Why's that?"

"'Cause they loved me."

"It's a pretty specific statement for somebody to remember," Raney said, referring to a statement made by a family friend during an interview.

"I refuse to believe it. I don't think Joshua or Tabitha would say that."

"No, it's just Tabitha. If I remember right."

"She wouldn't say it."

"And this is the one that's like, Mom doesn't love us anymore and wants to get rid of us."

Robin refused to concede and, when she couldn't change Raney's mind, deliberately changed the subject. They began talking about the groups of people from whom the detectives had obtained their information.

"The killers," Raney said of the witnesses that would negatively impact Robin's defense, "are, for the most part, the ones that you talked to that you lied to."

"Well, that's all right. That's my whole life," Robin confessed, self-deprecatingly.

"Lying?" Raney asked.

"Uh-huh. Probably, my whole life's made up of lies."

"Well, you can turn that around. Now's a good place to start," Raney said jovially, slapping his knees.

"Well, my life's real simple," Robin began. "There's physical abuse, sexual abuse, lack of a mother's love, and looking for a father. My whole life. That's it." Robin condensed the whole of her dysfunctional background into a single sentence.

"Nah," Raney said, shaking his head. "That's like sayin' I'm a cop 'cause I went to high school, went to college, went to police academy – now I'm a cop," Raney laughed.

"Yeah. 'Cause I worshipped the ground my father walked on…hated my mother for sending my father away. So I did whatever I could to hurt her. Plain and simple."

"How old were you?"

"Eleven. And my dad was everything to me…"

"Is this the final get-even?" Smith asked.

"No," Robin answered.

"See, we're reaching for some connection here between either you getting back together with your mother or your trip to New Hampshire, and I guess we wanna think that something triggered this," Raney surmised.

"I don't have anyone to get at right now. My mother and I more or less reconciled."

"There's gotta be something that triggered this…I'm still hopeful that you really didn't mean to kill 'em, that it was just an arson."

"The fact that you came back says there's something more," Smith added.

"I'm not gonna talk about it," Robin sat stonily resolute.

"That's unfortunate."

"My lawyer would kill me."

"Not talking is more likely to kill you," Raney suggested.

"I can't," Robin's vacant stare tunneled through Raney.

"Without anything else, I've probably gotta go for the best evidence... that you were going after the insurance money."

"Well, you hafta do your job. That's all I can say," Robin said shrugging her shoulders and flashing her empty palms.

"The other thing that keeps coming up is that a lot of people have commented about how cold you are."

"How cold I am?" Robin said in disbelief.

"They really think you're a cold-blooded murderer. 'Cause you don't show any emotions."

"You can't show emotion if you don't feel it or have it sent to you. My mother never hugged me."

"You don't have any remorse for killing your two kids and your husband?" Raney pounced.

"Now you're trying to put words in my mouth. I just SAID that you don't know what I feel," Robin arched her eyebrows and smirked.

"But that's 'cause you won't tell me."

"And I won't tell anyone. My feelings are personal. I mean, 'you don't display your feelings,' as my mother would say. And I won't cry in public," Robin said defiantly, still smirking.

"I don't see how any reasonable mother, no matter how she was brought up, can talk about the death of her two children the way we have and –"

"That's because you don't know me," Robin interrupted.

"Well, let me say, I've met thousands and thousands of people, many of whom were in circumstances not as bad as yours, and anybody out there has enough life experience to say that you're not reacting the way a normal person would react or even reacting in a way that's understandable...It makes you out to be the cold-blooded murderer."

"They don't know what I do in private, Raney." Primly, Robin interlaced her fingers in her lap.

"Don't bullshit me, Robin!"

"I'm not. I'm being honest with you." Robin wore her familiar smirk. If she was angry, she didn't show it.

"You're not gonna convince me that you didn't set the fire."

"Well, see, it wouldn't matter what I –"

"You could convince me about anything else. Unless you convince me that Danny set the fire. But that's the only other person – 'cause then he woulda had to have been, like, laying down in the car when you were driving."

"Danny wouldn't do something like that. Danny's a decent human being."

"Did Bernard set the fire? Bernie?" Smith asked.

"Bernie? No. He wouldn't do that either."

"Did Joan set the fire?" Smith went down the list to see if Robin would implicate someone else.

"She wouldn't do that either."

"Did anybody else have access to your car that particular night?" Smith asked.

"No. There's only one other set of keys, and Randy had 'em."

"Kinda narrows this whole thing down to one person then," Raney concluded, sharing a short laugh with Smith.

With Robin looking at the floor, a long silence settled over the threesome.

Smith broke it. "Why would someone in yours and Randy's financial condition – why would you have $140,000 worth of life insurance on the children?"

"There isn't that much on the children."

"The way it looks is you have, I don't know, it's gotta be pushing $200,000," Raney calculated.

"Actually," Smith said triumphantly, "as of Friday, it was $400,000, with double indemnity. There was one updated on February 1."

"Of this year? I don't think so. None of 'em are double indemnity," Robin corrected Smith. "There is NOT $400,000."

"Well, why would someone in your financial condition have $100,000 worth of insurance on –"

"Because that was offered through the bank and we purchased it."

"– six? Seven? Eight policies…all are obtained while you're on welfare. Randy has the accident, you guys are absolutely strapped, and you're maintaining these policies."

"But they weren't very much," Robin said.

"I think they were a lot. I don't have $100,000 on myself," Raney pointed out.

They continued to debate, with Robin evasively latching on to the most minute and trivial particulars.

"There's only one policy that you're not the SOLE beneficiary on," Raney said accusingly.

"I'm sorry?" Robin pretended she had lost her hearing for a moment, allowing herself time to readjust her armor.

"There's only one policy that you're not the sole beneficiary on," Raney repeated, locking his eyes on Robin's face.

"Well –" Robin faltered.

"The way those policies stand, if you and Randy die, the kids are not the beneficiary of Randy's policies. Randy and the kids hafta die for those policies to be paid."

"There aren't that many," Robin fell back on her same refrain.

"There's five on my desk, and we found, like, four more. That makes nine total."

"I honestly don't think there's that many."

After a ponderous pause, Raney said forbiddingly, "It's gonna be ugly."

"You already told me that." Annoyed, Robin brushed him off. "I used the dental plan too. That's how I got my teeth fixed."

"You're arguing fine points. The overall picture is really, really ugly."

"You've already told me that. Many, many, MANY times." Robin vented her pent-up aggravation.

"Ellie Matthews is probably booking his appearance on Geraldo as we speak," Raney joked.

"Why do you say that? Why Geraldo?" Robin said testily. "I don't even watch him, when you've got Oprah Winfrey."

"I mean it's just the kinda things that you hear about on Geraldo. Psycho mother kills her family and gets the death sentence in Idaho. I mean, you take a 34-year-old woman who has quite a bita con man in her –"

"Whatta you mean?"

"Well, it just flat takes some con man to do all this embezzlement. And not that you haven't changed." Raney made sure to sprinkle the crow with a little sugar so Robin could swallow it easier if she wanted to back away from her rigid stance of innocence.

Robin didn't seem the least bit offended at Raney's characterization.

Laying out a scenario, Raney waxed combative. "At age 18 she loses a baby under somewhat suspicious circumstances."

"It was never suspicious, NEVER," Robin said firmly. "And I resent that."

"There are –"

"Go on, you're just doing your job," Robin said bitingly.

"I'm just telling you what to expect. SIDS and 15 months old don't go together."

"Well, they couldn't find the cause of death."

"Next year," Raney continued his scenario, "you go to prison…come out to California and your son dies in an extre-e-e-mely suspicious fire that everybody in California bills as 'a murder that we couldn't prove.' And then you come to Idaho…Something at some point either snaps or you can't keep it up any more, and suddenly, the four kids that you ever had in your life all die, and is your husband there with the kids or are the kids there with the husband? Either way, it makes a great tabloid story. Right?"

"If you say so…"

"Based on that theory," Raney interrupted, "the FBI classifies you as both a serial killer and a mass murderer. I think it takes three people for each. Three people for a serial killer and three people for a mass murderer.

"And then you're going back to a mother that doesn't show emotion."

"But if I sat here and cried, you'd tell me it was all put on, so I don't bother." Again, Robin, whether subconsciously or by design, missed the bigger picture. She appeared less concerned over Raney's depiction of her as a notorious killer than she was at looking the part of an unemotional mother.

"And I showed affection towards my children."

"You have a strong opinion that we're the ones that you need to be concerned about in this whole deal."

"Then who is?"

"The general public and the twelve people that are gonna sit. I'd have a really, REALLY good case. 'Cause that's exactly the theory. I gotta throw in the insurance, the $25,000 insurance in California...umm, paying premiums while you're on welfare down there. Then you come up here; you're on welfare making premiums, take out all these policies...falls into the same pattern – another house fire."

"But you're going to policies that were taken out a couple of years ago."

"That just makes it sound worse to me," Smith threw in. "I mean, it doesn't make it sound better."

"Oh, okay. Whatever," Robin said, wearing the same pasted-on, sardonic smile the detectives had become accustomed to.

"Two of the basic rules of being an investigator are that coincidences usually aren't coincidences and hunches are usually more than hunches," Raney said.

"Do you have any more questions? Other than the ones you know I'm not gonna answer?"

"Are you looking for a deal or –"

"No, I'm not looking for anything."

"And there's nothing that you can think of, no circumstance or situation that would cause you to –"

"What? Confess?" Robin asked, her voice rising in disbelief.

"Yeah."

"No," she said flatly.

"Confession is –" Raney began.

"Is good for the soul? Is that what you're gonna say?" Robin ridiculed.

"Works well in crime just like it does in the Catholic Church. And most people wanna confess because they live with guilt. And you're not showing any guilt."

"You don't know what I feel."

"Do you feel guilt?" Smith asked.

"I feel a lotta things. None of which I'm gonna share because they're my personal feelings."

"Well, just as a general observation, obviously some of the things you've been told all your life don't seem to be working real well. Maybe you oughta try some alternatives," Smith laughed.

"He's got a point," Raney added.

Raney was getting tired of getting nowhere.

"I guess the summation would be that we've probably spent ten or twelve hours together now, and when I get asked on the stand was there ever any sign of remorse, I'd have to honestly answer, not one damn bit! I'll tell you the one thing about a confession is, that's the number one sign of remorse, and the more I talk to ya, the colder I think you are. I guess I'm starting to believe what everybody else thinks." Raney was fed up.

"You're entitled to your opinion," Robin said patronizingly.

"When somebody does something bad, if they've got a conscience, they feel guilt. And from the guilt they feel remorse over what they did. Are you with me?"

"Uh-huh."

"It's unfortunate. 'Cause I still don't think you're that bad – but you're starting to convince me."

"Because I don't show my feelings."

"Ahhh…that bullshit!" Raney was pissed off with Robin's mantra.

"No, that's what you're saying, though," Robin protested.

"Well, you're fulla shit!" Raney fumed. "You're starting to play this off on all this poor me, I was raised not to show my feelings and –"

"I'm sorry," Robin said haughtily. "You're entitled to your opinion."

"So are we done?" Raney asked.

"I guess so."

"I uh…as much as I enjoy these…"

"I won't call you again," Robin pouted.

"You can call me again if you have a serious question. Call me during the day."

It was after 3 a.m. The detectives were tired and frustrated. They had let Robin talk freely. They had learned that if they let her talk, her habitual lying would allow them to pick up on inconsistencies.

Detective Raney had used his most effective methods and creative psychological maneuvers to elicit a confession from Robin, to no avail. This woman was not normal, he thought. She was not responding or giving in to normal human emotions, no guilt, no remorse, no sorrow.

Chapter Eighteen

After the interview following Robin Row's arrest on Thursday, February 13, Detectives Raney and Smith were fairly certain that they were not going to get a confession. They would have to take a different tack.

They had a good circumstantial case, but not a great one. They had evidence of Robin's embezzlement of YWCA bingo money, insurance policies that she had taken out on her family, her inconsistent stories of abuse, and the suspicious fires that had occurred in her past. They also had found two people who claimed to have seen a car similar to Robin's near the scene of the fire in the early morning hours of February 10. But they had no hard evidence linking Robin to the fire. They had motive, means, and intent, but no opportunity. The investigators had to keep digging.

Raney and Smith thought that the key to this puzzle might lie with the person who was closest to Robin – Joan McHugh. It was going to be difficult, maybe even impossible to get Joan to cooperate. She hadn't hidden evidence or misdirected the detectives, but she was extremely defensive of her friend. During the days after the fire, there had been several discussions with Joan in which they would pose questions about Robin's inconsistent behavior. Although she countered with arguments and still believed her friend incapable of murder, Joan was listening. They had even begun to soften her loathing for the police.

After his suspect was in custody, Raney had wasted no time in contacting Joan. It was essential to the investigation to get as much evidence as possible as quickly as possible so that their prime suspect didn't somehow slip through their fingers. The Friday following the fire and the day after Robin's arrest, he went to the McHughs' apartment and knocked on the door. Even though he wasn't optimistic about the results, he presented Joan with his idea to connect a tape recorder to her telephone.

* * *

Joan had already had telephone conversations with Robin in the short time since her arrest; however, she battled with herself about whether putting a tap on her phone and recording those dialogues would be a betrayal. She had made it clear to Raney that she desperately wanted to prove Robin's innocence. Raney had argued that the tapes would prove it one way or the other.

A newspaper article printed Friday morning was a catalyst that convinced Joan to cooperate with the police. The article reported that officials in New Hampshire and North Carolina were cooperating in the investigation. She didn't know anything about Robin being in trouble in New Hampshire, and the only story she had about Robin doing time in North Carolina was that Robin had been picked up for prostitution. According to Robin, it had all been a big mistake. She and her husband were all dressed up and out on a double date. When the two men left their dates on the corner to get the car, Robin and the other woman were arrested for soliciting.

When she had asked Robin about the newspaper story while visiting her earlier in the day, Robin appeared baffled. Joan was confused and upset that Robin was being tried in the press. It seemed to Joan that neither the press nor the police were getting the facts. Joan wanted to do everything within her power to get Robin out of jail. It was unbearable seeing Robin through a sheet of glass, wearing a jumpsuit with a number stamped on it, looking rough and unkempt – caged like an animal – and hearing her tearful whispers. Her conviction that Robin did not belong in that place helped make the decision for her.

If letting the police tap her phone was an avenue to the truth and to free Robin, she would do it. She agreed to let Raney connect the equipment. She thought to herself that when Robin gave recorded proof of her innocence, she would save a copy of the tape. In case the police didn't release Robin from jail, Joan planned to give the recording to the press herself. She would beat the police at their own game.

* * *

"It's really hard to let you see me," Robin told Joan when she called the next day. Unbeknownst to Robin, their every word was being recorded.

"I know," Joan answered sympathetically.

"It's just so lonely."

"How many people are in there with you?"

"Oh, we're so crowded we're using cots in here. Everybody around me has been in here less than a week – but, of course, I'm the most famous," Robin said with a burst of pride.

"I guess you would be. Is there anything you need in there?"

"No, I'm fine.

"The children – Joan, I miss them – so-o-o much." Robin's words sounded unnatural, forced. She seemed to crave Joan's sympathy.

"I'm sure you miss them. The whole thing is just so terrible. Is there anyone you want me to call or anything?"

"Has my family called?"

"Not yet."

"When they do, just simply tell them I'm in jail for questioning. Don't tell them anything else, please. They don't need to go through all the agony."

"Okay."

"As far as everything I own in that storage unit in Meridian and my car and stuff, you're welcome to have. Randy was moving things out there, so I have no idea what's out there…you can keep it all. Things like my doll collections and stuff, um, I'd like those kept."

According to neighbors and Randy's family members, Robin had sent Randy and the children to the storage unit on several occasions to store items that were important to her.

"Okay. I'm always here, Robin, so call, please."

Robin took Joan's offer to heart. Her calls came often, sometimes several a day, especially during the first week she was in jail.

* * *

"Can I talk to Bernie?" Robin asked when she called later that same Saturday evening. All her conversations with the McHughs were now being recorded and would be until March 20.

"Sure," Joan answered and handed the phone to Bernie.

145

"Hi, kid. Howaaya?…I know it's a lousy place. Hey, a day at a time, you know. Things will work out. As Joanie said, anything we can do, you know I'm always here." Bernie tried to sound cheerful and enthusiastic, but there was an undertone of doubt and discomfort in his voice.

Danny sounded more uncomfortable on the phone than Bernie had. He was bewildered by the whole situation.

"How are you? Are you hangin' in there? They treatin' you okay there?"

"I'm okay, yeah…Danny?"

"What?"

"I'm sorry."

"For what?"

"Everything. I have messed everybody's life up…and that bothers me."

"Well, you'll be vindicated in the end, right?"

"I hope so. Just do me a favor?"

"What?"

"Keep smiling." Robin often asked that of Danny. "Let me remember you that way."

"Okay. You sound like you're never going to see us again."

"I might not. Thanks for talkin' to me."

"No, I don't mind talkin' to you. They [police] came and asked me something about taxes, and my head's spinnin'; I don't know what they're talkin' about."

"Taxes?" Robin said, suddenly quiet.

"Yeah. They asked me, and I told them how I'd done a rough sketch of your taxes and…then you were going to go home and figure out if you could do some medical deductions to try to bring it to a $1,000. And then they say, 'Well, who is Tara Row?' Which I don't know."

"Huh-uh."

"Do you know what that's all about?" Danny said, concerned.

"No, I don't."

"Isn't it this week comin' up when they're supposed to get all the lab results back?"

"Yep. Yeah."

"That's the part that should clear you, right?"

146

"He said that my clothes and my car wouldn't clear me. It's real hard for me to hang on to anything right now, Danny."

"Okay. All right...well, just try."

During her conversations with Danny, he clearly circumvented personal issues and, even though she was probably disappointed about not having any romantic dialogue, she at least got to hear his voice.

❋ ❋ ❋

"I talked to the detectives last night. They pulled me out at 12:10 to talk to me." Robin flooded Joan the next morning with a stream of chatter, about the interview Robin herself had requested with the detectives at about midnight.

"Did they say you're going to be charged?"

"Yeah, probably later this week," Robin answered in a no-big-deal tone of voice. "No insurance company's going to pay off. So he [Ellison Matthews] said use your cash donations and go to the county. He said you're definitely indigent now."

"Well, I'll get them buried," Joan offered. Somebody had to, she thought.

"It's not your responsibility. It's mine. And I can't do it...at least not from here."

"Maybe your family could help you a little bit."

"Maybe," Robin said with little feeling in her voice.

"He's [Raney] going to tell 'em right before he arrests me or right after...He kept askin' me if I wanted to confess, that it would be good for my soul. 'Well, Robin,' he says, 'you're not crying, you're not showing guilt, you're not showing remorse.' He said, 'You know what that sounds like to me?...It sounds like to me you're a cold-blooded murderer.' And almost everybody he says he's talked to said I'm a very cold person."

"I don't know; everybody sees a different person than I saw," Joan said sadly, not realizing she had used the past tense.

"And then he said he talked to some other people, and they told him that when I came back from New Hampshire that I looked happy, and I was wearing make-up and dressing up and stuff like that. And I said, well I was stressed out. And he said, 'No, I think it's more or less you made your decision of what you were going to do and you were happy with it.' I'm thinking the whole world is against me."

147

"You know what?" Joan changed the subject. She knew Robin had lied to her before. Would she tell the truth now?

"What?"

"Remember that Saturday that you went with Mrs. Washam?"

"Um-hum."

"And her husband and the sheriff's department, they went to the house when you found all the stuff broken –"

"Um-hum."

"– and everything slashed. Did they go back? You said Ellie was going to go there with a police photographer or something. Did they get all those pictures?"

"I don't know." Robin became irritated.

Getting no response, Joan pressed on. Were there other lies Robin had told her? "I mean, did they go to St. Luke's?"

"I don't know."

"And Saint Alphonsus and the Crisis Center?" Joan prodded.

"When I talked to him on Friday, they hadn't done that yet…" Robin changed the subject quickly. "And THEN he said, 'So what did you do it for, love and money? Or money and love?' He said this is going to be long and nasty."

"I knew it was going to be long –"

"And Ellie said that Idaho women don't have death row. If I'm convicted, I'll go to Nevada," Robin sounded indifferent.

"Dear God," Joan murmured, her voice breaking. Could Robin actually face the death penalty? The thought blindsided her.

✳ ✳ ✳

"How are you?" Robin asked Joan during a subsequent call.

"I'm old," Joan answered. "I always thought I would never get old, just older, but right now I feel old and tired…"

Robin was up and chit-chatty.

"It didn't dawn on me until I talked to Ellie today what they [the detectives] were doing, but they kept asking me; they said, 'Well, we know you did it, but tell us how.' He said, 'Robin, they're asking you that because they don't have any evidence, and they're hoping you'll confess to something, and then they have you.' And I told them, I says, 'I'm sorry, I'll be here for the rest of my life if I plead guilty to something I didn't do.'"

"There's a chance they're not going to charge you?"

"Ellie is trying to push them one way or the other, and he doesn't think that they're going to because they don't have any physical evidence. Because, Joan, I wasn't there. So how can they get physical evidence? I'm their prime suspect. But, apparently, all they have is circumstantial."

Robin cried in front of and claimed innocence to only two people, Joan and Danny. Throughout all her interviews with the detectives, she never once cried or proclaimed, "I'm innocent; I didn't do it."

"Don't underestimate their intelligence. All of the people I talked to at the sheriff's department, they're all very intelligent, articulate people. Like I always say, Robin, the truth will set you free."

"Another thing that I realized was that when they pulled me outta here Saturday, they kept sayin' to me, 'Well, we know you did it, but you need to tell us how.' And it just dawned on me today the reason why they're asking is because they don't know. They're playing cat and mouse."

"Yeah, well you could be outta jail in a coupla days then."

After they said their good-byes, Joan just sat on the couch and contemplated Robin's predicament. Lately, a pin-prick of doubt had pierced her loyal conviction of Robin's innocence. Her thoughts seesawed. Whenever she contemplated what others were saying about Robin, strayed too far toward the possibility that Robin had anything to do with the fire, her subconscious boomeranged her thoughts back to her certainty that Robin couldn't have done this horrendous act. The police had to be missing something.

* * *

When Robin called the next day, she was excited. "I got back the report today on the search warrants. Is Danny there?"

"Yeah."

"Would you ask him to go upstairs and listen on the upstairs phone so I only have to repeat it once?"

Once Danny was on the line, Robin chattered nonstop about what she saw as inconsistencies in the nine-page warrant.

The fire started in the downstairs closet. Whoever started it used gas, or accelerants of some kind. That's why they took my clothing and that's why they impounded my car. Well, my clothing and my car are both going to come back clean. So...we're disproving THAT one. The basis of searching your house was to get my clothes and any pictures that I might have had of the kids that I didn't want destroyed. They didn't find any pictures because I didn't have any there," Robin said with a note of pride in her voice. "The other one was…that you said the car was cold and had moisture on the window."

Robin was breathless, almost delirious about beating the rap. "I have to decide if I want 'em cremated or buried." Now that the coroner had released the bodies, the burial or inurnment could be scheduled. And Robin chattered about the arrangements as if she were redecorating a room or planning a party.

"And what did you decide?" Joan asked soberly.

"I haven't decided, to tell you the truth…It's been too hard."

"Yeah, I'm sure," Joan responded sympathetically.

"Sounds like quite a few things survived," Danny said.

"For a place that was supposed to be totally destroyed," Joan added.

"They told me, according to the report, the one fire was in the hall closet. They said the other fire had burned itself out and had burned a hole in the rug."

"What was the hall closet underneath?"

"Um, the stairs. Since they're searching for accelerant, I'm assuming that the fire was started with gasoline…[Randy] told somebody that I said to move all the valuables out to the storage shed. And I told Ellie, I said, I started moving my stuff out there a couple of weeks ago. I was moving my dolls, all my personal stuff, so he wouldn't know."

"What were the two fires that started simultaneously?"

"One of them was in the front – they're not even near each other from what I gather from the report – one of them was in the front room…and the other one was in the closet, which to me – I don't know much about fires – unless they were saying it was started by gasoline, it would have burnt itself out because of lack of oxygen."

"I don't know. I don't know anything about fires. I know it's hard to breathe in one," Joan said seriously.

✳ ✳ ✳

The next day, Robin continued their previous conversation.

"Hi," Robin began with her usual salutation.

"Hi," Joan answered. "What's happening today?"

"I guess Ellie is going to see you, and he's going to do a limited power of attorney. He told me, don't say anything more...because you don't know if her phone's not tapped or something...He gave me something to read – the two fires were started at the SAME TIME! Okay. How do you start two fires at the exact same time?"

"I don't know. How were they started?"

"They didn't say. And then, um, it was a definite case of arson. Their question was who did it. And I'm just their prime suspect. They didn't say that I did it. They just said that I was their prime suspect."

"And it was set in two places?"

"At the SAME TIME! I asked Ellie, 'How do you do that?' And he extended his hands out and said, 'Well, you put a match in this one, and a match in that one and you try to start them at the same time.' Well, how are you going to strike 'em, Joan? You need two hands to strike 'em," Robin exclaimed.

✳ ✳ ✳

"There's some things I want to tell you," Robin said when she got Joan on the line at the beginning of her second week in jail.

"I have to ask you something, too," Joan said firmly.

"I'm going to disappoint you now," Robin began.

"Why?"

"Because I'm going to tell you some things you're not going to want to hear."

"Okay," Joan said warily.

"Because of my life with Randy the last couple of weeks, I've done some things that I'm not very proud of."

"Um-hum," Joan's heart began to pound.

"I went to the house by myself."

Terrified at what Robin was leading up to, Joan couldn't speak.

"You went to the house?" Joan's heart tried to beat its way out of her chest.

"By myself. And Randy and the kids were there. And we talked. And things were still torn up," Robin sighed. "And, I don't know, I just needed to tell you that I guess."

"Okay." Joan felt as if she were walking between land mines. "Why didn't you take the children out of the house?"

"Because he wouldn't let me."

"What did he say?"

"It wasn't very pleasant, Joan. You've heard him before."

"Yeah." Joan recalled the many warnings she and others had given Robin not to go to the house alone.

"But I couldn't bring you there with me; I just couldn't do that. And I don't really know why. So I left early that morning and took the chance. I think then, that day, I realized exactly what he felt about me. You know, one minute he's sitting there telling me he loves me, and the next minute he's destroying my property. And the kids didn't want to come with me."

"They didn't want to leave him?"

"They didn't want to leave him."

"That hurts," Joan tried to be sympathetic, tried to curb the anger and hurt that was welling up inside of her. How could Robin have lied to her about something so important, putting her through all that agony? Making her think that the children were kidnapped and in danger?

"I couldn't tell ya," Robin's voice broke.

"I thought you could tell me anything," Joan said, Robin's tears softening her ire.

"And there were other things, too, Joan."

"You mean you lied about other things?" Things that Raney had told her flashed through Joan's mind. The media reports. What Robin had said and done that fatal weekend. Did any of it make sense? She began to think that she didn't know for sure about anything anymore.

"Yeah. Because I was afraid of what you'd do...you gotta understand – no, you don't understand because you weren't in my shoes. He could just say one thing to me, and I would submit and do whatever he said."

It was time to ask the question that had been haunting Joan. She was afraid to ask it yet afraid not to. Amazingly, the few words, impossible to form until now, came effortlessly and unadorned, a flood she couldn't have prevented.

"Robin," Joan said gravely, "did you start that fire?" She willed Robin to give an explanation. She would have believed anything. She would have believed any plausible account at this point.

"No, Joan, I did not," Robin said flatly, unhesitatingly, carefully enunciating each word.

"I mean, were you so angry with your children –"

"Oh, no, no –"

"– did you go crazy?"

"No."

Joan went on as if thinking aloud. "You know, people go crazy when those things happen. I mean it had to have hurt you terribly. I can't imagine them even saying it. I mean, did you just go out of your mind a little bit, Robin?"

"If I went out of my mind, Joan, I would have done something right then and there."

"I'm sorry they didn't want to go with you," Joan said with sincerity.

"They would have eventually. They just wanted to spend the weekend with him. And they didn't want to go over to your house with me. Joshua wanted to stay home with his friends. And I knew if you knew I went there, you would be so disappointed, and I couldn't bear it."

"I just would have felt bad that the children didn't want to go with you."

"They knew. They knew. 'Cause like Joshua said to me a coupla weeks ago, he said, 'Mom, Dad says you deserve it because you work all the time and you're never home.' And I used to have to say to him, 'Now, Joshua, who's the parent?'"

There was a long pause.

"Who do you think set the damn fire?" Joan asked in a quiet monotone.

Robin had stopped crying.

"You know, I still have that theory that Danny and us came up with before. But they said that didn't happen."

"Oh, you mean Randy, by accident?"

"Yeah, with the diary. He was so angry that day. But he did calm down and talk to me, and he didn't hit me..."

Joan's head was a jumble. She couldn't talk to Robin another minute; she needed to sort things out in her mind.

"Would you ask Danny to come and talk to me?" Robin asked.

"Yeah." Joan handed the phone to Danny.

Robin began crying. "Are you still my best friend?"

"Of course I'm your best friend. Of course I am."

"Okay. Thank you. I need a lot of friends."

"There's no need to cry. Calm down."

"Okay. Write to me."

"Okay. All right."

* * *

"Remember when you said you spent that Saturday with Randy?" Joan brought up a subject that had festered in her mind since their conversation a couple of days before. It was the same weekend before the fire when she and Robin had searched for Joshua and Tabitha because Robin had claimed Randy had kidnapped the children.

"Yeah."

"So he never kidnapped the children," Joan affirmed, tethering her anger. She had been mulling Robin's lies over and over and needed answers.

"Yeah, they didn't want to go with me, but he wasn't going to let 'em go with me either," Robin quickly added.

"But...I mean...they were right here in Boise. You knew where they were."

"That day I did. I didn't know after that when he called that night."

"Why did you lie?"

Robin let out a long sigh.

"I'd just like to know why," Joan said.

"Because you would have yelled at me. You would have been disappointed."

That wasn't good enough, Joan thought. Robin's explanation did not justify what she had put Joan through that weekend. And now, Joan was even more upset that Robin had not gotten the children out of danger when she'd had the chance.

"No, I mean, nobody was happy that he had kidnapped the children – I mean, I felt real bad for you. But then, like you spent the day with him. It just didn't make any sense to me. I was so afraid for the children."

"I was after that, too, Joan," Robin echoed.

"I mean, I just think your head was so screwed up you just didn't know what you were doing. So it wasn't true about a police photographer going up that day and everything," Joan stated, almost to herself.

"He tore my stuff up," Robin said feebly, referring to Randy.

"I'm just waiting for a lot of answers, that's all. And no matter what anybody tells me, I don't know what happened in that house." Joan hoped with all her heart that Robin could explain away her doubts.

"Someday they'll all be answered, Joan, one way or another," Robin said. "I'll talk to you later, I guess."

* * *

"I need to see her."

Joan McHugh pleaded with Detective Raney over the telephone for help obtaining permission to see Robin privately. She had heard so many unbelievable stories from Raney that she wanted to ask Robin about them directly, face to face, without a piece of glass and a telephone receiver between them. She wanted to gauge Robin's reactions and body language.

Raney saw an opportunity to do some bargaining.

"I'll do something for you, if you do something for me."

Despite Joan's efforts to hide her feelings of hostility beneath a veil of cooperation, Raney could tell she still believed completely in Robin's innocence. Even though Joan thought the police were one-track fools, in return for being allowed her visit, Joan agreed to carry a tape recorder in her purse when she talked to Robin, but she had no intention of it being audible.

* * *

When Joan arrived at the jail, Raney gave her a small tape recorder to put in her purse and led her into a private lawyer's conference room. The detective left, closing the door behind him.

Joan settled herself in a chair across from her friend. Almost the first words out of Robin's mouth were, "Are you wearing a wire?"

"Do you want me to lift my sweater and check?" Joan asked.

"No," Robin answered.

In spite of her answer, Joan set down her purse for a moment and lifted her sweater briefly to her chin.

Robin relaxed and began babbling about a police conspiracy; the cops were conspiring to take her down, she said.

"You're just paranoid. Why would they have a conspiracy against you? They don't even know you," Joan reasoned.

Joan was floored when Robin told her that Ellie had warned her she couldn't talk about the case because Joan was a prosecution witness. That possibility had never crossed Joan's mind; she assumed she would be a witness for the defense.

Robin assured Joan that she was not responsible for the fire. But she did an about-face, contradicting her previous claim of ignorance about fires, when she said that she had heard of two ways to start a fire that were undetectable. One way was to make a trail of gasoline with a "mouse's tail" (a wick) soaked in gasoline at one end, light the wick on fire, which in turn ignites the trail of gasoline (a crude delayed timer) which is connected to a larger source of accelerant that fuels the fire. The second way, Robin said, was to use a delayed timer.

The two friends had a long conversation. When Joan at last emerged from the small room, Detective Raney reached inside her purse to fish out the tape recorder. He popped the cassette into his recorder and, as he listened, his face fell. All he heard were unintelligible, muffled voices, the sound no clearer than voices heard through a bad speaker at a fast-food drive-through.

✳ ✳ ✳

As she left the jail, Joan smiled to herself. Still not trusting the cops' motives, Joan had thrust the recorder into the deepest recesses of her purse and had leaned her buxom torso on top of it while she talked to Robin in the attorney-client conference room. She figured she'd never hear from Detective Raney again.

CHAPTER NINETEEN

February 17, 1992

One week to the day after the fire, at 2:45 a.m., Raney and Smith revisited the scene. As if conducting a stakeout, the two cops sat in a cold, unmarked car at the intersection of Seneca and Blackhills overlooking the sad structure with a caved-in roof and gaping charcoal wounds. They positioned themselves where they could see and stop any cars that drove through the subdivision. They stayed until 4:30 a.m., well past the time when the fire would have been set.

During that period, four vehicles entered the subdivision from Five Mile Road. One was a milk delivery truck; another was a daily newspaper delivery vehicle; the third was a man giving an intoxicated friend a ride home; and the fourth was a woman who had gotten off work late. The latter two said they had not been driving in the area at that same time the week before. All four of the vehicles turned north on Blackhills rather than south onto Seneca.

This information was significant to the detectives. It proved that traffic that time of the morning in that neighborhood was almost nonexistent. The cars that did travel at that time drove in the opposite direction from Robin's house. And the car that was seen driving early in the morning on the day of the fire, described by a witness as being similar to Robin's, was headed in the direction of the Rows' home.

Anjanette Viehweg, Robin's cosmetologist, was next on Raney's list of people to question. He learned that during the past six months Robin had spent many hours at the Hair Doctor salon being pruned and groomed. The cosmetologist tallied her visits for Raney: a perm every eight weeks, $50 each; a haircut every three to four weeks, $12 each; hair color three times in six months, $35 each; a full set of false nails every other week, $40 each; brows waxed with each haircut, $5.50 each; pedicures three times over the winter months, $18 each; and nail polish every other day, $3.50 each.

Anjanette recalled Robin telling her about vacations and various purchases, including rings, a new bedroom set for herself and Randy, and a daybed and a bedroom set for Tabitha.

Most disturbing was an incident Robin had told Anjanette about a few days after it had occurred. Raney's ears pricked up when he heard the account: On February 2, just a week before the fire, Randy, Joshua, and Tabitha were relaxing in a hot tub. Robin was out of the tub when an electric radio fell into the hot, bubbling water. Randy jumped out with Joshua immediately, then quickly pulled Tabitha out. During Robin's retelling, she nonchalantly mused that there must have been a circuit breaker that saved them from electrocution. She claimed she was unaware of how the radio, sitting on a table near the tub, had fallen in.

"Did you ever see any unusual bruising or other signs of abuse on Robin's body?" Raney asked. As intimately and as often as Anjanette had worked with Robin, she had never seen or heard anything that would lead her to believe Randy abused Robin. Anjanette would definitely be subpoenaed to testify at the trial.

There were some interviews Raney conducted that didn't help his case one way or the other. One of these was with Mary Lou Weiner and her husband, Mort. She had been one of Robin's benefactresses when she first came to Boise. Mary Lou made it clear to Raney that she thought the police were on a witch hunt.

* * *

Although the embezzlement charge against Robin Row was no more than a side dish next to murder, seasoned investigators Detective Linda Scown from the Ada County Sheriff's Office and Idaho Health and Welfare Fraud Investigator Lynette Porter jumped into the investigation with both feet. Scown and Porter began their investigation by dissecting Robin Row's financial history, going all the way back to her arrival in Boise four and a half years earlier.

In addition to the embezzlement of the bingo money from the YWCA, they also found that Robin had misappropriated thousands of dollars of contributions donated to the YWCA. And although she was never charged with it, they found that she had committed welfare fraud as well.

Their investigation took a turn when Linda Kerr, the YWCA book-keeper, reported her findings. While looking through the YWCA bank statements, she noticed that a batch of checks, made out to different pay-ees, had been deposited into the same numbered account. A subpoena uncovered the rest.

That numbered account was traced to Robin Row. An additional six accounts in Robin's name were also discovered. The subpoenaed records showed that 38 checks, dating from July 1989 to January 1992, bearing the names of 21 different individuals, had been endorsed and deposited into one of Robin's accounts. Each check was stamped on the back, "FOR DEPOSIT ONLY."

Of the 21 names, Scown and Porter were able to associate only a handful with living, breathing human beings. Several checks bore the name of Teresa Blaser, Robin's landlady. There were two money orders signed by Barbara Fawcett that Robin had claimed were for expense reimbursements relating to loss of property as a result of the October fire at the YWCA. Ten checks, totaling $3,000, had been written by Bonnie and Ray Mason. The Masons were a generous couple who had given the money to Robin with the expectation that she would get the money to people in need.

Two of Bonnie Mason's checks had been made out directly to the YWCA. One was endorsed with a near-perfect imitation of Barbara Fawcett's signature. The other was endorsed with the signature of the YWCA's custodian. Neither person had ever endorsed a check written to the YWCA. Three more checks written by Bonnie Mason were made out to the Idaho Power Company, endorsed by Idaho Power, and applied to Robin Row's electric bill. Five additional checks written by Bonnie Mason had been made out to Teresa Blaser, the name Robin had given to the Masons as a mother of a needy family, and were found to have been deposited directly into one of Robin's accounts. The only monies the real Teresa Blaser had ever received from Robin Row were rent payments by checks drawn on Robin's own account.

Because of her charitable work, Robin was well-known at her banks, the Idaho Power Company, and other institutions. Consequently, no one questioned her when she deposited checks made out to someone else or paid her power bill with a check signed by someone else. When a contributor wanted to meet the person they were aiding, they believed Robin's considerate explanation that the people were too embarrassed to meet face to face.

The saddest case was a generous widower, Mr. Goody, who periodically and trustingly handed over between $6,000 and $7,000 in checks and cash to the soft-spoken woman from the YWCA. He lived in a small modest home, subsisting on savings and retirement income. Robin had convinced him he was helping one of her poor, suffering friends.

The 38 checks the investigators were able to track totaled nearly $14,000 in charitable contributions – all of which had gone directly into Robin Row's accounts. This was only the beginning of an investigation that would eventually uncover the many techniques Robin used to supplement her income.

Robin took in more contributions at teas and other functions sponsored by the "Albertsons wives." These contributions came from organizations and medical groups rather than individuals. Robin would make her plea, "We want to get this poor family into an apartment," and people would dig deep into their pockets and hand her cash. Most of her stories had the common ring of her own experiences. Scown and Porter guesstimated these donations to be in excess of $20,000.

Robin definitely had a variety of sources for her "income stream." Porter felt as though every time they turned over a rock, there were ten more beneath it. She noticed a great disparity between monies deposited into Robin's accounts and the total of her known income. Porter also discovered that Robin was experienced at another method for stretching her dollar, referred to as "kiting." The term was coined to describe a practice in which a person with several bank accounts would write a check on one account, deposit it into another account, and immediately write a check on that account, and continue that pattern. What existed, in reality, was just a paper trail of money but not enough funds to cover the checks written.

During the time Robin was coordinating the Harambee Center in 1989, she deposited $64,850 into her accounts, with $36,000 of that amount from unexplained funds; in 1990, her deposits added up to $29,000, with $4,700 from unexplained funds; and in 1991, while she was managing bingo, her deposits totalled $37,525, with $11,000 from unexplained funds. Not a bad "income" for a woman who had started out homeless and had begun working at just above minimum wage.

Reviewing the Health and Welfare files, Porter found that Robin had received AFDC (Aid to Families with Dependent Children) and medical assistance in 1987 when she first came to Boise, and she was on food stamps throughout most of 1990. The statute of limitations prevented Porter from using information older than three years to find evidence of welfare fraud. The only welfare fraud Porter could pin on Robin was in connection with her food stamps in 1990. Since ALL income must be reported when applying for assistance, even ill-gotten gains, Robin was in violation for not reporting her fraudulent income from 1990 on. In the past, the State of California had also used this legal quirk against Robin.

Since the fraudulent check deposits did not account for all of Robin's extra funds, the investigators dug deeper. Porter found that the profit on the bingo pull tabs, which Robin had ordered, was cut-and-dried. There were a certain number of tickets at a set price. To figure a precise net profit, one would simply subtract the cost of the tickets and the payout of prizes. Porter estimated over $20,000 had been embezzled via pull tabs. Robin had told the YWCA executive director that the unused pull tabs, which were later found in her storage unit, could not be returned for reimbursement, which was untrue.

It didn't take long for Scown and Porter to realize Robin's figures didn't add up. There were discrepancies regarding the number of bingo players and paychecks made out to nonexistent employees. This creative bookkeeping added another $10,000-plus to Robin's take, money intended for the needy that would never be used to benefit the truly deserving.

Since the YWCA didn't have adequate checks and balances in place, Porter felt anybody could have pulled off the bingo embezzlement. Robin's real talent was her ability to network and solicit charitable donations. That took charm and pretense, and Robin was good at both.

The bingo embezzlement alone represented an approximately $36,000 loss for the YWCA. There was no way to estimate the future loss resulting from damage done to their reputation. "Robin Row hurt us," Director Janice Johnson said, "personally, mentally, financially, and spiritually."

When Porter asked why there was no system of checks and balances, the answer was that Robin was so honest...so honest. Unfortunately, the YWCA, whose job it was to accept and help people unconditionally, had to learn to be suspicious. From this point on, they would contact references, hire locally, and do criminal background checks.

Also uncovered were Robin's frequent garage sales. Many of the items were new household items, including small appliances still carrying their price tags. It was suspected that these items were originally ordered in bulk for the YWCA's Harambee Center where Robin had worked helping people like Joan McHugh set up new households and find jobs.

Early in Raney's investigation, he was contacted by a local radio station that promoted a yearly charitable giveaway during the holidays, the K-106 Christmas Wish. It was the same station that had sent Robin "Roe" donated gifts in 1989, in response to an anonymous letter. The station faxed this letter and two others to Raney.

The second letter, dated November 16, 1990, written by Robin Row as "herself," explained that she now worked for the YWCA with people in need. She knew of a family of four in which the father had been in an accident, could not work, and was not eligible for workmen's compensation. She further explained that due to the YWCA's guidelines, she was not allowed to give out the name of the family. "Graciously," she offered to administrate the wish.

The third letter, handwritten by Robin was sent November 18, 1991. It was another sad tale of a family in need and bore a striking resemblance to Robin's family. Again, she did not give out the name of the family.

Robin had received cash, property, or gift certificates in response to all three.

It would have been impossible to track all the money that Robin Row had embezzled or swindled. Porter estimated Robin's total take while in Boise, above and beyond her regular pay, was in the neighborhood of $80,000.

* * *

The coroner's office had released the bodies, Randy Row's family planned a second ceremony to bury the ashes of Randy, Joshua, and Tabitha. It was scheduled for February 27, 1992, nearly two weeks after the memorial service. Robin's attorneys requested permission for her to be at the inurnment in her own clothing and without shackles. The court vehemently denied the request, saying, in effect, for Robin to attend the ceremony would be akin to a person who kills his parents then throws himself upon the mercy of the court because he is an orphan. Robin was not allowed to attend.

On February 21, Robin sent Danny McHugh a letter asking about his feelings for her and if they had changed. Enclosed with the letter were messages she wrote to Randy, Joshua, and Tabitha. They read as if Robin were speaking directly to the deceased. She wanted Danny to read the letters at the graveside and place a rose on each marker.

Joan knew that the Row family had planned the ceremony and did not want her family there because she believed in Robin's innocence. The Row famiy never doubted Robin's guilt, Joan was the enemy in their minds. While it hurt the McHughs to exclude themselves, out of respect for Randy's family, Joan, Bernie and Danny did not attend the inurnment. The McHughs comforted themselves with the memory of the memorial service and the knowledge that they would visit the gravesite many times.

CHAPTER TWENTY

March, 1992

With much of the local work done, it was time for the investigators to delve more deeply into Robin's past. Undersheriff H. Dee Pfeiffer traveled to New Hampshire while Detective Gary Raney flew to northern California. What the two men discovered was enlightening and cemented Raney's opinion that Robin Row was exactly where she should be. Keeping her locked up would be a challenge.

❊ ❊ ❊

On September 12, 1957, a baby girl named Robin Lee Cornellier was born in Nashua, New Hampshire, a small industrial town with a population of roughly 40,000. She was the first-born of five children to 16-year-old Virginia and 17-year-old Charles Augustus. Following her in birth order was sister Terry Ann, then brother Charles Augustus Jr., followed by brother Kevin Scott, and last, sister Tammy Lynn born in 1964.

The Cornellier family was poor. Virginia worked at Sprague Electric bringing home a small but regular paycheck. Her husband, Charles Sr., did not bring in a steady income. When he did work, much of his take-home pay was spent on booze.

By all accounts the fact they were poor didn't seem to bother any of the kids except Robin. She always wanted nice clothing, furnishings, cars, things her family could not afford. Even though the Cornellier kids' friends were poor, too, Robin was still embarrassed to bring pals home. As an adult, she fabricated a story that her family had been very wealthy and had lived in a big house, which they eventually lost because of her father's problems.

The Cornellier household was fraught with conflict and lacked unconditional love and nurturing. Neither parent was affectionate, nor was the maternal grandmother who sometimes cared for the children.

By the time they entered their teens, frequent clashes between Robin and her sister Terry, and between Robin and her mother, added to the turmoil. When Virginia filed for divorce and won custody of the children, the tensions were exacerbated. Terry, in some ways, was happy her father was leaving. She would not miss his weekend binges and the violence that erupted when he came home. Robin, however, had always identified with and sought her father's attention. She missed him.

Eventually, Charles Cornellier landed in the New Hampshire State Penitentiary for murdering an antique dealer during a robbery attempt in 1975. Robin seemed to love her father in spite of his downward spiral and self-destruction. Predictably, her relationship with her mother deteriorated more rapidly after Charles' arrest. She hated her mother and blamed her for her father's absence.

With the exception of Tammy, all the Cornellier children began getting into trouble – lying and stealing. At 14, Robin was pregnant. Her mother took her to New York for an abortion. At 15, Robin ran away from home and ended up in juvenile hall. Pregnant again at 16, this time Robin gave birth to a baby boy named Keith. Her sister Tammy recalled Keith's father was a boyfriend of Robin's named Mitch who lived in Litchfield, just a few miles north of Nashua.

In October of 1975, just a little over a year after Keith's birth, Robin Cornellier had another baby. Kristina Mae was a wide-eyed, sweet-faced child. Robin's family didn't know the identity of the newborn's father. Robin's sister Tammy doubted if Robin even knew for sure. Robin was 19 years old, on welfare, and living in an apartment with Keith and Kristina when a group of friends introduced her to 17-year-old Wayne Hamilton.

This clique of juveniles had a nasty pastime. For entertainment and a little extra cash, they set fire to cars. In December of 1976, one of the group's members gave a statement to investigators that implicated Robin and Wayne in their pack's "fire for hire" schemes. It appeared that Robin coordinated the jobs and made the payouts, typically $50 to $75 for the firesetter.

Obtaining insurance money for torching a car was a first offense for Wayne. He was young and impulsive, eager to go along to prove his masculinity. His choices when he got caught were simple: Either go directly to jail or join the military. He chose the latter.

Robin and Wayne didn't have much time together before he joined the Marines and left for New York. Since she was a prolific letter writer, their relationship continued on paper. Still very much a boy, Wayne was thrown into a man's occupation and was understandably lonely. He couldn't explain his attraction to Robin except to say that she was somewhat of a mother figure who showered Wayne with nurturing attention.

After Wayne left, a fire broke out in Robin's apartment complex that required her and her children to move in with her mother. Robin's 14-year-old sister Tammy, who was also living with their mother, turned out to be a convenient baby-sitter. She took care of Kristina much of the time. Robin didn't like being tied down with a baby.

The night of January 30, 1977, Kristina had slept in Tammy's room, which was not unusual. The next morning, after Virginia had gone to work, Tammy took Kristina into Robin's bedroom, leaving the toddler with her mother, then got dressed and left for school.

A couple of hours later Tammy was called out of her classroom for a family emergency. When she got home, Tammy heard Robin's version of what had happened. Leaving Kristina in her bed, Robin said she had gone into the kitchen to get some milk for her daughter. When she came back, the dog was in the bedroom and Kristina was lying motionless – dead at 15 months of age.

Kristina Mae Cornellier was buried amongst a sea of headstones in a shoddy section of the Woodlawn Cemetery, patches of weedy grass and dirt surrounding her tiny grave. No headstone marked her resting place.

Detective Raney heard the story about Kristina from Tammy. Her death was ruled SIDS, and Robin had emphatically reasoned that the dog's hair had caused Kristina's death. Raney recalled a theory espoused around 1977 linking animal hair to SIDS. He also knew the current definition of the syndrome specified that the phenomenon occurred in the first 12 months of life, the peak age being 3 to 4 months old. A fine or indistinguishable line is said to separate suffocation and SIDS. Raney was more than a little eager to see Kristina's death certificate and to talk to the pathologist who had performed her autopsy.

Raney could not locate the pathologist, but he did uncover indications that the man was not as thorough or accurate in his investigations as was expected. In one case of the autopsy of a woman found dead in her crumpled car, the pathologist had noted that the victim's injuries were consistent with a car accident. He concluded her death to be a result of internal injuries. The police, who had been treating the accident investigation as a possible homicide, elicited a confession from the woman's husband. He had strangled her, put her body in her car, and run the car off a cliff. The probability of an inaccurate autopsy was another clue that supported Raney's suspicion that Kristina's death was not caused by SIDS.

* * *

Wayne Hamilton was on operations when he got notification from Nashua that Robin's daughter Kristina had died. He was filled with sadness and concern for Robin. His fondness and sympathy for her grew with each emotional letter she sent. When the Marine Corps transferred Wayne from New York to a new post at Camp Lejeune in North Carolina, Robin and Keith would join him. But before she left for North Carolina, Robin took time to "hang some paper." She was detained briefly for passing bad checks and then released. Robin was still a teenager, 19, when she toted 3-year-old Keith with her to North Carolina to be with Wayne.

Not quite two months after Kristina's death, March 19, 1977, Wayne and Robin were married. The new family lived off base in a small mobile home. A few weeks into the marriage, Wayne went to bed before Robin in the only bedroom at the back of their home. The couple shared the room with Keith, who was already asleep. Robin had decided to sleep on the couch, something she had never done before.

In the middle of the night, Wayne awoke with a start. He thought it must have been the loud noise – a bang, a pop – that woke him. Flames were shooting into the dark from the top of the dresser. Although panicked, he kept his head long enough to beat out the fire, then flew into the living room.

"What the hell is going on?!" Wayne roared.

Robin was sleeping, she said; she didn't know. Robin even suggested 3-year-old Keith might be responsible for the fire.

At the time Wayne didn't dwell on the incident. It had to have been some kind of bizarre accident, he had thought. There was a can of gun powder on top of the chest of drawers which had fizzled and flashed causing the sound that woke him. In retrospect, however, he thought it strange that the dresser, near the door on the wall that separated the kitchen from the bedroom, would spontaneously ignite.

They didn't call the fire department. Wayne felt lucky that he had awakened soon enough to extinguish the flames. Had he perished in a fire, the Marine Corps would have sent $10,000 (a hefty hunk of cash in 1977) in life insurance benefits to his next of kin, his wife Robin. This incident was the beginning of a quick slide into divorce.

❄ ❄ ❄

In the beginning, Wayne thought Robin was a good wife and mother to her son Keith, a cute, blue-eyed blond child with a mischievous twinkle in his eyes and an irresistible smile. But one evening soon after the fire, Wayne came home to an empty apartment – no note, no calls – Robin and Keith had just disappeared.

After a day and a half, she returned with a far-fetched story of where she had been. Wayne was beginning to question his judgment in marrying this woman whom he hadn't really gotten to know.

After Robin's unexplained disappearance, Wayne noticed her wedding ring was missing. When he asked her about it, she said she had lost it in the backyard while playing frisbee. It just slipped off, she explained. Together they combed through the grass searching for the shiny ring. It was never found.

It was later Wayne found out the truth about Robin's day-and-a-half disappearance. She had been arrested for writing bad checks – forgery. He was beginning to see through her lies and reasoned that she had probably hocked her diamond ring to make bail. The relationship unraveled quickly.

Robin was convicted of the forgery and sent to the North Carolina state penitentiary with a four-year sentence. Wayne took care of Keith at first, but the burden of caring for a toddler while performing his military duties became too much. He finally had to send the little boy back to New Hampshire to stay with Robin's sister, Terry.

While she was in custody, Robin wrote a letter to Judge John Webb dated September 8, 1977, asking for immediate work release. She used Keith to tug on the judge's heartstrings: "My 15-month-old daughter died in January. My son is beginning to realize that she will not be coming home. Lately my son has been asking my sister if Mommy is dead. Every time I talk to him on the telephone he cries and says…I want to go home."

In March of 1978, Robin made parole. By that time, her husband had finally come to his senses and emphatically told Robin to get out. Too many strange things happened when she was around, he said, and there were too many lies. Robin moved back to New Hampshire.

✳ ✳ ✳

Back in Nashua, Robin and her sister Terry traded baby-sitting. According to Terry, she took care of her 5-year-old nephew, Keith, most of the time. She was used to caring for him during Robin's stint in prison. She lived with her own daughter, also named Kristina, in a two-bedroom apartment. Terry occupied one bedroom, the children the second. Although Robin didn't live there, she had a key to Terry's second-floor apartment.

Terry was jarred awake one night by Keith and Kristina screaming. Then she heard another terrifying sound – the crackling and spitting of fire. Looking desperately toward the only two avenues of escape, one through the kitchen and the other through the living room, Terry saw both routes out of the apartment were blocked by fire. Boldly, carrying the two children, one under each arm, Terry ran through the flames in a daring escape.

Incredibly, because of the cries of the children, they all made it out alive. Afterward, Terry realized she hadn't heard the smoke alarm, which was located in the hallway near the bedrooms.

The fire department had difficulty finding the cause of the fire. For lack of specific evidence, the cause was listed as "electrical." Terry remembered Robin's advice to her: It's a good idea to have life insurance on your children.

CHAPTER TWENTY-ONE

Detective Raney had only a few days to talk to people about Robin's four and a half years in California – the last leg of her transient trail before coming to Boise. During his flight to San Francisco he planned his strategy. He would first gather Robin's history in Redding and then move on to Pine Creek. From Pine Creek Raney would drive to Summerville. He later described the "town" as "three cabins and a ranger station." This was the site where Robin's first-born, Keith, had perished.

In January of 1980, Robin Cornellier Hamilton and her son moved to California at the invitation of a friend. Debbie Green gave Robin and her son a temporary home in a vacant cabin she owned in the small community 23 miles from Pine Creek. The 800-square-foot shack was old and constructed of porous, pecky cedar and roofed with corrugated sheet steel. A bare light bulb hung from a single wire with a switch attached.

Robin didn't have a car or a job. Welfare was again providing for her subsistence. She was stuck in a situation she didn't like – reminiscent of her childhood – no wheels, no money, and lousy accommodations.

There wasn't much to do in Summerville. In addition to a lodge and a few cabins, there was a quaint roadside cafe/bar, the River Bend Inn, the local hot spot. Miners and loggers came in to unwind, and tourists and locals patronized the bar when they didn't want to drive into Pine Creek.

On Thursday evening, June 19, Robin went to the bar to play pool and mingle with friends, and she took Keith with her.

Thursday had been a hot one, in the 90s. Because of its lower elevation, Summerville was always hotter than Pine Creek. The evening had been clear and calm, a near-perfect summer night.

When mother and son arrived home after midnight, Robin put Keith to bed in an enclosed porch in the southwest corner of the cabin. Keith's "bedroom" had two doors, one to the outside and one off the living room area. He slept with his favorite blanket, a large quilt, and his kitten. They also owned another cat.

Around 1:30 a.m., Mr. and Mrs. Willard Brown were startled from sleep by a frantic pounding on their door. They found their neighbor, Robin Hamilton, who lived only a hundred feet from their residence, standing on their porch in a nightgown and shoes, screaming and practically incoherent. Smoke spewed from Robin's little shack. When they asked where Keith was, Robin was so frenzied, it seemed an eternity before the Browns could get an intelligible answer from her.

She finally told Mr. Brown that her son was trapped in the bathroom. Having no other choice, Mr. Brown broke out the bathroom window. When he poked his head inside he saw nobody, nothing but flames. By this time, Mrs. Brown had calmed the hysterical mother. Robin now said Keith was actually in his bedroom. Mr. Brown tried the outside door to Keith's converted porch/bedroom, but it was padlocked from the inside.

Heroically, Willard Brown did not hesitate to enter the structure which was rapidly being consumed by flames. Crawling, he started through the living room toward the other door that accessed Keith's room. There was a couch against it, but the interior door was partially open. Unable to see through the smoke, he wormed his way across the bedroom like a snake, frantically searching the floor for the child. He got to the head of the bed. He felt nothing. Then the smoke became too thick for him to breathe, and he had to withdraw. Once outside, he saw a cat run from the structure.

The U.S. Forest Service, the first agency to respond to the fire, watered down the inferno. Detective Chuck Sanborn followed the one fire engine allotted for emergency services to the scene. He called the Fire Marshal in Redding and, after determining there was a casualty, also called the county coroner, George Files.

Only a small portion of the cabin was still standing. Fire Marshal Gale Hawthorne joined Sanborn and, as the ruins were being sprayed down, they talked to Robin and the neighbors. When she talked about Keith and the fire, Robin was emotional and distraught. Hawthorne noticed she used every adjective conceivable associated with such a tragedy. She explained that she had come home at 12:30 or 12:45, made Keith's bed, and put him to sleep. She went to bed in the other bedroom. Shortly before 1:30, her cat jumped on her face and woke her up. She smelled smoke and saw fire in her son's bedroom and tried in vain to get into his room, then went to the next-door neighbors for help.

The volunteer ambulance attendant who transported Robin to the hospital was told he was picking up a hysterical lady and that she would need to be treated for shock. Despite her emotional condition, she indicated her attraction to the attendant, Doug Trowbridge, whom she would later insist pulled her burned body from the inferno, saving her life.

The structure had burned to the ground, but was still cooking when Robin left. It was 8 a.m. before the firemen had it cooled down enough for the investigators to step into the blackened mess and search for Keith and the cause of the fire.

The only evidence that just hours before a home had stood on that spot were pieces of concrete, pipes and wires, metal from the roof, twisted melted appliances, and some heavily charred stringers. The floor was burned completely through; the roof had fallen to the ground.

Between them, Sanborn and Hawthorne had over fifty years experience investigating crimes. They had learned that the best way to find dead people in a house so thoroughly destroyed was to back away from the ruins and just look. Usually some part of the body, a skull for instance, would stand out from the debris. Their trained eyes would pick up something recognizable. Finally, through the dissipating smoke and steam they saw, sticking up over a big pile of rubble, a small backbone. The flesh had been burned away. Part of the cabin roof had fallen down on top of the small body.

Coroner Files joined Sanborn and Hawthorne, and all three stepped carefully into the ashes and gingerly pulled away some of the debris. They found Keith's charred body lying on its right side at the foot of the bed only inches from where Willard Brown's frantically searching fingers had reached. Keith was headed away from the door as if he had made an attempt to get out and, finding the door locked, was trying to reach the other exit door.

The investigators discovered a portable electric heater with what looked like clothing or bedding stacked up against it. They took a closer look. The severely burned heater was pushed up against the middle of the bed with the mattress overlapping it. It was plugged into an extension cord and was in the fully "on" position. In a chair about five feet from the bed, they discovered the burnt bones of a small animal, Keith's kitten.

The investigators determined the electric heater was the source of the fire and that it had ignited the mound of cloth material that had been piled against it. The fire had burned extremely hot and fast, as evidenced by the "alligator" charring on the building's stringers.

Pictures were taken, and what was left of the disfigured body was sent to the county morgue for autopsy. Sanborn observed that a little boy Keith's size would burn quickly in a fire as hot as this one had been.

At 2 p.m. that afternoon, Robin Cornellier Hamilton reappeared at the scene. She acted confused and didn't have much to say when questioned by Sanborn and Files. She did explain that Keith knew how to operate the heater in his room and sometimes played with it "by turning on a light switch which gave power to the electrical heater from a service cord." She said he slept with "bedclothes" and a favorite large quilt. She also told the investigators she was poor and on assistance. When asked if she had insurance, Robin claimed she had none.

Even though the investigators felt Robin was evasive and learned later she had made some contradictory statements, there was nothing specific at that time to prove foul play. Nothing inconsistent turned up in the necropsy report. However, the boy was too charred for testing of carbon monoxide or drugs. "Accidental" was listed under cause in the coroner's report.

* * *

The coroner who conducted Keith's necropsy listed cause of death as "incineration" because the body was so extensively charred it was difficult to determine if the child had died of smoke inhalation or another cause prior to the fire. What the examination did show was that Keith's body weight (approximately 8 pounds) and his length (21 inches) were roughly the same at death as they had been at birth. The report went on in detail:

> The specimen consists of the head, neck, vertebral column with exposed organs and pelvic bones. There is extensive charring of the specimen without recognizable identifying features. The head has no hair; the frontal and

parietal bones have been completely burnt and disinte-
grated; there is a small plate of relatively intact occipital
bone. All facial features are absent and replaced by extensively charred, cooked tissue. The neck is intact. The tho-
racic and abdominal walls are completely burnt, leaving
exposed organs and the vertebral column. The vertebral
column is bent 90 degrees in the mid-thoracic region,
with a fracture of the invertebral disks in this area. The
arms consist of two stubs extending from the shoulder
area; the forearms are completely missing. The legs are
also completely missing.

Within the bag in which the remains were placed are
several burnt, broken bone fragments...similar to burnt
charcoal. Both lungs are exposed within the pleural cavity and are markedly shrunken and covered with extensively charred external surfaces. The normal-sized heart
has a completely charred external surface. The brain is
largely exposed and covered with completely charred
tissue. X-rays were performed on the entire remains; no
bullet or bullet fragments are identified.

Sanborn wasn't willing to let it go so easily. He had a queasy feeling, a feeling with which most good cops can identify. Something wasn't
right. Robin had expressed the gamut of grief-stricken reactions, from
tears to shock, but his instincts told him she was conniving and elusive.
Were her emotions a major performance?

Sanborn, Hawthorne, and Files all felt it was unusual to have a heater
turned on full-boil in the middle of summer. Things just didn't add up. But
their feelings wouldn't count in court. In order to get a conviction, they
needed to prove beyond a reasonable doubt that a crime had been committed, and the district attorney felt there wasn't enough evidence to build a
case. Sanborn, however, was not finished with Robin Cornellier Hamilton.

Services for Keith were held in Pine Creek four days after the fire. It
was a Catholic service. The casket was closed for the ceremony, Keith's
remains snugly wrapped in a blanket inside. His cremation – Keith's
fourth and final experience with fire – followed the service.

Robin's mother paid the $593.05 that was owed for services and cremation. Robin paid $18.41 for packaging and shipping Keith's remains to New Hampshire where her mother took care of the arrangements at that end. On July 1, 1980, Keith Douglas Cornellier's cremains were sent in a metal urn via the U.S. mail to Nashua, New Hampshire, traveling full-circle, to rest beside his baby sister Kristina. As with Kristina, no marker for Keith was placed on the site.

* * *

Bells went off in Detective Raney's head when he learned more about Keith. In his short 6-year life, the little boy born to Robin Cornellier had lived in three locations in the United States and had been involved in house fires in all three. Raney thought it an unbelievable record for a boy just starting out his life; most people don't experience even one fire in a lifetime.

Subsequently, Gary Raney spoke to a former California neighbor of Robin's, Cindy Teal, who reiterated everything she could remember that Robin had told her about Keith. Robin had been insistent, she said, about teaching him fire safety rules. When a fire broke out at her sister's house, Keith had been able to wake everyone up, and they all got safely out of the house because of him, Robin had told Cindy.

Robin also explained about the California fire, adding an interesting fact unknown even to the California investigators. A girlfriend who was being battered by her husband had moved in with her, Robin told Cindy. They had put a lock on the inside of Keith's bedroom door, the door to the outside, to keep her safe from her husband. The lock was too high for Keith to reach either to lock or unlock. Robin told Cindy the firemen said Keith was found by the door and the lock had been latched. She felt bad, she had said, because Keith was trapped in the bedroom and couldn't reach the lock to unlatch it and escape.

In fact, Keith was not found by the door. He was found on his bed on the other side of the room. He might have been looking for another escape route after finding one door locked and the other blocked by the couch. That Robin might have locked her own son in his room to die that night was a chilling thought, and Raney couldn't dismiss it from his mind.

He would hear a different version of the California fire from Joan McHugh. "It was a terrible accident," Joan reported. "Robin tried valiantly to save her little boy. She would not give up, and the firemen had to pull her from the burning structure. She still carries guilt because she couldn't save him, because she lived and he died."

✳ ✳ ✳

Detective Sanborn learned from Coroner Files that Robin had requested several certified copies of Keith's death certificate. In July, he discovered that Robin had taken out a $14,000 life insurance policy on Keith in May of 1980, just one month before the fire. Subsequently, she had added a double indemnity clause that brought the total accidental death benefit to $28,000. When Sanborn learned that a claim had been made on the policy, he became extremely agitated. There was no law against insurance policies, but one taken out one month before the fire? He was going to keep his eye on Robin Cornellier Hamilton.

The Row family, *clockwise from left*, Robin, Randy, Joshua and Tabitha

Randy Row, age 34, killed in house fire in 1992

Tabitha Cornellier, age 8, killed in house fire in 1992

Joshua Cornellier, age 10, killed in house fire in 1992

Left, Keith Cornellier, age 5, died in house fire in 1980. Death was ruled accidental.

Right, Kristina Cornellier, age 9 months, died in 1977 at the age of 14 months. Death was classified as SIDS.

Both Keith and Kristina's deaths were considered suspicious, but there was not enough evidence to pursue an investigation.

177

Master bedroom window where firefighters laddered in to find the body of Randy Row

Left, closet area beneath stairs where concentration of accelerant was found and fireman fell through to the crawl space

Right, pour pattern in living room near the base of the stairs where the front door blocked the firemen's access to the second floor

Left, master bedroom where Randy Row was found dead on the four-poster bed and Tabitha Cornellier was found dead under debris on the floor at the foot of the bed

Below, pour pattern caused by large amount of accelerant snaking its way across the living room floor to connect to accelerant in the closet area

Robin Row with son Keith, circa 1976

Robin Lee Row when she was arrested in February 1992

Ada County Sheriff, Former Lead
Detective, Gary Raney

Ada County Lead Homicide
Detective, Ken Smith

Left to right, Former Prosecutor, Judge Kevin Swain and Chief
Deputy Ada County Prosecutor Roger Bourne

Former Fourth District Court Judge Alan
Schwartzman

Chapter Twenty-Two

Homeless and alone after the fire, Robin moved into the Whispering Pines Apartments in Pine Creek in July of 1980. Being jobless, she was still receiving public assistance and waiting for the insurance settlement from Keith's death. Angela Cheney, a county social worker, was counseling Robin, helping her deal with the death of her child.

Robin didn't grieve long. She called Doug Trowbridge to thank him for saving her life. He had only driven her to the hospital, he thought to himself; he hadn't even been at the scene of the fire. But the flattery was not disagreeable. Robin was insistent that Doug had saved her life and persistent about getting to know him better.

In 1980, Robin had long, straight hair and weighed around 125 pounds. Although not a raving beauty, she was considerably more attractive than the short, pudgy Robin who would arrive in Boise seven years later.

Doug thought Robin was pleasant and friendly. There weren't many single women in Pine Creek, especially women who made themselves "available." Robin set her sights and artfully ingratiated herself into Doug's life. She was approximately the same age, but much more cunning and sexually experienced. By August they were deep into an affair.

Early in 1981, Robin finally received $28,000 from Keith's life insurance. She spent $12,000 on a slick new black and silver Toyota Celica Supra with a T-top. She also put money down on a double-wide mobile home and settled, for the time being, in a trailer court in Pine Creek just off the highway.

Robin's younger sister Tammy, now a 16-year-old sophomore, came from New Hampshire for a visit. Life wasn't good at home, and California looked inviting. So it was decided that Tammy would stay and go to high school.

To explain her recent fortune, Robin told Tammy that she had received money from the landlord's insurance because of the fire. To Robin, her new financial situation was opulence – a new car, a new place to live, and extra cash. However, the interpersonal side of her life was not faring as well.

Several months into the relationship, Doug wanted out. He noticed Robin was a habitual liar and very secretive. He hadn't seen any evidence supporting the story she had told about an ex-husband chasing her. Above all, it was unnerving the way she could change her personality.

Robin wasn't going to let Doug go without a fight. To keep her finger on the pulse of his life, she befriended Doug's coworkers. She attempted suicide with pills. Whether this was genuine or feigned, Doug couldn't be sure. Coincidentally, or by design, he was the one sent out on the ambulance call to her home. Robin told him she was pregnant with twins, insinuating he was the father. Another suicide attempt followed, again, with pills. Unbeknownst to Doug, Robin had begun to cast out her net in other waters. She moved swiftly and purposefully toward her next victim.

* * *

Robin went into the CETA (Comprehensive Employment and Training Act) office for help. This federally mandated program provided grant funds for the unemployed or unemployable. Robin was placed in the CETA office itself as a clerk/typist. Shortly after she started, she announced she was pregnant and began wearing maternity clothes. Valerie Truitt, who worked closely with Robin asked, "Is this your first?"

Robin told her about Kristina and went into great detail about crib death. Robin said that Kristina had been blind. She would later tell Joan McHugh that Kristina had breathing problems and someone else that her daughter had had multiple sclerosis.

"Are you the mother of the child that died in Summerville last year?" Valerie asked.

"Yeah, that was my son," Robin answered casually.

Valerie was not as sympathetic or trusting as others in the office. She felt uneasy about Robin almost from the day she had met her.

One day Robin didn't show up for work. Her explanation was that she had gone to Our Lady of Hope and had been diagnosed with breast cancer. Later, rejoicing, she exclaimed that she had experienced a miracle! While doing a surgical procedure for the twins she said she was carrying, the doctors found that the cancer had disappeared. Valerie thought something was fishy when she heard the story.

Some weeks later Robin disappeared again. She phoned her office on a Monday morning and told the director she had been in San Francisco over the weekend and had delivered premature twins. One was dead and the other was in the neonatal intensive care unit. Her hospital bill was $3,000 for a 24-hour period. Robin claimed that the second baby had died within a week of its birth and that both babies were buried in Whiskeytown in a pauper's burial ground.

"She's lying! That's MY story!" Valerie stormed when the administrator told her what Robin had said.

Valerie's own daughter had been in a neonatal intensive care unit in Redding at a charge of $3,000 for a 24-hour period. Valerie hadn't put it together until now. She discussed with her administrator the "coincidences" in Robin's excuses for being absent from work and her suspicions that Robin was adopting other people's experiences, modifying them slightly, and using them as her own. In addition to incorporating the facts from Valerie's story into hers, Valerie recognized that Robin used another scenario based on an incident in Angela Cheney's life. Cheney, Robin's counselor, had been plagued with breast cancer and had gone to Our Lady of Hope.

Valerie decided to make a few calls. The hospital in San Francisco had never heard of a Robin Cornellier or Hamilton. There had been no premature twins born – in fact, no twins had been born during that time period. The cemetery in Whiskeytown verified that no babies had been buried either.

After the administrator confronted Robin with Valerie's findings, Robin never returned to work.

Valerie believed that Robin might have actually been pregnant and had either had an abortion or a miscarriage and didn't want anyone to

183

know she wasn't still pregnant. If that were the case, she must have become pregnant again. Shortly afterward Joshua Cornellier was born, December of 1981.

Before Joshua's birth, Robin convinced Loraine, a casual acquaintance, that her son Albert was responsible for her pregnancy. Loraine, feeling somewhat obligated and sorry for Robin, hired her to do the bookkeeping for her business, the Stitchery Barn.

Robin didn't risk letting all her paternity options ride on one man. After Joshua's birth, she told Doug about twins being born, leading him to believe they were his. This time, her story was that one twin had died at birth and the other had lived, a baby boy named Joshua. Doug didn't know if he was the father or not.

Still holding on to Doug while using her pregnancy as leverage with Albert, Robin began courting another attractive young man. Steve Voigt was in his early 20s with dark hair and piercing blue eyes. Sensitivity, innocence, and honesty gave him an all-American, apple-pie quality.

Steve had been working in a convenience store when Robin came in and struck up a friendly conversation. The next night, she invited Steve to come over to her place and talk. They talked until 5 a.m. She was a good conversationalist and made him feel like a friend. Steve was on the rebound, his broken heart making him vulnerable and impressionable.

Robin soon pressured Steve into moving into her mobile home. He acquiesced, but kept his own apartment where he stored most of his belongings. The speed with which Robin moved the relationship to its next level left Steve a bit dizzy and uncomfortable. Nevertheless, he moved forward with their relationship because Robin was very persuasive.

During the time Steve lived with Robin, she was pregnant and domestic, made home-cooked meals, and was fastidious in keeping her home spotless. She shopped often at Montgomery Ward where she purchased household items such as orange and brown velveteen floral couches. Steve was surprised that on her limited income she could afford the new home and all its accoutrements, as well as the new car she drove.

It wouldn't be long before Steve would get the surprise of his young life.

CHAPTER TWENTY-THREE

Detective Chuck Sanborn met Detective Raney at his favorite Pine Creek restaurant. He hadn't forgotten Robin Cornellier – never would forget her.

"There was nothing left, it went right to the ground." Sanborn clearly recalled the fire in Summerville and his strong suspicion that grew with time that Robin Cornellier Hamilton was responsible for starting it. "I can't arrest anybody or do anything at all on a suspicion, other than just kind of sit back and hope that nobody else gets hurt," he told Detective Raney.

Raney integrated the new pieces into his puzzle while he listened to Sanborn relate a past incident about Robin's new Toyota. Apparently, having spent all of the insurance money from Keith's death, "She had a little financial problem and needed some cash. She took it back and tried to sell it to the Chevrolet dealership, and they weren't interested in giving her what she paid for it. [Then] the car was 'stolen.'"

Sanborn continued, "She heard it drive away one night, called the cops and the cops just couldn't find it, so she called the insurance company right away. And I'll be damned if we didn't find it a few days later, way down the canyon by the lake," Sanborn said with contempt, taking a gulp of his coffee. "It was almost a brand new car, so the insurance company refused to total it, and they fixed it. That really pissed her off.

"After the Toyota got fixed, the car got 'stolen' again. Robin said, 'Oh, my God, somebody drove off with my car last night; it's gone again.' Well, we found it the next morning behind the lumber company, over the bank, and it had been burned to the ground. She called up and said, 'I heard you found my car.' She said her sister walked by and saw us looking at her car. I said, 'I think you better come down and talk to us.'"

Sanborn gave Robin a polygraph test. "She came back halfway evasive about a few subjects. It was a tossup because she screwed up the test; the graph wasn't worth a damn because she knew what she was doing. And the polygraph examiner was good, an expert, and he says the girl's nuts – she lied like hell, but it's not showing anything. She's a compulsive liar. She has no emotions, just cold – just cold. I know damn good and well she had that car burned out there because the guy that burned it also wrecked HIS car up on the top of this mountain up here."

Taking another swig of his now lukewarm coffee, Sanborn said, "It was an insurance job, bigger than hell. The insurance company couldn't keep from paying her. There just wasn't any evidence.

"Robin's sister, Tammy, I think was scared to death of Robin, intimidated by her and afraid to say anything to the police. She's a nice girl," Sanborn explained, flagging the waitress for more coffee. "She took care of herself, finished high school. She was a strong-willed individual, but she was not like Robin; she wasn't cold. If you closed your eyes and listened to her talk, she had that same New England accent that Robin had.

"Right about this time Robin supposedly gave birth to twins," Sanborn recalled. "They were stillborn and buried at Whiskeytown Cemetery...Crock of shit, I think."

* * *

Cassandra Ryker was a young married woman, pregnant with her first child, when she met Robin in the winter of 1981. Robin fostered a relationship with the 19-year-old who lived next door to her at the Five Cent Gulch Trailer Park. Cassandra didn't hear about twins; in fact, she was not even aware Robin was pregnant.

One night, early in December, Cassandra heard sirens and saw lights next door at Robin's. The next day Robin told her that an ambulance had taken her to the hospital because of a burst cyst. Now without a car, Robin asked Cassandra for a favor.

While at the hospital she had run into a friend who had just given birth and was trying to decide whether to adopt the baby out. Robin said she had offered to care for the infant until her friend made a decision. Robin wanted Cassandra to drive her to the hospital to pick up the baby. After transporting the baby boy home, Robin asked Cassandra if she would watch him that night so that she could go to Summerville to see friends.

Eventually, Robin confessed that the baby boy was her child; his name was Joshua Cornellier. An evaluation written by Child Protective Services (CPS) about Robin after giving birth to Joshua contained this insight:

"Displayed ambivalence about it [baby], and hospital referred to CPS...Appears to be cold and calculating and compulsive as well as a psychopathic liar. Is now telling people that he is her baby but took baby home with her under guise of him being friend's baby. [CPS is] concerned about child's safety despite adequate care and appearance."

Cassandra baby-sat for Robin often and noticed something was "off" with Robin's interaction with Joshua. Though Robin attended to his needs, she didn't seem bonded with her baby boy. Tammy, also, noticed that Robin was never affectionate with Joshua and believed that her sister didn't possess any maternal instinct.

The more Cassandra got to know Robin, the more uncomfortable she became around her. She began to sense that Robin had a definite purpose in befriending her. Robin once gave Cassandra an article with a section highlighted about a method people used to abuse children using bare wires. Cassandra didn't want to read it and promptly gave it back. Robin also told her she had had nightmares about Tammy and baby Josh dying in a trailer fire.

There were other strange things about Robin that Cassandra couldn't exactly put a name to, events or behaviors that were off-center and disturbing. For instance, Robin played a tape for her of Keith before his death, reciting loving phrases like, "Mommy, I love you so much." The performance appeared to be staged, as if Robin had prompted her child to stand in front of the camera and repeat scripted sentences.

Robin also kept a double 3-by-5 frame, one side of which held a picture of Keith smiling brightly, holding a Winnie the Pooh stuffed animal; the other side displayed the following poem written in an adult's cursive script:

> *To Mommy*
> *When you cry – please know that I cry, too*
> *When you hurt – please know that I hurt, too*
> *When you feel that nothing else in the world matters*
> *Know that you are all that matters to me*
> *When you feel as if you don't want to live*
> *Cuz I'm not there to love you – know that I do love you still*
> *Merely because you can't hear my voice –*
> > *or look into my eyes*
> > *or touch my face*
> > *or comb my hair*
> > *does not mean we are parted or that my love*
> > *has gone*
> > *It merely means we are in two separate places*
> > *for a time.*
> *I love you Mommy,*
> > > *Keith*

CHAPTER TWENTY-FOUR

Robin's bookkeeping job at the Stitchery Barn included paying bills, reconciling bank statements, and picking up the mail. During the winter of 1981, Loraine left Robin a number of signed, blank checks with which to pay bills. Loraine generally didn't look at the bank statements.

Around the time Joshua was born, in December, Loraine had begun to receive past due notices and calls from her suppliers claiming they hadn't received payment. When questioned about the delinquent payments, Robin assured Loraine they had been paid.

Eventually, while reviewing her accounts, Loraine became puzzled by the large sum of money that had been transferred from a cash reserve account to cover outstanding checks and asked the bank to investigate. Between September 31 and December 31, a total of $2,000 had been transferred. Upon closer examination of her statements, Loraine found a canceled $200 check made out to and endorsed by Robin.

Since Robin was now on maternity leave, it was mid-January of 1982 when Loraine finally confronted her with the bookkeeping discrepancies. Robin at first denied any knowledge about them, blaming the disparity on bank error, but a letter dated January 24 that Loraine would later turn over to the authorities, told a different story:

> Loraine, this will probably be the hardest letter I've ever written. I'm not asking you to understand or forgive me, but I do think I should explain it. The bank isn't wrong about your cash reserve. I did it. When you were in China I had a body scan done. It had shown that the

growth was growing and spreading. The chemotherapy isn't working anymore. Dr. Zidensarai said that surgery was not recommended as the cancer had spread too close to my heart and if I had the surgery I would most likely not survive. I guess I didn't want to face it all, so I decided to seek another doctor's advice…[he] came to the same conclusion. I wasn't just going to sit around for 6 to 8 months and die when my daughter needed me. So I saw four more doctors. One in Oregon, Sacramento, Seattle, and San Francisco. They all ran their own tests and they all wanted their money up front.

I took it from your cash reserve, and I was going to put it back when the insurance money came in.

When Tara was alive it all mattered to me. I had to be okay for her. She needed her mommy. Now that she's gone, it doesn't matter any more. I know the reason she is dead is because God is punishing me for what I did to you. I've excepted [sic] the fact that I am going to die and probably won't see…my 25th birthday.

I don't want anyone to know – not even you. When people tell me I look like hell, I tell them I have the flu. I'm using make-up to cover my pale face – you noticed it when you commented on my blush last week. My sudden weight loss I say is from water pills, but it's not. I stopped the treatment completely now.

I have no real good reason for what I did. You were probably the best friend I have. I'm sorry that it's now gone. If you turn this matter over to the Sheriff's Department, I can't blame you. I will send you some money each month – if I should die before you are all paid off, I have two insurance policies…one for $2,500 which as of last week will go to you…

You were a good friend to me and I betrayed your friendship.

Fondly, Robin.

Tara, the fictitious surviving twin who, according to one of Robin's versions, initially lived then died, was used by Robin as a strategy for gaining sympathy and the attention of Loraine's son Albert. (This was also the name Raney would find on Robin's tax return years later.) Loraine was not fooled this time. She contacted Dr. Zidensarai, who had never heard of or treated Robin Cornellier. Still, it was two months after Robin's letter before Loraine finally went to the authorities with evidence of embezzlement.

She showed Detective Sanborn the proof she had uncovered and proffered a deal: If Robin would pay her at least $750 by March 28, 1982, so that Loraine could pay her retirement account and would agree to begin paying back the money she had stolen, estimated at $5,362.50, Loraine would agree to take a lien on Robin's mobile home and not press criminal charges. If Robin refused this offer, Loraine requested that the situation be handled as a criminal matter.

Detective Sanborn was more than happy to catch Robin doing something he could prove. The same day they took Loraine's statement, he and Undersheriff Laffranchini took a short drive to the Five Cent Gulch Trailer Park.

Robin was evasive and curtly told the men that she had worked the matter out with Loraine and had until the 28th to come up with the money. Sanborn asked if she had the $750. Robin admitted that she probably would not have it by the 28th. She also stated that she hadn't taken anywhere near the $5,000 that Loraine had claimed. Robin said she took the money to pay her medical bills because she had not been paid by the insurance company for a vehicle she had lost to auto theft.

Sanborn shot back that his information showed that she had received over $5,000 from the insurance company for the Toyota. Robin, unperturbed at being caught in an out-and-out lie, muttered that it was possible that was the amount.

Sanborn offered Robin a choice: Come with them to be booked or he would return with an arrest warrant. Robin Cornellier, a.k.a Robin Hamilton, was taken to the Pine Creek jail and booked for a violation of Section 503. Joshua, for the time being, was left in the care of Robin's neighbor, Cassandra.

When Steve found out Robin had been arrested for embezzlement, he was shocked. He also knew Sanborn wouldn't arrest anyone without proof. Robin's finances had always been a mystery to him. Even though she was on welfare, she always seemed to have money and nice things.

After Robin was taken into custody, Cassandra remembered a manila envelope she had hidden for Robin. Inside were invoices, bank statements, and checks that Robin told Sanborn she had destroyed. Sanborn found handwritten records of deposits not made and checks not mailed, all drafted in Robin's unmistakable hand. He also found blank checks penned with Loraine's signature, as well as checks made payable to Robin Cornellier or to cash. A total of $5,362.50 reflected unaccounted-for funds.

Robin was really beginning to hate Sanborn, who was always sticking his nose in her business. Every time she turned around, there he was, stepping on her shadow. He was as annoying as a Chihuahua and as tenacious as a bulldog.

If Sanborn hated Robin in the end, it was something that had evolved over time. "I didn't dislike her, but the first time I met her, it was just something that told me whoaaah – just the way she came across – that maybe she'd met her match with me or maybe I'd met my match with her because we're both stubborn people. I interrogated her for five hours once and still didn't get her to confess on the Stitchery Barn embezzlement."

After Robin was released on bail, her boyfriend Steve confronted her.

"I got bills," Robin grumbled.

"We could have done something if you needed money. We could have paid the bills without you doing that," Steve countered.

Robin made it clear she didn't want to talk about it.

"I'm not comfortable living here anymore," Steve told her before moving out.

He thought they had a good relationship and didn't want to just throw it away. Maybe, he justified, this was just a one-time mistake Robin had made. They agreed to work on their relationship, partly because of Joshua. Steve adored him, thought he was a terrific kid. He continued to visit Robin and her son.

Steve and Sanborn held a mutual admiration for each other, but their relationship deteriorated after Sanborn advised Steve to stay away from Robin, that she was bad news. After searching Robin's home, Sanborn's warnings to Steve intensified, but Steve wouldn't believe Robin would intentionally hurt anyone.

"I saw life insurance policies," Sanborn recalled. "One of them was on Steve, one of them was on the kid [Joshua], and one on her sister. It caught my attention. I thought, Holy Smoke!"

Tammy was with Sanborn when he searched the mobile home she shared with her sister. The policy bearing Tammy's name as insured and Robin as beneficiary was an incredible shock to the teenager. Her belief had always been that Robin had killed Kristina, and she also had her doubts about Keith's "accident." The policy with her name on it was a clear warning that Robin intended eventually to kill her. Why else would she waste her money on life insurance for a teenager? Scared and angry, Tammy confronted her sister. Robin calmly explained that the policy was to be a graduation present.

Sanborn was concerned about Tammy and Steve – anyone, for that matter, who was close to Robin – but most of all Joshua, who was totally dependent. "I felt she was neglecting and abusing the baby. I called CPS. It went to Superior Court, and they placed the child in foster care." That was when Joshua went to live with Jack and Alyce Woods.

One day before work, Steve stopped by to visit Robin. She had her luggage packed. "Where are you going?" he asked, amazed that she was leaving when she had criminal charges pending.

"My Dad's real sick, and I gotta go see him," Robin claimed.

It was too suspicious. Steve went to Sanborn and told him he thought Robin was going to jump bail.

"She was going to split," Sanborn recalled. "While she was in jail she was writing some real weird stuff on yellow-lined paper. It was something about some guy – two or three different people – Rocko and Rico, you know, rough sounding punks."

Sanborn went on. "I said to her, 'My God, you must have a big family,' and she said, 'The Mafia is bigger than you'll ever imagine…we're all family.'

"I said, 'Don't give me that horseshit. You're just low-rent, for crying out loud. You'd be a throw-down for the Mafia.' She had a hell of an imagination," Sanborn chuckled.

"She implied that she had Mafia ties…and that my kids would be in danger. That's when I told her, 'You come around my house, and I'll kill you.' She's hard, you bet your life. You mention my name to her, and you watch her bristle up like a hairbrush. She hates my guts, and rightfully so because I picked on her because she was up to something.

"I had her thrown back in jail, had the bond pulled out from under her. That really made her angry. She was going to Florida. She had made reservations on an airplane for two people." Sanborn didn't know who the other person was. He didn't believe it was her sister or Steve or Joshua, who was in foster care.

Robin pled guilty to a felony charge of grand theft and was sentenced to state prison for three years. In the end, she had to serve nine months in county jail, followed by three years probation and an order to cooperate with any plan for psychiatric or psychological counseling. Under her probation order, Robin was required to make restitution to Loraine at $150 per month or more until the $5,362 was paid in full.

Jack and Alyce Woods brought baby Joshua to the jail to visit his mother every two weeks for eight months. By the end of Robin's jail term, Joshua and the Woods had become inseparable. They had fostered him for almost all of his first year of life. He was their baby boy; they had become "Mommy" and "Papa."

While in jail, Robin continued seeing social worker Angela Cheney. Cheney's initial evaluation of Robin indicated she had definite reservations about returning Joshua to his mother:

> Robin has a serious problem with psychopathic lying...Out-patient counseling does not seem to be adequate to effect a significant change...I do not feel that her mental condition is such that she can be assured of providing reasonable care to Joshua until she has a period of intensive mental health treatment and evaluation...
>
> Results of the MMPI (Minnesota Multiphasic Personality Inventory) test given to Robin in September were not positive:
>
> The patient is likely to show a history of social maladjustment and seriously disrupted interpersonal relationships, particularly with the opposite sex...may show antisocial acting out, defective judgment...poor

work history is also likely. Although the patient may appear sociopathic, the possibility of a psychotic or pre-psychotic condition should be considered...minimal response to treatment. Prognosis is poor...faced with frustration she may become irritable, aggressive or impul-sive...Test results on this patient are strongly suggestive of a major emotional disorder...resembles those of psychiatric outpatients who later require inpatient care.

Angela Cheney wrote a more positive report which gave a green light for Robin to get Joshua back in 1983:

[I see] no evidence of active psychosis or other disability that would indicate she is unable to care for herself or Joshua. She has expressed a desire and will-ingness to continue in counseling...Although major changes are not expected in therapy, she would probably benefit from this contact.

Based on Robin's MMPI, in December after her release from jail, another psychologist gave an almost identical psychiatric evaluation as the first, concluding with:

She has her own unique way of dealing with her world, which may or may not coincide with accepted standards of behavior. She is not likely to change this style and would be a poor psychotherapeutic risk. Test results are strongly suggestive of a major emotional disor-der. She is not likely to be predictable in her behavior, stable in her moods, or rational in her thinking.

When Robin got out of jail, she sold her mobile home (some of the money went to Loraine for restitution) and moved into a tiny house at the end of a dirt road named Mill Street. Many of the people Robin knew felt she had paid her dues. Loraine even gave her a little work.

195

Despite clues in Robin's MMPI of her volatility and instability, her son was placed back in her care. The day Alyce had to give Joshua back to a woman she really didn't know was one of the hardest in her life. When she left him, Joshua pressed his face up against the window and called, "Mommy, Mommy!" Driving back down Mill Street, Alyce's heart was like a weight being dragged through the dirt. Her tears blurred her vision, the cloud of dust behind the car veiling the little face in the window of Robin's house.

Robin allowed Joshua to visit the Woods at least one week every month or whenever she needed a break from motherhood. Alyce was even able to get Robin to warm up and trust them a little and, eventually, they became friends.

The Woods hoped Robin could turn her life around and wanted to do everything they could to help. It seemed she was trying to be a good mother. She wasn't affectionate to her son, but her home was always immaculate, and Joshua was always clean – almost too clean. She didn't allow him to do anything that would cause him to get dirty, which included just about everything the tyke wanted to do. Alyce noticed that Robin appeared frigid with her child. What she didn't fully recognize at the time was the block of ice that was the center of Robin's soul.

Robin hounded Steve to come by and see her. They weren't dating, but he came by off and on to visit, to see Joshua. On one visit, he noticed men's clothes in a heap on Robin's bedroom floor. When he asked her about them, she claimed they belonged to a "fellow agent."

Before her arrest for embezzlement, Robin had confided in Steve that she was on a top-secret and delicate mission. She was working in Pine Creek for a secret government agency investigating the sheriff's department. Later, after she went to jail for embezzlement, she explained to Steve that this was all part of her undercover investigation. Robin said there were also two women agents, Susan and Regina, who would eventually explain everything to him. She had told this story so convincingly that it had seemed absolutely believable to Steve. Now, she was using the same story to cover her affair with a man whom she had met shortly after her release from jail.

Robin had met blond-haired, blue-eyed Jim Hutchings at a dinner club while on a double date. He was a 22-year-old, newly-divorced construction worker. As was Robin's habit, she moved full speed ahead in pursuing their relationship. Unbeknownst to Jim, he was Robin's "fellow agent."

Except for one unfortunate occasion, Steve Voigt didn't have anything to do with Robin sexually after her incarceration and release. It was a cold night in January when Robin seduced him into spending the night.

Looking back later on his experience with Robin, Steve realized that she had used any way she could to control him. He used an analogy that Robin had been saddled with before: "She's like a black widow. They're really nice…and then they eat their husbands. That's how I feel about Robin now."

Roughly two weeks later, Steve heard through the Pine Creek rumor mill that Robin had tested positive on a pregnancy test. Steve believed that Robin had made sure to tell many people about the pregnancy in hopes that it would get back to him.

He had begun to doubt her stories. He knew she had been seeing "agent" Jim Hutchings, and he had never been introduced to the other "agents," Susan and Regina. Considering the swiftness of the pregnancy and the fact that he knew he had been intimate with her only one night just days earlier, Steve felt certain he had not fathered the child Robin was carrying. He had gotten on with his life and didn't get in touch with Robin. Steve wouldn't hear from her until after the child was born.

Jim, too, ended his relationship with Robin. He had begun to feel uncomfortable around her. He learned that she was unpredictable. He never knew if or when she would do something crazy. As they were driving down a twisting mountain road one night, she had grabbed the wheel in anger, swerving and nearly causing an accident.

As birthing coach, Alyce was the only one by her side when Robin went into labor. Together, they walked up and down the sterile halls. It was a quick delivery, an hour at most; Robin was strong and had babies easily. Alyce cut the cord on a healthy baby girl. The moment she saw her, Alyce knew she would love Tabitha as she loved Joshua. Alyce believed, because of what Robin had told her, that Steve Voigt was Tabitha's father.

Robin phoned Steve when Tabitha was 2 months old. It was not a pleasant call. She demanded child support. When Steve suggested getting a blood test, Robin went through the roof. She yelled into the mouthpiece at him and slammed down the receiver. Three or four months would pass before they would speak again.

She took another shot at getting child support for Tabitha, this time hitting up Jim Hutchings. His first inkling that he might be a father was when he received papers from Health and Welfare's family support office. Doug Trowbridge had also received papers charging that he was Joshua's father. The three men continued to question their paternity and asked for blood tests, which Robin always refused to have done.

Even without the tests, there were definite physical similarities between Doug and Joshua. And in the end, even though he never saw Joshua and felt that Robin had deliberately kept him away from the boy, Doug paid child support.

Robin contacted Jim's family, who lived in Marysville, California, and sent them pictures of Tabitha. Although Jim still wasn't convinced he was the little girl's father, he acquiesced and began paying child support for Tabitha because his mother and sister convinced him that Robin's little girl looked exactly like him. Both were blond, plump, and round-faced.

Steve Voigt didn't bear any resemblance to Tabitha, but he would have taken parental responsibility if he had believed she was his child. When Tabitha was a few months old, Robin tried to put the relationship back together with Steve making comments such as, "If you lived with me, you could have home-cooked meals every day." He declined her invitation. Steve visited Robin occasionally until she moved to Redding in 1985. He always worried about the kids' safety.

Sanborn was sure that Robin held a sincere hatred for him because, "I would tell it like it is," he said. "She's sharp, but she's not pretty," Sanborn described Robin. "Kind of a large, stocky woman, probably half an axe handle across the back side. She's clever and witty; she'd come off the wall with one every once in a while just in passing conversation."

Sanborn also saw another side of Robin: "She's a very cold, calculating woman; made me very nervous. Kind of curled the hair on the back of your neck, you know – just nasty – colder than a hooker's heart."

Robin had told Sanborn that she was working with the New Hampshire police on a case. There was a serial rapist that was tracking her, she'd said. He'd killed the other four victims, and she was next. When Sanborn called the police in New Hampshire they had a different story.

Sanborn recalled, "They had warrants for her, like misdemeanors, but they wouldn't extradite her. They called her a low-class whore and said, 'We don't want her back here; she's just a pain in the butt.'" They also described Robin's father as a small-time punk.

With gusto Sanborn recited what he'd say, if he ever got the chance, to his antagonist from the past. "I told you I'm going to get you. I told you some day it's going to catch up with you."

In the early 1980s Sanborn told Robin how he thought karma would affect her future: "Somebody is going to get you. Some day it's all going to catch up with you, and you're going to spend a long ride to the bucket because of the things you've done."

Robin didn't appreciate his insight. "Get fucked, Chuck," she had responded with a cold stare.

That was the last time he saw Robin Cornellier.

※ ※ ※

When he put Robin's file in a container he had labeled the "asshole box," Sanborn had felt a degree of satisfaction. Her file joined others of an especially nefarious nature, criminals Sanborn had run into during his career, all waiting for the day someone would call looking for the information. Everything he had on Robin was in that file. When Detective Raney called, Sanborn had reached right over, opened his desk drawer and pulled out the folder labeled "Robin Cornellier Hamilton" and made copies for the Idaho detective.

"You got a homicide there, boy," Sanborn had said. "I don't know what happened but...where was Robin when it happened?"

"She was at somebody else's house," Raney answered.

"Did she get herself all cleaned up real good before she came in to talk to you?"

"Well, I think so. She said something about taking a shower and doing some laundry."

The advice served only as confirmation of what Raney had already suspected.

CHAPTER TWENTY-FIVE

Summer

Alyce and Jack Woods wanted to give Robin and her children a new start. They felt Robin had endured a bad childhood and had just gotten off at the wrong exit early in life. Hearing stories about her past chilled Alyce's blood and stirred her sympathies. For instance, Robin told her that she had been gang-raped at the age of 16, becoming pregnant with Kristina.

Characterizing her mother as uncaring and emotionally detached, Robin claimed that when her labor had begun, her mother had just dropped her off at the front door of a clinic to give birth by herself, saying, "Just call me when you're done." Robin also said that her father was confined in an institution and often thought he was Hitler's son or Jesus Christ.

When Robin moved to Redding, a medium-sized city in northern California, Jack and Alyce thought she was getting a handle on her life. They decided the best way they could help her was to put money down on a nice mobile home for her, with the understanding that she would pay them back in monthly installments. The Woods were not wealthy, but they wanted to help Robin and her children. Their generous offer also showed the depth of their faith and trust in Robin.

In June, Robin and her children moved into a beautiful new 14-by-70-foot mobile home with an expanded living room tip-out. It was set up in a mobile home park on a frontage road between the cities of Redding and Anderson, with pines and manzanita shrubs camouflaging the park.

It could have been a new start for Robin. She had paid the restitution to Loraine and her probation was over. However, she had been on some form of assistance ever since she moved to California, and she continued that practice.

Tabitha was a toddler still in diapers, and Joshua was three and a half when they moved into their new home. Robin initiated a relationship with her neighbor Ruth Montgomery, a struggling single mother with two daughters. Robin and Ruth often shared coffee and conversation and eventually traded baby-sitting. They discovered they had bingo in common. It was the first time in a long while Ruth had gotten close to someone as a friend.

Robin was a helpful neighbor and often offered to pick up Ruth's mail or post payments for her. It was very thoughtful, Ruth felt, and she gave Robin her mailbox key.

Sometimes when Ruth went out on a date, Robin would watch her children, occasionally keeping them overnight if Ruth planned a late evening. Robin didn't seem interested in men, never dated as far as Ruth could tell. Her passion was bingo.

Initially, it appeared that Robin took good care of her children. Even though she was not well-dressed, the kids were always neatly dressed and clean. And she kept a clean house. Robin fostered the illusion that she spent every dime on her children. She rarely cooked meals, leaving that chore to baby-sitters.

After she came to know Robin better, Ruth noticed she had an extremely low tolerance level for the normal activities of children and seemed to be constantly screaming at Joshua and Tabitha. She would put them outside for extended periods of time. Sometimes Ruth would take the children to her house just to get them away from those situations.

To make ends meet, Ruth sometimes held two jobs. She always tried to keep a well-stocked kitchen. When Robin would complain about running out of food or losing her food stamps, Ruth would insist that she come over and get something to eat.

There came a time when Ruth paid Robin to care for her 9-year-old daughter, Shelly, while she worked a part-time night job. Ruth gave Robin a key to her mobile home in case she needed anything. Ruth trusted Robin implicitly. One evening when she had to work, Robin suggested that Shelly spend the night at her place.

"Fine," Ruth said. "I'll just pick her up in the morning."

When Ruth got home from work, she couldn't find Shelly's dog. He was a small dog and had never gotten out before. She assumed Robin must have taken the dog to her house to sleep with Shelly. Ruth was tired and went to bed in the back bedroom.

About half an hour later, a loud BOOM! startled her awake. She leapt out of bed to find Shelly's bedroom was on fire. Ruth smothered the flames with a blanket. Only after the fire was out did the fear of what could have happened set in. Relief that her children had been out of the house was followed by bewilderment. The firemen couldn't find any accidental cause for the fire, which had broken out behind the white fiberboard cabinet in Shelly's room. Curiously, a piece of cloth was found trailing from the cabinet. The investigators believed the fire was arson, but couldn't conclusively prove anything. "UNKNOWN" was listed under cause.

Ruth was baffled. If the fire wasn't electrical, how had it started? And why in such a strange place? She felt as if the investigators suspected she had started the fire for insurance. If they did, they had hit a dead end – she had no insurance on the mobile home and certainly had nothing to gain by destroying her residence. It would be months before Ruth would suspect the truth.

Ruth and Robin often shared the expense of buying bingo cards and then split their winnings. On one occasion, because Robin had told her that her food stamps had been stolen, Ruth offered Robin half of her own winnings to buy groceries. On another occasion, Robin put the winnings in her cigarette case, telling Ruth she would split the proceeds later. The next day Robin claimed her brother Charlie, who was living with her, had stolen the money.

Robin's sad tales about money problems increased. More and more often, Robin would find reasons to justify keeping the winnings. Ruth believed her. She saw an innocent, little-girl quality in Robin and felt sorry for her continuing misfortune. Ruth never had reason to doubt what Robin told her – until she got a call from her bank.

She was flabbergasted. Her account had been drained. After examining the cancelled checks, she pieced together the truth. On November 6, 1986, Ruth Montgomery contacted the Redding Police Department and spoke to Investigator Pat Tennant. Ruth showed him several checks she believed Robin had forged and told him she deduced Robin had been intercepting her bank statements from the mailbox. Tennant recognized the unusual handwriting as belonging to a woman who was making restitution on her own bad checks.

At first, Tennant had found Robin to be enjoyable to converse with, seemingly a friendly person who had just screwed up and was truly sorry. Subsequently, after being placed under arrest for another matter, Robin had remarked to Tennant, "If this is about Ruth Montgomery's checks, it is just a mistake that I can explain."

Looking askance, Tennant explained that it wasn't about Ruth Montgomery's checks. Later that day he questioned Robin about Ruth's checks, and she had replied coolly, characteristically deadpan, "I don't know what you're talking about."

Ruth had a clear picture now. Robin must have used her key, rifled through her house, finding her checks in the bottom dresser drawer buried beneath books. The missing checks were taken from a single pad and replaced beneath the other pads in a box of checks. Night after night Robin had gambled Ruth's money away at bingo games. When Ruth asked where she was getting the money to go so often, Robin had responded, "Oh, I'm winning," or she would say someone was paying her way. Ruth found out, too, that Robin had been selling food stamps for cash. To cover the forged checks, Robin was tearing up payments that Ruth had trusted her to mail.

Ruth had lost about two months' pay to Robin's addiction, her credit rating was damaged, her utilities were shut off, and her space rent checks bounced. She would have lost her car if Tennant hadn't spoken to her creditors on her behalf. Ruth felt victimized and embarrassed that she had unwaveringly believed in and helped Robin for over a year.

When Ruth found Shelly's dog a few days after the fire, eight miles from her home she concluded that Robin had taken the dog from the house. She shuddered when she thought about the fire in her home and would always believe that Robin had started it to cover up what she had done.

It became obvious to Tennant as the process chugged along that Robin was in more than just a "little trouble" and was not a remorseful single mother who had just made a mistake but a hard-core con.

He staked out her house and monitored her every move. He spoke to Detective Sanborn in Pine Creek. When he mentioned Sanborn's name to Robin she exploded.

"Oh, he'll lie to you! All he'll do is lie to you!"

Tennant concluded that Robin fit the profile of a sociopathic personality, as do many con artists: compulsive and manipulative, enjoying a feeling of tremendous superiority. They don't reveal much about themselves and tend not to have "tells" (body language that gives them away) because they don't feel guilt. Consequently, they are often able to beat a lie detector test. They are too smooth, too glib, and have a hard time pulling off a sincere show of remorse, acting out rather than feeling true emotion – like a wax reproduction of a peach, more perfect in some ways than the genuine article.

Experience with these mimics had taught Tennant that it was more than money that drove a con; it was the game. No matter how much money they got, it would never be enough. It was a mistake to get hung up on motive because their thought mechanisms and emotional circuitry diverged dramatically from the norm.

During the preliminary hearing, Robin claimed Ruth had given her permission to write the checks. Her friendly facade fell away entirely. She had gotten hard. At 29 years old, she had gotten heavier, now carrying 190 pounds on her 5-foot-2-inch frame. The hearing revealed that Robin had cashed Ruth's checks at several charitable bingo centers.

Robin was released on bail April 2, 1987, and ordered to return for trial August 10, 1987. She convinced her sister Tammy and her new husband to post bail. Ruth was appalled that Robin was free and again living as her neighbor. In confirmation of her fears, after Robin's release, Ruth found sugar in the gas tank of her car.

The presentence investigation report submitted to Judge Joseph H. Redmon recommended that Robin Lee Cornellier be denied probation, that she be committed to state prison for a term of three years and eight months with a subsequent three-year period of parole, and that she pay a restitution fine of $1,000. In fact, Robin herself stated to the probation officer that she considered herself a compulsive gambler. She also promised that if probation were granted, she would complete it successfully. "I plan to…finish my degree in accounting," Robin stated, telling them what they wanted to hear. "I am...trying to establish a stable home for myself and my children. I also plan to go back into therapy."

The report summarized: "Ms. Cornellier appears to be a compulsive gambler and to supplement her gambling income, stole from the victim, a victim who was herself having financial difficulty. The defendant's prior record indicates she has had problems before in taking what is not hers...Neither probation nor jail has served as a deterrent in preventing the defendant from victimizing others...Ms. Cornellier denies wrong-doing and attempts to present herself as the victim...It is this officer's opinion that a state prison commitment is in order and, further, that the aggravated term be imposed."

When interviewed by the Shasta County Probation Department in July, Robin gave an entirely different account from Ruth's:

> "One day she [Ruth] got her income tax back...[and] wanted to treat me to bingo for watching Shelly...She told me if I won we would pay her back for what she spent and split the rest. And that's how it all started...
>
> She was winning 3 to 4 times a week but never gave me money for feeding and caring for her daughter and she wasn't splitting either. She said she couldn't, that she had to pay for this or that.
>
> When she started working at Greyhound it was nights so she couldn't go to bingo...so I started having Shelly at nights...This is when she told me to go to bingo and if I won buy the check back. She would write the check before going to work...Then a couple of times she wouldn't come home and would call and tell me just to write out the check. I voiced concern over this...She told me she was having problems at work because money was coming up missing out of her cash draw [sic].
>
> On Oct. 22nd she asked me to keep Shelly and the dog overnight even though she was home. I thought that was strange...In the middle of the night I was awaken [sic] by fire trucks. Ruth's house was on fire.

Later I found out she put the fire out before calling for help. The first question she asked them when they came to talk to her at my house, was the fire arson. They told her no…Ruth started talking about the fire and how she could remodel etc., that's when I started to wonder.

Then on Halloween we went to bingo and I paid for it. Ruth won $250. When they paid her she told me she would split it when we got home. She never did…

I told her I was angry over the $250 and being her free baby-sitter etc. I told her I also knew she started the fire herself and I was going to do something about it, but I didn't have a choice, she reported me on forgery [first].

After I bailed out of jail she told a neighbor she feared for her life – that I was going to hurt her…I asked her why? She told me…if she had me arrested and I went to the fire marshal everyone would think I was seeking revenge…it's my word against hers and my past is dirty but hers cleaned [sic]."

At first glance the details seemed plausible. Robin's version of the truth was amazingly similar to her victim's account – except the roles were reversed. Upon closer scrutiny, Robin's story unraveled.

Using some of Ruth's own words about Robin, Robin characterized Ruth as an irresponsible mother, a gambler, and a thief. The irony of casting Ruth as the villain in her intricately woven web of deception revealed itself when Robin pled guilty to felony forgery.

There were continuing aftershocks for Ruth. Robin was out on bail, living close enough that anything was possible in the name of revenge. Ruth was truly afraid. She left everything and moved away. It would probably take a lifetime before she would be able to forget completely about her "friend" Robin Cornellier.

Robin left Redding, too – hastily. Without telling anyone her plans, Robin loaded a few belongings and her children into the car and stole away without a word.

In her leaving, Robin had left a trail of unanswered questions, unresolved problems, and broken promises. Her "men" in Pine Creek were left wondering about the true paternity of her children. Jim Hutchings continued to pay child support, as did Doug Trowbridge, who had planned to try to get custody of Joshua. Jack and Alyce Woods, who had expected to have custody of the children, were left with payments due on Robin's mobile home space. And Tammy lost the money she had put up for bail.

Robin drove east. Her car made it as far as Nevada, where it broke down. She left it at a service station with most of her possessions inside and bought bus tickets for Boise, Idaho.

CHAPTER TWENTY-SIX

If Detective Raney hadn't been positive before his trip to California, he was certain now. The details he had gathered – Robin's past criminal record, the suspicious fires that seemed to follow her, and the yet unproven YWCA embezzlement back in Boise – confirmed his initial gut feelings. Raney was dealing with a skilled grifter and vicious murderer.

His gut feelings and Robin's past wouldn't be of much help to a prosecutor back in Idaho. However, the facts a prosecutor might be able to work with were: No one had ever seen any tangible evidence that Randy had abused Robin, and all the Seneca residence doors were locked and only two people had keys, Robin and Randy. Based on this circumstantial evidence, would Raney be able to convince a prosecutor to try this entirely circumstantial case? And, if he did, could they convince a jury beyond a reasonable doubt that a mother could do something so heinous to the babies that came from her womb?

Raney needed something that would show a window of opportunity for Robin to set the fire. He needed to find something that could prove Robin was away from Joan's house when the fire started. Unfortunately, his chances were slim to none on Joan's end, considering she still believed Robin had been asleep on her couch when the fire started.

* * *

Raney was talking to Joan at least once a day, relentlessly trying to convince her of Robin's guilt. Joan was still trying to prove her friend's innocence. Some of the stories Raney told her about Robin's past were so wild they were just unbelievable. But Joan couldn't seem to wipe his words out of her mind.

When Joan confronted Robin with specifics, Robin would deflect and use Joan's distrust of the police to reinforce Robin's argument that she was being framed. But the number of facts against Robin was increasing faster than Joan could repudiate them. Some could not be explained away as easily as others. One instance was the existence of several insurance policies, proving that Robin had lied about having only one.

That Robin lied was not impossible for Joan to swallow. She was aware that at times Robin could be a cold, miserable bitch. But she had suffered a terrible childhood and had experienced frightening things as an adult. Robin had even told Joan about being gang-raped as a teenager and about being raped, stabbed, and left for dead under a bridge by a serial killer.

Joan wasn't going to give the police anything to use against her friend. They didn't understand her. With shoulders set and dark eyes flashing, Joan announced to Detective Raney, "Even if she did lie about being abused by Randy or taking money that wasn't hers, that doesn't make her a murderer!"

The taped conversations Joan was having with Robin were not particularly noteworthy from an investigative standpoint. Not only did Robin phone the McHugh residence often, she frequently wrote letters to Joan and Danny, trying desperately to cling to both relationships.

* * *

Robin had turned Danny's life into a fatal attraction nightmare. He was horrified he had considered this woman his friend. He tried to avoid her phone calls. When he did have to speak to her, he tried to break the connection by being distant.

When Robin found out he was considering moving back to Massachusetts to be with his son's mother, Cheryl, she flipped out. While she sat in jail, Robin's perception of their brief affair grew out of proportion. Danny had become vital to her existence. Robin was obsessed, pleading with him through letters and gifts. Danny did not respond.

Robin was preparing to appear in court on her embezzlement charge. She wrote a short letter to Joan, going over the events of the weekend regarding the bingo money, making sure Joan "remembered" it the same way she did. If read between the lines, Robin's letter reinforced that the way she remembered the events was the way she wanted Joan to remember the events – if Joan didn't want her to "do any time." What Robin hadn't counted on was Joan's honesty, her instincts, and her memory. Later, when the fog of stress and confusion lifted, Joan realized that Robin's letters contained mostly concern about herself and nothing about the loss of her family.

✳ ✳ ✳

Joan was experiencing a roller-coaster of emotions. She spent much of her time and energy thinking about Robin's predicaments. Her belief in her friend was reaffirmed every time they talked, but she would hear stories from Raney. Joan could not arbitrarily dismiss what he said. Still, Joan could more readily believe that Raney would lie to solve his case than that Robin had killed her family.

Raney was always sensitive and compassionate with her. If Joan had a question, he urged her to call anytime day or night. Joan called with all her questions. She rationalized everything the cops alleged, posing possibilities that might negate Raney's facts. Rather than dismissing her thoughts, he listened, checking out the possibilities she raised.

In the end, Raney would interrupt her and say, "Rule Number One, Joan."

"We all live by rules. For most of us it's 'do unto others' rules: we don't kill people; we don't steal from people; and you care for your children and your family. Robin has no rules – that's Rule Number One." It was the rule he used to define sociopaths.

Joan thought, I don't care how many rules Raney comes up with; I know Robin could never kill her family. He should be applying his rules to the person who committed the crime. Outwardly, however, she listened. She was open to hearing everything Raney said so she could find a way to free Robin.

"Joan," Raney began, "I've got an idea that would help us prove one way or another what might have happened at your house around 3:30, a way to find out whether or not Robin was there. It's gonna be a little bit of a ruse, but it's just a way to get to the truth because it will come from Robin not from you or the police; it comes from Robin herself."

When she heard Raney's suggestion, at first, Joan was incensed. She felt he was trying to trap or trick Robin. Her initial reaction was to tell

210

him to get out of her house. Alternating between giving Raney piercing
looks and pacing, her mind raced trying to figure out how to respond.
Then it struck her: She felt certain that what he was suggesting would
be the irrefutable proof that Robin had nothing to do with the fire. The
police would be forced to release Robin.

Over the phone, Joan posed to Robin the scenario and question
Raney had suggested, certain her response would clarify everything.
Joan was shocked when Robin didn't have an immediate answer, but
instead beat around the bush. When Robin called back and Joan pressed
harder to get an answer, Robin's reply made her dizzy. Shocked beyond
belief that her good friend could not come up with an answer to the
simple question she had asked – Where were you in the middle of the
night of the fire? – Joan now knew with 99 percent probability that
Robin HAD been out of the McHughs' apartment when the fire was
started. Robin's final words left Joan reeling and speechless. Shaking,
she hung up the phone and went directly to the bathroom to vomit.

In a stupor, Joan popped the tape out of the recorder. Holding it
in her hand she paced like an expectant father. Time and space were
suspended as she walked the living room floor wrestling with the worst
moral dilemma she'd ever had to face. She could toss the tape in the
trash and no one would ever know. If she gave the tape to the police,
they would have the evidence they needed to prosecute Robin for murder. Would her act ultimately put Robin to death? If Robin did start the
fire, did she really mean to kill her family? Could there possibly be an
explanation? Was it just a horrible accident?

As she looked at the tape she held in her hand, Joan thought of the
nearly one hundred calls Robin had made to her since she had been
jailed. She could have endured a hundred more of the same – but not
this last one. Robin had sworn passionately to her even today that she
didn't have anything to do with the fire. This tape proved to Joan that
Robin had been lying all along. When she finally decided to do what she
had known she must, she called Raney and told him to come quickly
before she changed her mind. She hoped she would be able to live with
her decision.

"Please don't let anything happen to that tape. I'll be right there!"
Raney exclaimed.

Raney took the tape to the prosecutor's office and listened to it with deputy prosecutors Roger Bourne and Kevin Swain.

"Do you want to go ahead or should we wait and see if something else comes up?" Bourne asked.

"I want to go ahead," Raney said, sounding more confident than he actually felt. "I want to do it for the psychological advantage with Robin and Joan."

If they waited, Raney thought they might lose a lot of the positioning they had gained over the last month and a half. And if he didn't move now, possibly Joan could be swayed back to Robin's side by the same crafty manipulation he knew his suspect was capable of exerting.

Raney and Bourne went to the courthouse where the prosecutor read to Judge Morden probable cause for three counts of first-degree murder and one count of aggravated arson. The judge issued a warrant for Robin Row's arrest on those charges and ordered that she be held without bond.

* * *

Robin heard in advance about the Friday press conference announcing that murder charges had been filed against her. She placed a tearful and forlorn phone call to Joan.

Prior to the announcement to the press, Raney had contacted Judd Ray with the F.B.I. Behavioral Analysis Unit in Quantico, Virginia, for a personality profile on Robin. Ray also indicated that the suspect might display flirtatiousness toward detectives. Raney had experienced this in the interview room. Also indicative of the spectrum of personal involvement in dealing with the detective, others noticed Robin referred to Raney warmly as "her detective" at times. At other times she would become hostile and rant about how much she hated him.

Raney escorted Robin into a small, quiet courtroom adjacent to the female section of the jail. Reading the arrest warrant out loud, he informed Robin she was under arrest for three counts of first-degree murder. Across her countenance, Raney didn't discern a flicker of emotion – the one-upmanship at play again, the familiar I-knew-you-were-coming routine. He let her read the warrant.

* * *

A few days after the tape recorder was disconnected from Joan's telephone, Robin called her acting as if they'd never had that last conversation. Coincidentally, Raney was there and asked if he could speak to Robin.

He hated what she had done to her family; it was so cold-blooded. He was frustrated with her, too. He had his evidence; he had given her the warrant; as far as he was concerned, the jig was up, the game was over. But Robin continued playing. His frustration boiled over into contempt.

"Hey, Robin, how's it goin'?" Raney was more animated than ever. He talked about her daughter Kristina, her son Keith, and her other carefully guarded, dark secrets.

"Hey, you know what your sister in California said? You know what Tammy told me, Robin? Tammy told me that you killed Kristina, and she wants you to rot in hell."

After Raney finished, Robin rebutted, not with the expected, vehement denial of murder but with a simple correction regarding a minor detail. As she had responded to Joan, her reaction to Raney's accusations was totally out of context for the mood of the exchange. But "her detective" must have pushed some buttons because she hung up without saying good-bye.

Raney knew they would never talk about the murders again. As an investigator he expected to be lied to, expected Robin would never confess, but it personally irritated him that she lied about insignificant details. He asked Joan if he should put a block on her phone to stop Robin's calls. She gratefully accepted.

CHAPTER TWENTY-SEVEN

In the days leading up to the trial, those close to Robin noticed her behavior had changed, culminating in a call from Robin to *The Idaho Statesman* reporting her own suicide attempt. Her cellmates and jailers observed that she had become more touchy and depressed. She never laughed and sometimes would cry out in the night, appearing to be talking in her sleep. Once she woke other inmates with exclamations, "I'm innocent! I'm innocent!" She never went out during recreation time or to church on Wednesdays and Sundays. She stayed on her bed most of the day curling into the wall, creating her own private fetal darkness. However, being in her cell so much would eventually drive her "nuts." Robin would then convince one of the "nicer" jailers to allow her out to sit in the booking room where she would either talk to the guard or write letters.

One of the recipients of her letters and her erratic mood swings was Robert "Bobby" Baer. Robin had met Bobby when he was doing time. After his release, even though he visited her every week, Robin wrote Bobby a steady stream of letters filled with declarations of her obsessive love, sexual fantasies, and pity-provoking dialogue. He was a well of sympathy. Bobby like her, he said, and it didn't matter to him if she had committed the murders or not. Robin told her cellmates she and Bobby would be married when she got out. In spite of her depression, she gave the impression of being fairly positive about gaining an acquittal. Robin appeared to need Bobby. Her only visitors besides him were her court-appointed trial attorneys, Gus Cahill and Amil Myshin; and Mary Lou Weiner, from Saint Michael's Episcopal Church, who had given Robin her first break and believed in her innocence.

Those in Robin's cell observed what preceded her call to *The Idaho Statesman*. One night before the trial, Robin got out an envelope. Without trying to hide what she was doing, she got a glass of water and appeared to swallow a fistful of pills. After a few minutes she began to stagger, then collapsed upon another woman who was asleep in her bunk. The guards were called, and Robin was rushed to the hospital. Upon her return, Robin wore a sneaky smirk and let everyone know that she had called the newspaper to report the incident because none of her cellmates would do it for her. She was segregated from the others inside a glassed-in isolation room off the main cell where she just stared through the glass at the other inmates.

Josie, one of Robin's cellmates, recalled that before the alleged suicide attempt Robin had said to her, "Everybody is mean to me; I just can't take it anymore." Josie acknowledged that inmates could be cruel to each other. Robin was called by some inmates "baby killer" or "baby burner." When she tried to elicit sympathy, it was often thrown right back in her face with remarks like, "Get off your pity party, Robin."

Many, including Detective Raney, presumed Robin's suicide attempt was staged for public sympathy. The hospital didn't find enough drugs in Robin to have done much damage.

❋　❋　❋

Joan's life was falling apart. She was fighting with Bernie. She couldn't find another job. She was diagnosed with posttraumatic stress syndrome. She realized this experience would never go away completely – Robin had infected every segment of her life. Joan was beginning to feel that she and Robin were inextricably bound by some perverse fate that insisted on being played out. Questions possessed her waking hours and nightmares haunted her sleep. What if her testimony put Robin on death row? What if Robin were acquitted and decided to seek revenge on her family? More than once she thought about running away, moving to a different state, but she knew she couldn't run from her thoughts. She would ultimately have to face Robin in a trial.

The stress Joan had suffered before her last contact with Robin, when she was still certain her friend was innocent, was different from the anxiety she had to deal with now that she knew the horrible truth. Back then she felt she was fighting for a good cause, a good person.

Embarrassment, betrayal, and fear replaced the righteous campaign she had waged for Robin.

Joan was now convinced Detective Raney was telling her the truth about her friend. Robin had deliberately built Joan's trust in her with a wall of lies, brick upon brick with a little mortar of truth between. When it all started, Joan remembered her mantric phrase to Robin, "Don't worry, the truth will set you free." Instead, she felt the truth had made them both prisoners. Now, more than ever, Joan was determined to revere the truth.

The facts pointed to Robin's guilt, but Joan was still tormented by the gnawing thought – What if she didn't do it? What if there's a perfectly logical explanation that's eluding everybody?

CHAPTER TWENTY-EIGHT

February 8, 1993

The trial, which was originally set to take place in August 1992, was postponed and rescheduled more than once. Judge Alan Schwartzman bent over backwards to give the defense all the time they needed. When the case actually came to court, they would not be able to complain they hadn't been given sufficient time to prepare.

Robin's newly-appointed lawyers used part of that time for Dr. Craig Beaver to evaluate Robin's mental condition. In his evaluation, Beaver concluded that he had found no evidence of psychosis or schizophrenia, which ruled out any possibility of an insanity defense. He did, however, characterize Robin as a pathological liar and a sociopath. He noted that while she was clearly depressed, she was competent to stand trial.

A trial date was finally set, and jury selection (voir dire) began on February 1 – almost a year after the fatal fire. While checking the list of prospective jurors, the jury commissioner's clerk tripped over an improbable fluke. Incredibly, Randy Row was slated to serve jury duty during his wife's trial. Some wondered if this was a message from a higher power or if Robin's husband was speaking from the grave. If Randy could have served from the hereafter, what verdict would he have pronounced?

The day before jury selection *The Idaho Statesman* ran a two-page story of the defendant's history. The article, which was thoroughly researched, lacked input from Joan McHugh. She had declined the reporter's requests for an interview to avoid compromising her testimony. However, the article, which contained certain details that would not be admitted during trial, severely hampered the voir dire process. Nearly half of the approximately 100 potential jurors would ultimately be disqualified because they had read the story.

The prosecution looked for people who could make hard decisions, think logically, and had some life experiences. And above all, they wanted people who understood that parents can and sometimes do kill their own children. The defense attorneys wanted jurors who were open-minded, people who wouldn't assume that Robin committed murder simply because she was a liar.

Each side was allowed to dismiss up to ten potential jurors for cause. Eventually, a jury of nine men and three women was selected with two alternates. They ranged in age from 29 years to retirement. Professions ran the gamut: a retired high school English teacher, an installation supervisor for a cable television company, a port-of-entry officer, a manager of a receiving dock, a bank secretary, a partner in a construction company, and a United Postal Service employee.

* * *

At 9 a.m. Monday, February 8, 1993, almost a year to the day after the tragedy, the trial began.

Robin Row chatted with the female marshal who had escorted her into the courtroom. Her casual demeanor obscured her identity for the moment. The judge had allowed her to wear street clothing and to be free of handcuffs.

Sandwiched between her attorneys, Cahill and Myshin, Robin slumped in her chair at the defendant's table near the jury box. She looked matronly, older than her 35 years. Her hair hung limply, as devoid of style as her clothing. She sat silent and stoic. Her expression did not betray her thoughts as she listened to the opening statements of the trial that would decide her fate. She appeared to have less interest in the proceedings than did the onlookers in the gallery.

Her lawyers had known Robin to be quite pleasant at times. They noticed a definite change in her demeanor in the courtroom. Her emotions were frozen, suspended. The prosecutors, too, noticed a change in her personality – from independent and in control, as she had appeared on the police videos, to quiet and dumpy in the courtroom. They speculated that she might not want to be perceived as a high-class killer with a quarter of a million dollars, but more like somebody's mother, a pathetic and abused housewife.

Before the jury was brought into the courtroom, the judge denied the defense's request for a change of venue. Then he denied the prosecutor's request to have Detective Gary Raney present, explaining, that as a key witness, he should not be a spectator at the proceedings.

After the jury was seated, Judge Alan Schwartzman's voice thundered to a half-full courtroom with a capacity for over one hundred people, "This case charges the defendant, Robin Lee Row, with three counts of murder in the first degree and a fourth count of aggravated arson."

Robin pled not guilty on all counts.

* * *

Deputy Ada County Prosecutor Roger Bourne gave the opening argument. The 40-year-old Bourne was a career prosecutor and had no aspirations to change professions. Generally, when there was a homicide in Ada County, he was one of the first to be called.

For Bourne and his co-counsel, Kevin Swain (who was making his debut in a murder trial), the case wasn't starting today but had begun almost a year ago. They had looked at every piece of evidence under a microscope. Bourne estimated that in many cases, this one in particular, it took a day of preparation for every hour spent in the courtroom.

Propped up in front of the jury were two visual aids. A large calendar displayed dates of significant events beginning with Christmas 1991. The other listed Robin's insurance policies in bold print and how much she thought they would pay off.

Adroitly as a chess master, Bourne set about to convince the jury that the defendant had murdered in cold blood, with the premeditation and cunning of a predatory animal. His piercing dark eyes rarely drifted from the jury box. With all eyes fixed on him, he built a framework for his case with a whisper.

"Robin Row needed a reason. She needed a really good reason…to be outside of her house at 4 o'clock in the morning on February the 10th, 1992. She needed…a really good alibi. An alibi that everybody would understand and nobody would question…because she knew that she was going to burn that house to the ground on that day with her husband and two children in it." Bourne's hushed tone intensified. "For love

219

and money. She loved a new boyfriend and she loved insurance money – life insurance money – more than a quarter of a million dollars worth of life insurance money on two children and a man who didn't work, that she supported economically."

Leaning toward the jury box, he spoke personally to each attentive juror. "Ladies and gentlemen, let me tell you how she tried to create the perfect crime and how it almost worked."

Bourne continued for several minutes to a rapt audience, giving a skeletal overview of his case.

"Now, Sunday night was not a good one for Joan," Bourne went on, describing the night before the fire. "Joan is worried...sick about the children...will they be able to get him [Randy]? Will the kids be safe?...She heard the defendant up in the night taking a shower, using the washing machine.

"And then at about 5:00, 5:30 in the morning the defendant came into her bedroom all dressed and said, Joan, I haven't been able to sleep all night...I have a terrible feeling something is wrong at Seneca Street. Will you go with me?...Joan jumped up, got dressed, and they went down and got in the defendant's car. It was a cold, dark, foggy night...

"Robin's car started cold and ran cold..." To deflate the impact, Bourne made sure to tell the jury about the cold car before the defense did.

"Before they ever got to Seneca Street the defendant said, 'Joan, I have a feeling the terrible thing at my house is that it's on fire.' And Joan said, 'You know, you can't know that the house is on fire; it's dark out. I'll bet everything's going to be fine and we'll go to breakfast.' But the defendant was right. The house was on fire."

Bourne told the jury how the fire started and how the smoke was sucked into the cold air duct return above the closet, distributing carbon monoxide upstairs where Randy, Joshua, and Tabitha lay sleeping. He also told them about the pour patterns which showed a flammable liquid was dispersed throughout the living room blocking both escape exits.

Bourne used Robin's own words to illustrate discrepancies in the defense's case. He pointed out that when Robin spoke to detectives after the fire, her story regarding her whereabouts over the weekend differed from what she had told Joan. To Raney, she mentioned nothing about any kidnapping and claimed to have no insurance other than a small policy through the YWCA.

Bourne's tone again rose to a whispered roar. "Detective Raney began his investigation...and ladies and gentlemen, this is what he found:

"He talked to Mr. Healy next door about the rape [that Robin had claimed Randy had committed] and coming in and untying her [Robin] and finding her naked. Mr. Healy didn't know anything about that...So the detective checked the records of the sheriff's office...No record. No police report. No dispatch run sheet...Mental Health had never heard of Robin and Randy Row...He wasn't being committed.

"How about the CT scan? Surely the CT scan is going to show she's got a bruise on her brain wall. She had a CT scan – it was normal. There was nothing wrong with her.

"Well, [what about] the friend and her retired sheriff's deputy husband...who went on Saturday morning with her to Seneca Street to find...knickknacks had been broken up and her clothing slashed? The husband is a retired truckdriver. He'd never been to Seneca Street. The sheriff's department didn't go there on Saturday morning to act as a civil standby.

"Well," Bourne's voice began its crescendo, "how about Sue Fellen then? Sue Fellen must have spent Sunday morning talking about the rape, counseling with her. No. Sue Fellen didn't have anything to do with her on that Sunday morning, hadn't seen her at all.

"Robin Row needed...an alibi, and she created one out of whole cloth. It was a pack of lies," Bourne seethed, unsuccessfully containing his loathing. "Except for one thing.

"She did have $2,500 worth of life insurance on the children through the YWCA. What she didn't tell Detective Raney about was that she had five other policies through four different insurance companies, that if they had paid off, if this scheme had worked, would have paid her over a quarter of a million dollars worth of life insurance on two children and Randy Row.

"I'll submit to you," Bourne concluded, "that the State will put evidence before you to convince you beyond a reasonable doubt that this defendant planned and premeditated the murder of her husband and two children and that she did it because she loved somebody else and she wanted the insurance money.

"It almost worked because everybody thought that Randy had done it. At the conclusion of this case…the People of the State of Idaho will ask you to find proof beyond a reasonable doubt that this defendant committed the crime that she's charged with. Thank you."

Bourne had given the jury and the gallery an encapsulated version of a long and complicated story that spanned almost four years. Digesting the drama unfolding before them and sifting through the testimony and evidence would be a mammoth task. A vast array of witnesses would help get to the truth. The prosecution expected to call roughly 50 witnesses, the defense around 30.

Lead counsel August "Gus" Cahill Jr., who was in his early 40s, and Amil Myshin, in his late 40s, were well-respected by colleagues and considered the best advocates in the public defenders office. No lawyer in Ada County had defended more murder cases over the past ten years than either of Robin's defenders.

Their goal was to get an acquittal. Their tactics were, one, to point the finger of guilt away from their client and offer up one of the victims, Randy Row, portraying him as unbalanced and suicidal; and, two, to put the Ada County Sheriff's Office on trial in an attempt to nullify the circumstantial evidence by insinuating Robin Row was set up. Above all, in order for the circumstantial pieces of the State's puzzle to fall apart, the defense had to tear apart the most damaging witness, Joan McHugh, the prosecution's frame. Their ace in the hole was that the jury would have to find their client guilty beyond a reasonable doubt.

Amil Myshin was not a tall man. His wire-rimmed glasses and wavy salt-and-pepper mane and whiskers gave him a serious, doctoral air. He stepped up to the podium and began his opening statement, "Robin Row did not set the fire that caused the death of her family," Myshin began soberly. "What a tragedy. A mother's worst nightmare. Imagine losing your family so suddenly and then being accused of setting the fire that caused their deaths."

The trial would be emotional, Myshin warned, and they should not let it stir their passion or sympathy. He explained that the once harmonious family had deteriorated dramatically after Randy Row was disabled in a motorcycle accident and left brain damaged. "This was not a perfect family. This family needed counseling, there's no question about it.

"He had to be raised like a child for a while," Myshin said about Randy. "Not only did she have to support the family," he nodded toward his client, "she had to care for Randy…and probably worst of all, adjust to the personality change that occurred. Randy was a different person, and it does appear that Robin was the one who had to bear the burden of that.

"Well, I think when that burden became so great, Robin decided it was time to separate, and it was time to divorce. Randy didn't like this. Randy began calling. Randy made threats. Randy was abusive. When that got to be too much, Robin decided that divorce was the only way out. And, in fact, even called a lawyer about it. A divorce by legal means. Not a divorce by murder as the State would have you believe.

"Robin Row loved her children, and now they're gone. She had a friend that she trusted and relied on. A friend that manipulated her…a friend who turned on her – Joan McHugh…I ask you to view this witness with caution…look at the motives she had for doing the things that she did, for saying the things that she said, for helping the police investigate the case, for helping to create a circumstantial case against Robin Row.

"After this fire, the police decided that Robin Row was their primary suspect. And you will see that everything they did after that was designed to build a case against Robin Row."

The defendant sat still, round-shouldered and slightly pitiful. She seemed to be just tolerating the court process until she would surely be found innocent. The prosecutor didn't have a shred of physical evidence tying her to the murders.

CHAPTER TWENTY-NINE

Prosecutor Roger Bourne and his second chair, Prosecutor Kevin Swain, had screened over 100 potential witnesses. Their challenge was to put the bits and pieces of their circumstantial case together in a way that the jury would understand. They were confidant that Robin Row was their perpetrator, but the jury would not hear all the things they knew about her. Bourne's credo was that he had to be absolutely convinced of a person's guilt before he ever stepped a foot into a courtroom. In this case, he was beyond certain. The proof that tipped the scales had been the information gleaned from Joan McHugh's final conversations with the defendant.

From the beginning, Joan had impressed Bourne as an honest person with integrity. He was confident that if they could convince her of the truth, she would make a good witness. Though she had been outraged when he and Raney had initially talked to her, Bourne had seen a trace of a question beneath her indignant stance.

* * *

In the basement, Joan paced the length of the small witness waiting room, still stewing about the trial that had caused her fitful sleep. Though she had argued and pleaded with Bourne, he insisted she had to be the first witness. She was the puzzle's frame, he explained, the witnesses following were the pieces.

During the days leading up to the trial, Joan's opinion about Bourne had changed dramatically. When she had first met him at the magistrate's hearing, she had thought he was a fool, a mouthpiece for that cop Raney who sat next to him feeding him lies about Robin. She found out after getting to know him better that he was kind, gentle, and patient. Joan regretted her earlier clash with Detective Raney and Prosecutor Bourne, when she had still thought of them as the enemy.

* * *

"It's time. You'll be fine." Although Bourne's voice was calm, it had little effect on Joan McHugh's shaking knees.

Although she was anxious, it was not obvious. Now that the time had finally come, Joan was determined to tell the truth and get through the ordeal with as much grace as she could muster. As she made her way toward the witness chair, pangs of guilt tempted her to turn and run. What if her testimony put Robin to death? She had wrestled with her moral dilemma through many sleepless nights.

Joan walked past the defense table where her former best friend was seated. She lightly brushed the wood with her fingertips, maybe to connect with Robin or just to feel something solid, real. When she turned, her eyes met Robin's for the first time in many months. They smiled at each other before Joan raised her hand to take the oath. It was an odd moment as she began to testify against the woman she had so staunchly defended for so long.

Joan quietly stated her name and spelled it for the record. Detecting a slight quiver in her voice, Bourne tried to set her at ease. "You nervous?"

"I guess so," Joan answered.

"You should have seen some of these jurors when we were questioning them. Take a deep breath," Bourne smiled comfortingly and prompted her to relate her story.

She repeated the story she had told so many times during the past year. Repetition didn't make it any easier. As she spoke, some of her nervousness moved over to make room for melancholy. As concisely as she could, she told about moving to Boise and explained how Robin had become so inextricably woven into the fabric of her life. She explained their work at the bingo center and told about the closeness of the two families. She testified about the abuse stories she had heard from Robin. She managed to keep her emotions in check. Joan was afraid she might not be able to close the floodgates if she started to cry.

Feeling awkward referring to her as Mrs. McHugh, a woman whom he'd been on a first-name basis with for months, Bourne asked, "You don't mind if I call you Joan, do you?"

Even within the jaws of her agonizing situation, a little of Joan's natural humor escaped. Responding with a shy smile, her facial strain eased a bit, "No, as long as I can call you Roger." She pronounced his name, "Rah-jah."

Observers quickly realized that the woman sitting in the witness chair radiated intelligence and candor. Her inner strength was evident as she carefully articulated her answers in her Bostonian accent, lightly skipping over the "r's" in the middle of words, pronouncing them "ahh," and adding them to words ending in "a." The jurors cocked their heads and leaned a little closer.

Roger had never spoon-fed testimony but had always told Joan just to answer in her own words. She had to make an effort not to be sarcastic or flippant, her usual communication style. In some quirky way, Joan got strength by looking at Robin. Mostly, Robin looked back impassively. Once, however, she smiled warmly, giving Joan a glimpse of her "old friend." What am I doing? Joan thought, wanting to flee. Then, like liquid quick-frozen, Robin's face was a mask again.

Joan's credibility was enhanced by the fact that she related her experiences from the perspective she had held at the time the events had occurred. Even though she knew better now, her memory still retained her original perception.

For instance, when Bourne asked Joan why Robin didn't go to work with her on that Saturday evening before the fire, she responded, "Well, she was pretty upset. I mean, you know, her husband just kidnapped her children…"

Joan was transported back in time as she spoke from the witness stand. She had thought the tremendous ache in her heart had scarred over, become calloused. But all the old emotions were stirred up by recalling the past she'd shared with Robin.

"How did she tell you she'd spent the day on Saturday?"

"She told me that she got up and went to Albertsons, and while she was at Albertsons, she bumped into someone she knew. She told the woman what was going on because she was a friend of hers – how upset she was…Robin said that she wanted to go home and get some clothes, and the woman's husband said that she shouldn't go there alone…in case he was there."

"So what happened then?"

"So the husband went with Robin and they called and had someone from the sheriff's department meet them there."

"What did they find at Seneca Street when they got there?"

"Robin's clothes had been destroyed; they had been cut with something. The side of the mattress that she slept on was all cut up. The woman's husband was very upset and said that what Robin needed were pictures. So he called someone because he was retired from the sheriff's department...a police photographer, and he told Robin to call her attorney...and she told me that Ellie had agreed to meet the police photographer there."

"Did she describe certain of her things that had been destroyed?"

"Yes. All of her clothes. There were clothes in the living room; there was something that was burnt; and there was something that was slashed; and her mattress was slashed and all the clothes in the closet."

"Did she say anything about her knickknacks?"

"Well, they were broken."

Robin sat stone-faced as Joan retold her stories.

"Now, Sunday morning when you got up, was Robin in your apartment then?"

"No."

"When did you see her on Sunday, if you did?"

"I think it was around noontime, maybe a little bit after."

"Did she tell you where she'd been that morning?"

"Yes. She went to see Sue Fellen, the woman at the Crisis Center, because she was really distraught about the children."

Again, Joan remembered what she thought had happened and what she thought had been Robin's mental state at that time.

"Now," Bourne continued, "that Sunday evening at 6-ish or thereabouts, did Robin stay at your apartment the rest of the evening so far as you knew then, until bedtime?"

"Yes."

"What did she do during that time?"

"I don't remember. I think we might have watched a little TV. We were probably doing laundry because I was always doing laundry on the weekends. We just sat around visiting."

"Okay. Did she have a shower that afternoon or evening, there at your house?"

"I think she did – yeah, I think she did," Joan remembered.

"Wash her hair?"

"I think so. I can see her in her housecoat."

Joan told the Court about Randy's call late Sunday evening when he said he was going to lock Robin out of the house. Joan said she had slept fitfully that night, worrying about the children and a possible confrontation with Randy the next day and had heard the washer and shower running during the night.

"At sometime early Monday morning, the 10th, did Robin Row come into your bedroom?" Bourne asked.

"Yes. She woke me and said that at 3 o'clock she had this terrible feeling that there was something wrong at her house. And she tried to ignore the feeling, and she just kept busy, but she couldn't go back to sleep. And the feeling was just getting stronger, and she thought there was something wrong, would I please go with her."

"Did she say she'd been up with the washing machine and the shower and such that night?"

"In the course of conversation she told me that she had just been trying to keep busy and, you know, did a load of clothes and took a shower and the feeling just – the feeling just didn't go away, so she woke me up."

"When she came into your bedroom, was she dressed in clothes or was she still in her night clothes?"

"No, she was dressed."

Joan testified it was about a quarter past 5:00 when they got into Robin's Mazda and headed for Seneca. She also answered honestly that the car was cold and that Robin had trouble keeping it going, which was a boon the defense could use to imply Robin hadn't taken the car out earlier.

"Okay. From the position on Five Mile that you were when Robin first started talking about the fire, can you see Robin's house or the duplex from where she began talking about that?"

"I couldn't see much of anything. I mean, it was very dark and it was very foggy."

"Could you see flames or fire or anything like that?"

"Oh, no. No."

228

"All right," he continued, "as you kept walking towards her apartment there on Seneca Street, as you got closer, were you able to tell what was going on at the house?"

"Yes."

"What could you see as you got closer?" Bourne moved slowly from the lectern toward the jury box. When he had advised Joan ahead of time to look at the jury, she said it would be rude not to look at the person asking her questions. He knew better than to push Joan and cleverly got around the issue by positioning himself in front of the jury. When answering questions, she now had to face the jury to look in Bourne's direction.

"I could see the flames coming out of Joshua's bedroom, and right after that I could see black smoke coming out of Robin's bedroom," Joan answered numbly, tears pooled in her eyes. A mist from the past crossed her face; the courtroom vanished and she was right back on Seneca Street. The graphic memories would never fade – huge, billowing flames leaping from Joshua's window, the cloud of blue smoke furiously surging from Randy's and Robin's bedroom, the involuntary urge impelling her to charge into the inferno and drag out the people. Robin is so lucky she went into shock, Joan remembered thinking.

"What happened then? What'd you do?" Bourne probed gently.

"Well, Robin started to run, and I was trying to help the policeman to stop her from running, and she was – she was just saying, 'my…my' – I'm sorry," Joan apologized, her voice quavered, then broke. Her composure melted away. She couldn't stop the flood of tears. The two women looked at each other, reliving the tragic evening. For the first time the defendant appeared to show some emotion. Joan wondered for whom Robin shed her tears.

"'– my children are in there,'" Joan continued. "And the policeman stopped her, and she started to go down to her knees, and I guess between the two of us we held her up and she said she wanted to go to her children."

"Where did you go from that point when you were standing out on Seneca Street?"

"Paramedics or police – I have no idea who they were – they came over and they walked Robin over to…the back of a truck…I think they sat her down and they told her that they had gotten Joshua out of the house. They could see Randy and he was dead, but the floor was too hot and they couldn't get to him, and they couldn't find Tabitha. And Robin suddenly remembered that for some reason Tabitha used to get up in the middle of the night and go into Robin's room and sleep on the floor. Robin almost stepped on her a couple of times…"

"Did you think Randy had done this at that point?"

"Oh, absolutely – yes."

"And was that based upon the things that Robin had told you had been going on for the last month?"

"Yes."

"Did Robin tell you that she feared being blamed for this?"

"Yes."

"When you were talking to Robin about being blamed, did she tell you something about the burning bed syndrome?"

"She said they were probably going to blame her because it was their thinking that it was the burning bed syndrome."

"What was that?"

"There was a movie about a battered wife. After years of abuse, while he was sleeping, she set the bed on fire."

He then asked if she and Robin had discussed insurance. Robin had told her about only one small policy through the YWCA, Joan said. Then Bourne elicited the incriminating words Robin had spoken to Joan just before Joan went to interview with Detective Raney.

"Was there a point…Robin made a statement to you concerning what would happen if you testified or what would happen to her if you testified?"

"Uh-huh."

"And what did she say to you?"

"That we were going to kill her. And I – I said, 'We're just going to tell the truth.' And she said, 'That's going to kill me.'"

Joan hoped Robin's words weren't prophetic. Hearing herself say them out loud underscored the possibility that her testimony could put Robin in prison for life, or put her to death. The faces of the jurors and onlookers reflected empathy for Joan McHugh.

Bourne went on to question Joan, between objections, about what she had seen in Robin's storage unit. She answered that she saw nothing of Randy's or the children's in storage.

The next line of questioning covered the tape recorded phone conversations between Joan and Robin and the tapes and letters that Joan had turned over to the police.

"Were you doing that to assist the police or to assist Robin?" Bourne asked about the tapes.

"I thought I was assisting Robin."

Judge Schwartzman called for a short recess to give the defense time to review the letters. When they reconvened, Judge Schwartzman, outside the presence of the jury, entertained an objection from Gus Cahill:

"The testimony at the suppression hearing through Detective Raney, not this witness, establishes that at the time these letters were received and turned over to the police, this witness was an agent for the police... funneling documents pretty much carte blanche at his [Raney's] request." Cahill stated one of the pillars supporting his defense.

"We have the defendant writing a letter to this gentleman, in essence you could call them love letters, and in some aspects they're graphic; they describe things that have nothing to do with this case. I think they are embarrassing...they're a lot more prejudicial toward the defendant's character than they are probative of any issue in this case. So I think they're suppressible – under the Fourth Amendment expectation of privacy from the jail. There's been a Sixth Amendment violation by the agent of the police in seizing them..."

An agent for the police!? Joan fumed to herself. That was the last thing she ever expected to be accused of. The lawyers obviously didn't know the first thing about her or her motivation.

Judge Schwartzman took the wind out of the defense's sails when he made it clear the letters were voluntary communication from the defendant.

"State's Exhibit No. 11, for want of a better word, is an ardent love letter from the Ada County jail to whom I presume has been described as the witness' son. In terms of its relationship to relevancy and Rule 403, in my opinion, this is clearly admissible – in terms of relationship, motive, and piecing together of this entire scenario.

"State's Exhibit No. 12 is another version of a love letter in less ardent form. Again, I will admit State's Exhibit No. 12."

Deciding that the ardent love letter got the point across that Robin Row was desperately in love with Danny McHugh and would do anything to be with him, Bourne withdrew his motion for the admission of the second letter, Exhibit No. 12.

Exhibit No. 14 was then played for the jury from a tape made from Joan's message service: "Tell her she better get her ass home or I'll be locking her out!…If she doesn't call, something bad's gonna happen that she doesn't want to happen." Randy's angry, bellowing voice sounded canned coming from the tape player.

Robin appeared shaken listening to Randy's profane threats, piercing through the stillness, eerily rising as if from the dead. Joan shuddered, but for a different reason. This time she wasn't afraid for Robin. She realized that it had all been choreographed – with Robin as director – to provoke Randy, to get him infuriated enough to call and leave angry messages which would support her claims of abuse.

Next, Bourne introduced the graphic postmortem photographs of Tabitha, Joshua and Randy. To diminish the shock he had given Joan and Bernie an advance look. After looking at them for the first time in Bourne's office, feeling sick, Joan had gone to the bathroom and sobbed until her well of tears went dry. After the shock wore off, she was surprised. Randy and the kids were not burned beyond recognition like Robin had described when the two women had decided cremation would be best. Tabitha's arm, the one that was up over her head serving as a pillow, in rigor mortis appeared to be stiffly reaching. To Joan it looked like a sign from the child – Tabitha was reaching for someone to help her.

Bourne was through with his direct questioning and released his star witness. Opposing counsel would now have their turn to question Joan.

CHAPTER THIRTY

Gus Cahill jumped up quickly. He was eager to divert the jurors' attention from the impact of Joan's testimony. Unable to contain his contempt for Joan, he swaggered up to the lectern to begin his cross-examination.

"Ms. McHugh, as I understand it, you had a limited power of attorney that was drawn up so that you could assist with burial arrangements. Correct?"

"And it said and other personal, too, whatever that means," Joan answered openly. She wanted to volunteer that Robin had needed her to take care of her business affairs.

"And from that, you ended up with the title to this vehicle that you and your husband are driving now? Is that my understanding?"

"Yes."

"And as a matter of fact, Ms. Row's attorney sent a demand letter to you within the last month asking you to turn that car back over, did he not?" Cahill snapped.

"In January. Yes, he did," Joan answered without apology.

"Yes. Then you sought legal counsel and haven't turned that over yet, right?"

"That's right."

"You also cashed Robin's tax returns last spring, did you not?"

"Yes, I did."

"And put them in your account?"

"Just as she told me to do."

Cahill went on to insinuate that Joan's son, Danny, had more than one alias. She explained her son's alias was sometimes going by his middle name.

233

Cahill tried his best to shake Joan, with little success. He questioned her veracity, her memory, and her eyesight.

"Now, do I understand that you lied to the people that you worked with concerning Robin's condition? Correct?"

"Yes, I did." In Joan's voice was a hint of indignation. How dare Cahill have the unmitigated gall to compare her protection of Robin's dignity and privacy to the lies told to cover three murders.

"Now, as I understand, you actually observed what Robin reported to you as marks on her body that were caused by Randy's abusive behavior, correct?"

"Yes. Well...I saw the bandages and I saw the Band-Aid. I mean, I saw when she had her face covered, and I saw that her wrist was wrapped up. I didn't actually see the bruises...she told me that she was in pain, and I had no reason to doubt that."

"You also testified, did you not, on two prior occasions that you saw red marks on her neck from where –"

"That was the night she came to my house in her night clothes, and I could see red marks on her neck, yes."

To dispel any testimony that would tend to show his client as cold and unfeeling, Cahill questioned Joan about arriving on the scene. "What I'm curious about is you've said that when Robin started to approach the house she was restrained?..."

"By the policeman who had been at the corner," Joan answered.

"And she screamed stuff about her children being there, that sort of thing, correct?"

"Yes, she did."

"And was pretty upset, correct?"

"As far as I could see."

"Now, did I understand that you – after Robin was arrested – that you cashed one of her paychecks. Is that right?" Cahill tried again to paint Joan as a turncoat friend whose only concern was getting Robin's money.

"Yes, I did."

"Do you know how much that was for?"

"$1,026 and, I think, 36 cents."

"And you deposited that check into your account?"

"Yes, just as she told me to do."

"You indicated that you paid bills with that?"

"I put money in her account; she told me to pay my rent and to pay my phone bill, and I did what she told me to do."

To point out that there were things in storage that could have belonged to the children, Cahill asked if Joan had seen Tabitha's vanity, a backpack, and some dolls (which were actually a collection of Robin's).

Cahill didn't miss making a point about Robin's Mazda running cold. He readdressed her demeanor, pointing out that Robin appeared panicky when they approached the corner of Seneca.

"You never heard Robin Row leave your house at all that evening until you left with her around 5:00 in the morning, correct?"

"That's correct."

"Pass the witness."

Although Joan had been prepared to answer difficult questions, she was still surprised at how vicious Cahill was during his cross-examination. It felt to her like an undeserved personal attack. She had just told the truth. She had also noticed a smug, "gotcha" grin on Robin's face during Cahill's questioning.

Bourne's redirect examination would be a chance to repair any damage done by the defense. He started with the inferences that opposing counsel had made about Joan not being ethical in regard to money matters.

"Counsel's questions makes you sound like Ma Barker…is that what was happening at all?" Bourne asked.

"Object to that, Judge," Cahill interrupted.

"I'm going to sustain the objection to the form of the question who Ma Baker is," Schwartzman ruled.

"It's Barker," Bourne corrected.

"Take a different tack, Counsel."

"Now, let's talk about the paycheck that you got for Robin, and we're talking about the $1,026 paycheck. Was that her last paycheck from the YWCA?"

"Yes."

Did she direct you about what to do with the money?…"

"Yes, she did."

"Was that conversation had on tape-recorded telephone calls?"

"Yes."

"Just in general, what do you recall her telling you to do with the check?"

"First call she told me to give $200 to Ellie, $100 to her and pay my bills with the rest. And then in a later conversation she said not to give anything to Ellie, just to bring up some money to put on her account and to pay my bills."

"With part of the money that you got, did you use some of that money to pay bills connected with the Chevrolet car?"

"Oh, I paid off the car so that she wouldn't lose it. That was $600."

"Okay. Now this business about the car itself – now does she tell you what to do with the Chevrolet car on the phone calls?"

"She told me to take the car. She told me to take everything."

Joan didn't get the opportunity to explain how much a part of her family Robin was. They were pooling their resources. It was important to both Robin and Joan that the bills be paid, that she have a place to come home to and a car to drive when she got out of jail. After all, Joan had still believed Robin to be innocent at that time.

Bourne called for the evening recess in order to prepare the tape-recorded phone calls for the next day.

CHAPTER THIRTY-ONE

Bourne awoke at 6 a.m. on the second day of the Row trial. Alongside his breakfast was a conspicuous reminder that the press was watching his every move. PROSECUTOR: ROW KILLED FOR LOVE, MONEY was blazoned in bold print across the front page of *The Idaho Statesman*. This trial was going to be long. For probably a few weeks he wouldn't see much of his family: he would be getting up before dawn and dropping into bed late. Knowing he had to get to the office by 7 a.m. to prepare for his 9 a.m. court appearance, he swallowed his orange juice and darted out the door.

✳ ✳ ✳

Robin Row was escorted into the courtroom wearing a smug expression on her face. She was dressed in a short-sleeved, flowered top with polyester slacks. Day two began with a startling, but tactically typical, motion from the defense.

Cahill puffed up like an angry rooster. "I'm moving for a mistrial."

"All right, Counsel," Schwartzman sighed.

"I asked Joan McHugh about her going out to the storage shed...Her response, 'I went out there to get the stuff back from the YWCA that Robin had taken,' was nonresponsive. That does implicate matters that this Court had deemed previously were not admissible, and that is the defendant's alleged theft from the YWCA. And I think it's prejudicial, and I'd ask the Court to declare a mistrial based upon that."

Joan McHugh's verbatim response to Cahill's question actually was, "I met Gary Raney and Janice Johnson because Robin had told me to give back all the things to the YWCA that belonged to them that were in that storage shed."

"Counselor, the statement is absolutely de minimus; no one picked it up with that interpretation – I think, Counselor, in all honesty – other than yourself, and there's no implication of any impropriety in that remark, and I'm going to deny your motion for mistrial," Schwartzman pronounced.

Joan was called to return to the stand. Bourne continued his redirect examination of her.

"Now," Bourne proceeded, "did you discuss with her at one point the question of whether the children had chosen to stay with Randy or to go with her during the weekend before the fire?"

"Well, she told me that she had something to tell me and that she had gone home that Saturday…and she had a lot of trouble with Randy, that he had destroyed her things…first he talked nice to her, then he was angry with her, and she was upset because the children wanted to stay with Randy."

The lawyers continued to play legal volleyball with Joan's reputation and memory until she was physically worn out. Judge Schwartzman finally dismissed Joan, informing her she was subject to recall when the controversial tapes were introduced.

As she stepped down, some of the jurors gave her a smile of understanding and encouragement. Robin flashed her a grin, and a guard stepped quickly between the two women. Joan smiled wryly. The idea that Robin would attack her, or vice versa, was ludicrous. Joan finally understood that Robin was a coward. She betrayed people indirectly through lies and deceit while presenting a needy facade.

Her shoulders sagged; she didn't feel her hand pushing through the swinging doors. Bernie waited just outside. He held her and the dam broke.

"Oh, Joanie." Bernie said, wishing he could trade places with her. There were no words.

✳ ✳ ✳

Collateral prosecution witnesses reinforced Joan's testimony. Randy was characterized as docile and obedient. Robin was described as a dominant wife who was rude to and belittled her husband. The children were portrayed as loving Randy and wanting to stay with him in the event of a divorce. More than one witness testified that Robin spoke of

Randy kidnapping the children; ironically, she had also been emphatic that he would never hurt Joshua and Tabitha. Witnesses also refuted Robin's accounts that Randy physically abused her.

* * *

The testimony continued with Patty Coler and her husband Dave, who were bingo players who had become friends with Robin and Randy. Patty characterized Randy's behavior around his wife as that of a "whipped puppy" and said that she had never seen him treat Robin badly. Her impression was that Randy got along well with the kids.

Patty also heard stories of abuse. Robin told her of beatings, being kicked and pushed down stairs, and of her plans for divorce. Roger Bourne asked Patty the same questions and got the same answers he would get from witnesses to follow. Like Joan, Patty had not seen any marks or bruises, only bandages.

In between objections, Patty managed to describe how Robin fainted at bingo the night of January 28.

"She was behind the candy stand, and when she came out to go call bingo, she was in the doorway, and she fell."

"Describe what you saw and how did she fall?"

"Slowly. She went on one knee – I would say on the left knee – and then the body went to the ground."

"Did it look to you like she was truly fainting and falling down, or what did it look like?"

"Well, no…her body didn't look limp. It was very slow in movement."

"Does somebody call the paramedics?"

"Yes. Joan."

"How close do you get to her after she's fallen down?"

"Well, before the paramedics get there, I'm helping Dave; I'm holding her, and I have my hands around her. He's checking the vital signs."

"Has she told you that she's wearing some kind of a thing under her clothes in connection with the abuse?"

"Yeah. She was wearing a wrap around her waist."

"When you're checking her and helping her there, do you detect any sign that she's wearing some kind of a wrap?"

"No."

"Do you talk to her about the paramedic contact?"

"Yeah. A little later I go back to check and see how she's doing, and she's upset with the paramedics."

"Why? What's she say?"

"Well, apparently, she had to tell them that she had fallen down the steps and that she was in a wrap, and they wanted to check that wrap to make sure it wasn't too tight."

"Why did that make her mad?"

"She didn't want them to check her...she was mad because they didn't believe her story."

Myshin cross-examined Patty. "You told Detective Raney that Robin was 'happy-go-lucky' that night and was 'going to let her hair down' since bingo was coming to an end. Can you describe her behavior before the fall?"

Patty said she was watching Robin before her fall and she looked "out in space land" like she was "not really there."

Randy bigger than Robin?" Myshin asked.

"Randy and Robin are the same size," came back Patty's unexpected answer.

Bourne had one important question on redirect, which was buffeted by defense objections. "When Robin fainted there at the YWCA, did that look like the real thing or a fake to you?"

"No. It was very slow; it was not a limp type of fall."

"Did it look theatrical to you?"

"Yes. Very much so."

"That's all. Thank you."

The next witness, Linda Kerr, the accountant for the YWCA, recalled abuse stories Robin had told her.

"In January, she said that Randy had...held her captive in the house sometimes and that's why she would miss meetings...at one point she told me that he was very abusive and that they hadn't had any relationship for a long time, but that he had forcibly raped her twice within that week."

"Did she say she was taking any counseling as a result of the rape?" Bourne questioned.

"Yes. She said that she had been to the doctor and was talking with Sue Fellen...counselor at the YWCA."

"Did she talk about the sheriff's department being involved?"

"Yeah. She had indicated, too, that she would be leaving Randy or was contemplating that and that the sheriff was going to help her get her belongings because Randy wouldn't let her have her things..."

"While you were discussing these matters with Robin, did the subject of her having an affair come up?"

"She indicated to me that Randy was jealous of her relationship with Danny McHugh, but that there wasn't anything to it, that he was just a friend of hers..."

Linda never saw evidence of abuse on Robin's body, did not see a mark on Robin's face after her facial bandage was removed.

The day after the fire, Robin called Linda to inform her that the memorial service had been scheduled for the next day.

"What did she say about her life at that point?" Bourne asked.

"She had asked me about some insurance papers – a small policy that was carried as an addendum to a policy at the YWCA on the children. And she just said that she would like the information on that... She had some severance pay and vacation pay coming, and she wanted to pick them up early because she wanted to get the memorial service over and get on with her life."

During her phone call with Linda, Robin also confirmed that Randy had, indeed, kidnapped the children. Then, later in the conversation, she changed her story completely indicating that she and Randy had agreed to separate and that he was keeping the children on a temporary basis.

Myshin did his best to impugn Linda's testimony. "Did you take any notes of those conversations? Can you give me a time frame?" He grilled her on the size and shape of the Band-Aid on Robin's face and was intent on establishing Robin's tone of voice after the fire.

"Matter-of-fact, you know," Linda explained.

"She's pretty matter-of-fact all the time?"

"Pretty much."

"Could you describe her as having a flat affect?"

"Yes, she pretty much is. Yes, she is."

On redirect Bourne asked, "Randy being jealous of Danny McHugh is only what Robin told you?"

"Yes."

The parade of YWCA employees continued. Sue Fellen was up next. Sue directed the Women's and Children's Crisis Center and was the person who had hired Robin in 1988. She echoed what had been said by other witnesses. She also testified that she saw no bruises or abrasions when Robin removed the bandage on her face.

"On the Sunday before the fire…the 9th of February, 1992, did you spend that Sunday morning with Robin Row counseling her and discussing with her the state of her marriage and in particular counseling with her about her being raped by Randy?"

"No," Sue responded.

"Had you been out with her during January to assist her to get a rape examination done or anything of that type?"

"No, I did not," Sue stated firmly.

"Well, did Robin ever talk to you about her being raped by Randy and you giving her advice to file charges or anything of the sort in January?"

"I did not."

The defense had no questions for Sue Fellen.

The last woman from the YWCA to testify was Janice Johnson, the director at the time of the fire. In addition to testimony reiterating what other witnesses had said, Janice had her own experience with Robin's abuse stories.

"In one instance, she told me that Randy had put special locks on the windows and doors so she couldn't get out. On another occasion, she told me that he'd hit her on her back and she had marks on the back, and she'd gone to the doctor."

"Did she describe to you the reason she was wearing one of those elastic Ace bandages around her wrist?"

"Yes. She said that Randy had tied up her wrists together with some kind of rope or something and had drug her around the house. And that she had red marks on her wrist…she wanted to protect the wrist. I never saw any marks after the bandages were off, but that's what she told me."

"When the topic of the YWCA closing was discussed, did Robin ever give an indication that she was going to be leaving the YWCA's employment anyway?" Bourne asked.

"I advised her that the board had made a decision and we were going to close bingo. She could run it [through] the end of the week. The board had agreed to pay her salary through the end of February."

"And you told her all this on…January 31? So she knew a week in advance then?"

"Yes. And at that time she also told me that – she says, 'Well, you know, bingo isn't my life.' And she says, 'I plan to be gone by the end of March anyway.'"

"Okay. On Wednesday the 12th, which was the day of the memorial service, did Robin bring in payroll records and other things concerning the operation of the bingo game?"

"Yes, she did."

"All right. Did you hear her conversation with people at the front counter on the morning of that memorial service concerning her demeanor?"

"Oh, yes…She was visiting with our front desk receptionist and she was joking, they were laughing about something."

The pieces of the State's puzzle were beginning to fill in the frame, proffered to show the elaborate scheme they believed Robin devised to get at what she wanted – money and another man.

The next few witnesses appeared briefly, making small but significant contributions. A custodian of postal records stated that two change of address cards, one for Robin and Randy Row and one for Robin and Tabitha Cornellier, were signed effective February 10, 1992. This was a meaningful fact to the prosecution.

The kernel of suspicion had begun with a question: Why would Robin be concerned with changing her address on the very day her family had perished? If she were consumed with grief, rerouting her mail would be the last thing on her mind, Bourne had mused.

Then there was the newest life insurance policy on Randy and the kids that Robin had purchased about two weeks prior to the fire, using Seneca as a return address. This was about the same time Randy was supposedly breaking her ribs, raping her, and cutting her with a knife. She was also talking about cutting him loose and moving away with Joan and her family. Logic would expose Robin, Bourne reasoned. If you are going to divorce a guy and he's beating you up, the last thing you would do would be to buy a life insurance policy. That's money thrown down the drain.

Two weeks come and go, and Robin hasn't received the completed policy back showing it's in full force and effect. She might have expected it back sooner. But her lies are catching up to her; she's backed into a corner. Joan expects the police to pick up Randy for kidnapping, and the abuse allegations have all been told. It was time to act. So the day of the fire, she changes the address, and two or three days later the new policy arrives in Joan's mailbox.

Another witness, an employee of Ada County, testified that she found no criminal filings against Randy Row in 1991 or 1992, in fact, no domestic violence or kidnapping reports at all.

James Greenwell from the Department of Health and Welfare stated that he did, indeed, know Robin Row, but he found no mental health unit record of Randy Row and had never gone to the Row's home to give Randy a shot to calm him down or been involved in any kind of a mental commitment proceeding involving him.

Other than the fire on February 10, Pamela Babbitt from the Ada County Sheriff's Office found no evidence of any contact with the Row household regarding domestic violence, kidnapping, or missing children in the six months prior to the fire.

Mr. Washam, the man Robin had claimed was an ex-sheriff who had accompanied her to her home a week before the fire and was witness to Randy's destruction, stated he was a retired truckdriver and knew Robin through his wife. He had never been in law enforcement, had never been to 10489 Seneca, and had never discussed Robin's domestic problems with her. The prosecution was unraveling Robin's claims stitch by stitch.

Chapter Thirty-Two

February 11, 1993

Day three officially began at 9 a.m. The prosecution called Dr. Glenn Bockwell, the emergency room physician who had examined Robin after she had fainted at bingo. He spoke with certainty, testifying that Robin's CT scan, a special x-ray of the brain, proved to be normal. During his physical examination he found no sign of injury around her head and neck.

The doctor also said that the paramedics were frustrated because they didn't feel they were getting the straight story from Robin. They didn't think she looked ill. When they took her vital signs, they could find no significant problem.

The next witness would testify that she had an even closer look at Robin's head than the doctor. Even though Bourne had done a good job calming her nerves beforehand, Anjanette Viehweg, the young cosmetologist who had taken care of Robin's beautification needs for over a year, was still nervous when she approached the witness stand. She had had some sleepless nights after the fire wondering if Robin was responsible. One night, she sat up until 4:30 in the morning writing down everything she could remember. She would make an ideal witness for the State.

Her voice was timid and quiet, and the judge had to ask her to pull the microphone closer. She was especially afraid to look at Robin. They had been good friends; in the year before the fire, she had seen Robin two or three times a week. It was only after Anjanette had talked to Detective Raney and Robin was arrested that she had become uneasy. Then a terrible nightmare brought out an even deeper fear.

Anjanette and her husband had been trying for four years to have a child. In her dream, she was very pregnant and pushed her cumbersome body out of her chair to answer the front door. When she opened it, she was looking down the barrel of a gun, then past it into Robin's steely, wicked eyes. The explosion of the gun shattered her sleep and she awoke, her heart pounding.

By the time of the trial Anjanette had truly become pregnant and was due to give birth in the summertime – the same season of the dream. Her nightmare had seemed so real that to actually be pregnant made her go a little crazy. She insisted on putting five fire alarms up in her small home, the kind that used batteries that couldn't be turned off by the flip of a breaker switch.

Anjanette testified that Robin was dominant in her relationship with Randy. She likened it to a connection between mother and son. She also testified that she had never seen any indications of abuse.

Like a cat with a canary, Cahill set about to intimidate the seemingly fragile witness. He was condescending when he asked her to clarify minor details and asked more than once if Anjanette had ever been in the Row home. Then Cahill brought out an incident which had occurred two to three weeks before the fire. It was a story that could be incriminating to his client. Apparently, he was hoping it would incriminate Randy.

"All right. Now, during that same time frame, did she also talk to you about an incident where Randy had knocked a portable radio in a hot tub and almost electrocuted the children?"

"She said that Randy and Tabby and Joshua were all in the hot tub and that the radio fell in, but they all got out."

"Because the radio had turned out had one of those – like an electrical circuit breaker?"

"Right. I just remember because she chewed all her fingernails off." Anjanette chanced a quick glance at Robin who flashed her a rare smile. They had a standing joke because Robin often chewed her nails to the quick.

Robin looked like a stranger to Anjanette. She was shocked that her former client was so haggard and nasty looking. Before she left the stand, she had an urge to tell everyone, I don't do her hair anymore; I didn't make her look that way.

The court heard testimony from a few of Randy Row's relatives. A friend confirmed there was talk of divorce and that Randy was under the impression that Robin intended to move without him or Joshua or Tabitha. Two witnesses stated that Randy thought there was another man in his wife's life and that Robin stayed at Joan's house so much to give her a chance to be around her new boyfriend. The relatives corroborated testimony characterizing Robin as the one in charge. There was also evidence that Randy was told by Robin to put some things in storage and that he didn't know why but just did as he was told.

The defense tried to characterize Randy as mentally unstable and his personality as being fraught with mood swings. They hoped to paint this picture in order for Randy to take the fall as the arsonist.

Janet Gentry, Randy's older sister and a good friend of Robin's, refuted the defense's contention that Randy was mentally unstable after his motorcycle accident. She maintained he had forgotten his childhood memories but was otherwise okay. In addition, she had seen no sign of Randy being abusive, and her friend Robin had never mentioned abuse. Robin did say, however, when talking of divorce, that "she had had it with him, his baby attitude."

Janet recounted a phone conversation with Randy late in the evening the Sunday before the fire. He had called his sister around 10 p.m.

"Okay," Bourne asked. "On this night when he called, did Randy talk to you about his and Robin's plans for the next day?"

"He had called and told me that him and the kids had discussed that they weren't going to argue anymore; they were going to sit down and discuss it... everything looked like it was going to be fine. She was going to come home the next morning...he was happy...that everything was going to work out."

Myshin's cross-examination focused on Robin's goodness – her generosity toward Janet and others and her love for her children. He also extracted the fact that Janet had heard Randy swear.

"Well, he wouldn't hit...anybody. He just used bad words, you know, swearing...I've never seen him hit anybody.

The next witness, James Brown, was a contract hauler for *The Idaho Statesman*. His job was to drop newspaper bundles in strategic locations for delivery people to pick up.

After making drops on Seneca, Brown dipped into a cul-de-sac for a drop. When he came back out, he stopped at the intersection of Varian and Seneca to let a car pass. It was a few minutes before 4 a.m. when he pulled out behind the other car.

"Is it common for you to see traffic along that road at 4:00 in the morning?" Bourne asked.

"Not very common, no," Brown answered.

Brown noticed the car he was following was a silver-gray compact with rectangular-shaped taillights and a boxy trunk, similar to his wife's car and possibly a foreign make similar to a Toyota, Nissan, or Datsun. The illuminated silhouette told him that the driver was alone, wore short hair, and was of medium build. He couldn't tell if the person was male or female.

He followed the car east on Seneca out of the subdivision. It seemed peculiar to Brown that, when exiting the subdivision, the silver compact turned west from the intersection of Mitchell and Victory back toward Five Mile as if heading around the block. If the car's destination were west, the most logical, expedient way to have exited the subdivision would have been from the opposite end, from Five Mile.

"Have you ever seen that car again, that small gray car as you've described it, coming down Seneca like that?"

"No, I haven't."

Brown testified that the car he picked out from a sea of 140 cars, including some gray and silver compacts, looked a lot like the car he followed early the morning of February 10. When he had walked through the parking lot with Detective Smith, it was Robin's silver Mazda that immediately caught his eye – he had walked directly to it.

Cahill tried valiantly to discredit this eyewitness, questioning his memory and use of eyeglasses. The witness said he did wear eyeglasses for reading and had them on when he saw the gray car that night.

John Healy, the Row's next-door neighbor, testified that Robin was verbally abusive to her husband, often calling him a stupid idiot.

"Did you ever go to Robin and Randy's house, open the door and break in on what looked like must be a rape going on, where Robin was tied up or any kind of violence?…" Bourne asked.

"No."

"Were you ever around when Randy was being restrained by police and Randy broke away from the police and hit Robin or knocked her down or hit her head on the cement?"

"No."

"Did you ever have any reason to suspect that Randy was a physically abusive husband towards Robin?"

"No."

CHAPTER THIRTY-THREE

The courtroom was full every day now. About one third of the crowd that squeezed together in front of the double doors were bingo players, many retired, arriving a little after 8 a.m. to secure a seat. Joan and Bernie did not attend the trial during witness testimony because Joan was subject to recall.

Friday, day four, would produce only the beginning of copious evidence detailing specifics of the fire scene, the fire investigation, and the insurance policies held by the defendant.

Firemen were compelled to recall grisly details: finding the charred bodies, taking photographs of them, using a scoop stretcher to move the debris-littered body of Randy Row still in a sleeping position, and discovering Tabitha concealed in the ruins with a quilt covering her hands and head.

Through most of the description, Robin sat stock-still. But when Captain Robert Saum described finding Tabitha's body where he had been standing, on cue, Robin displayed emotion. She kept a hankie held up to her face, and with her head bent and body convulsing, the defendant appeared to be stifling sobs. Her demonstration starkly contrasted with the detachment she had been exhibiting. With his arm around his client's shoulders, Gus Cahill called for a break saying, "She's having a hard time."

When court reconvened, second-chair Prosecutor Kevin Swain questioned Coroner Lynn Bowerman about Robin's behavior when he notified her of Joshua's death.

"I told her that Joshua was on the lawn, that he was deceased. And I told her that we were presuming we'd find Randy also in the residence, but I was concerned that Tabitha's room was empty and she wasn't in her room."

"What was her demeanor when you informed her of the death of her son, probable deaths of the husband and daughter?" Kevin Swain asked.

"During the whole time I was with her she was calm; she was very quiet. She didn't ask me any questions. I did all the talking. She just kind of stared straight ahead."

Bowerman later recalled he had never encountered anything like Robin's reaction except in cases of shock when a trance-like period may follow a major emotional response. That night he had gone directly to the deputy to tell him of her strange response.

During the testimony about transportation of Randy, Joshua, and Tabitha in body bags and the autopsy testimony that followed, Robin was typically dispassionate.

Over Cahill's strenuous objection, the State moved for the admission of the three morgue photographs of Robin's family. Tabitha's showed the worst burning of the three, extensive third-degree burns over her upper and lower body.

After viewing the photographs himself, Judge Schwartzman sent the jury out of the courtroom before making his judgment known.

"Counsel, I want to make my remarks outside the presence of the jury. I'll try and control myself. Looking at photographs like this – they're obviously the two children, one rather severely burned, another looking almost natural. They're dead," Schwartzman said sternly. "The husband is burned rather severely…one picture bespeaks a thousand words and many emotions…the pictures are graphic and emotional and completely accurate.

"The jury is entitled to see them…it gives the absolute reality of the situation. We, as a society, are somewhat becoming inured to this – hardened – simply because we see it all the time…We are not going to sugar-coat the realities of the situation in terms of what this fire did and how it affected the victims. Nothing is more relevant as far as this court is concerned than these pictures…And I am a firm believer in the truth being presented, even if to the casual observer it may be hideous. It is life. It is death…and I'm not going to hide this from the jury. They will be admitted over objection of counsel." Schwartzman glared down from the bench, daring anyone to disagree. There was not a peep of argument or comment – nor even any discernible breathing.

* * *

Barbara Witte worked as an advanced emergency medical technician for the Ada County Paramedics. She had spent almost three hours with Robin Row in the early morning hours of February 10 and was the first to feel bad vibes from the mother while sitting in the back of Ambulance 49 with her.

"Okay," Bourne began. "For the first while after Mrs. Row got into the ambulance, how did she act in there?"

"She basically sat and watched the fire like she was mesmerized. I spoke to her, asked her if there was anything that I could do for her. I initially put my arm around her and took her by the arm and led her into the ambulance. She sat on the bench, and then she just was mesmerized by the fire," Witte answered.

"When she was watching the fire, what was she doing? My point, was she crying or hysterical or visibly upset?…"

"No, there was no emotion…I asked her for the dates of birth, told her that we would need them for the coroner, and she gave them to me without hesitation."

"Did you ask her if you could call anyone for her?" Bourne asked.

"Yes. I asked her if there were any friends or family of either hers or Randy's. And she stated that she did not want me to contact Randy's family; she couldn't deal with them right then. They were going to blame her for his death like they did his motorcycle accident."

"Now, at some point did…paramedics or some other person come to the ambulance where you were and basically give information that they couldn't find Tabitha?"

"Correct…Mrs. McHugh stated that she – maybe Tabitha had gotten out. And there was a look on Mrs. Row's face of – I perceived to be that of –"

"Objection. Speculation," Myshin interrupted.

"She can say what she saw, Counselor," Schwartzman ruled.

"What did Mrs. Row look like when that information was relayed or mentioned that maybe Tabitha got out?"

"It was…more like a look of terror."

"Terror," Bourne reiterated. "What happened next? Did she observe that you were looking at her?"

"Yes, she did."

"What happened then?"

"She just kind of went blank and she looked at me and said, 'No, Tabitha is dead.'"

"Then what happened?"

"We asked her if Tabitha did get out, where would she go. You know, is there a neighbor or someplace that she would run to…and she said, 'I know where she's at,' and hit her own forehead. She said that she was on a blanket on her side of the bed, that she went there often at night and slept."

"Did Mrs. Row cry or weep from time to time?" Bourne probed.

"No. She did not cry at all, the whole time I was with her."

"Are you acquainted with the medical process, the medical phenomenon of shock?"

"Yes."

"What are the physical signs?"

"The physical signs of shock are usually restlessness, anxiety, dizziness, nausea, vomiting, thirst, pallor, cold, clammy skin, that type of thing."

"Did you observe any of those…kinds of things about Mrs. Row on the morning that you've described?"

"No."

Amil Myshin cross-examined Witte about Robin's lack of tears, hoping to elicit the reason that Robin didn't cry was based upon her upbringing or that she was just in denial.

Witte was steadfast. "No. She was perfectly accepted to it. She stated that Tabitha was dead."

"Those are the words she used?"

"She looked at me and said, 'No, Tabitha's dead, too.'"

Witte was asked only a few crucial questions and, to satisfy the court, could only give short answers relating specific facts. Later when she was off the witness stand she had more to say about the time she had spent with Robin Row.

The night of the fire, Witte vividly recalled Robin's composed demeanor, which sharply contrasted with Joan's tearful grief. Thirty seconds after stepping into the ambulance to console Robin, the hair on the back of EMT Witte's neck stood on end.   As was her common practice and one method of assessing potential shock victims, she began by asking Robin the names, dates of birth, and Social Security numbers of her family members.   One sign of shock in a person is an inability to think quickly, a difficulty or incapacity to recall even familiar information.   Robin rattled off the answers with no hesitation. Throughout her career Witte had seen many different manifestations of shock including anger, crying, hysteria, and calm acceptance. However, Witte had never seen anyone like Robin, so devoid of emotion.

✴ ✴ ✴

A chilling find centered around an innocuous little box mounted in the garage. The box which held the circuit breaker panel generated lengthy examination. Fire investigator Captain Robert Saum and electrician Gerald Hudson testified that breaker #2 was in an automatic tripped position caused by the fire; however, breaker #14 had been manually turned off before the fire started. It supplied electricity to the children's bedrooms, the lights and fan in the upstairs bathroom, and the smoke alarm.

Myshin cross-examined Captain Saum and unsuccessfully tried to cast doubt when he questioned whether firefighters may have turned off the breaker during the suppression and rescue. Captain Saum was adamant that firefighters don't touch electrical evidence and explained that the undisturbed soot covering the breaker encasement proved the box had remained untouched.

The jury was dismissed for a four-day weekend, admonished by the judge essentially to turn off their eyes, ears, and mouths to anything regarding the case or news of other fires.

Chapter Thirty-Four

Day five of the trial began with testimony that revealed Robin Row was the policyholder on six out of seven life or accidental death insurance policies. She was beneficiary on all seven, all fully in force at the time of the fire. Robin had purchased one accidental death policy on her family July 12, 1991, six months before the fire, and another on January 24, 1992, only sixteen days before the fire. This last policy would be worth $12,000 and was effective immediately upon purchase. In 1990, the value of one policy on Joshua and Tabitha was doubled to $24,000 each; another was increased in 1991 from $10,000 to $15,000 on each child. With the exception of a life insurance policy with the YWCA, all the policies had two things in common: They were direct solicitation proffered through the mail and offered low initial premiums. No representative had ever spoken to or examined the insureds.

A beneficiary who accepted these policies at face value might think she would reap over half a million dollars. The fine print, however, indicated a total that was much less. In the event that an accident killed Randy and the children, Robin Row's insurance policies would pay her $276,500.

The defendant's brother-in-law, Robert Row, told jurors that he heard Robin say in 1989 that she would gain financially if Randy died from injuries he suffered in his motorcycle accident. During a conversation that took place while they were visiting Randy in the hospital, Robert remembered his dad expressing concern about how Robin and the children would cope if Randy died.

"And did Robin Row make some response to that?" Bourne asked Randy's brother.

"I'll be $100,000 ahead," Robert testified.

After the noon break, head held high, the defendant strode into the courtroom. She sat through the testimony with an empty stare in her eyes, magnified by her thick glasses, focused on anything and nothing. As usual, her face wore the subtle smirk that Joan recognized as her indignant look. Although she appeared to listen to the testimony, she seemed detached and unconcerned. She wrote little and conferred with her attorneys infrequently.

The next testimony was necessary to prove arson. Chief Deputy State Fire Marshal Donald Dillard and Doug McGrew, Assistant Chief of the Whitney Fire District, represented the Ada County Arson Task Force Team. With the help of expert William Dietz, Chief of Forensics from the San Francisco ATF (Alcohol, Tobacco, and Firearms) lab and Susan Williamson, State Department of Law Enforcement forensics analyst, Dillard's and McGrew's testimonies would extend into day six and provide details of the fire investigation evidence.

When debris was cleared away, the most conspicuous proof of foul play surfaced: Scorched pour patterns slashed a trail across the living room carpet leading to the most heavily burned area, the closet under the stairwell. Carpet samples that had been cut from the floor at the fire scene were entered into evidence.

Rubbing alcohol was the light distillate Dillard had poured onto a carpet sample which, when lit, whooshed a short-lived flame branding the carpet with a pour pattern similar to the actual carpet from the fire scene.

During testing by the state lab and the ATF in San Francisco, no accelerant was found on the living room carpet, but it was possible it could either have been there initially and burned off or have been there at such a low level as to be undetectable. Lab tests did show a heavy petroleum residue on the hatch door that made up most of the floor of the closet.

The closet door was burned completely off, and the hatch door in the floor of the closet, which led to a crawl space, had also burned through and had dropped into the area below. It was the only item out of seven tested that showed traces of accelerant; the test indicated the presence of heavy petroleum distillates such as kerosene, diesel fuel, or fuel oil.

Dillard described another smaller, heavily burned area in the living room where the firefighters had seen a small pile of clothing smoldering. Between it and the closet was another larger pile of clothing. It looked as if the pour pattern led from the smaller pile to the larger pile of clothing and then to the point of origin in the closet. Dillard deduced that the perpetrator had poured a heavier amount of accelerant on the small pile which was connected to the heavier distillate in the closet by the ribbon of light accelerant streaked across the carpet. By lighting the smaller pile, which upon closer examination was identified as the kids' underwear, this rudimentary fuse or "trailer" enabled the arsonist effectively to block both exits and safely escape.

The arsonist was well-versed in the field of fire. All exits had been covered, preventing Randy, Joshua, and Tabitha from escaping down the stairs and out the front door or through the garage door. But what was the reason for the clothing that was piled up on the portable heater found in the off position? Was it a decoy for the fire investigators? A contrived setup to establish an accidental cause?

A closer look at Robin Row's history revealed that the same or similar anomalies had been discovered in many of the fires in Robin's past. Trailing cloth was found in her sister's apartment fire around 1979, and also in Ruth's mobile home fire in 1986. A portable heater was found pushed up against bedding in the 1980 fire that had killed Robin's son, Keith. Similarly, clothing was found piled on a portable heater in the YWCA fire in 1989. These coincidental circumstances now looked more like staged scenes.

The pour patterns at the Seneca Street fire, estimated to have taken two to five gallons of accelerant, and the deliberate flipping off of the breaker switch which governed the hard-wired smoke detector upstairs, would have been enough to do the arsonist's job. But a third factor played a part in spreading the deadly flames more quickly to the upstairs bedrooms where Robin's husband and children were sleeping.

A cold air return vent directly above the door to the garage and adjacent to the fiercely burning closet area was in an ideal position to transport the fire. Within 15 to 20 minutes of its inception, the fire, coupled with billowing smoke, was sucked up into the vent which extended the flames and smoke rapidly into the second floor and provided more oxygen to the fire. Either by deadly coincidence or strategic design, the fan had been switched to a continuous running mode rather than the automatic on/off mode typically used in a residential dwelling.

The latch on the front door called a "hinge lock" or "swing lock" seemed, on the surface, to receive more attention than its size warranted. Pictures and testimony proved that the lock was in the open/unlocked position during the fire. The front door had one keyed lock and, as on a motel room door, one swing lock that secured the door from the inside. The fact that the first people on the scene found all the outside doors locked didn't preclude the swing lock being in an open position. This information negated what Robin had told Detective Raney. She said that the night of the fire Randy had told her that, by using the swing lock, he was locking her out so she wouldn't be able to get in even with her key.

The method employed by investigators to determine the position of the swing lock was elementary. Beneath the lock as it rested in the open position was its silhouette, where the wood was not charred, blistered, or soot-laden.

Most of the circumstantial evidence, comprised of small, sometimes ostensibly insignificant links, would ultimately create a damning chain that pointed only to two possibilities: Either someone from inside set the fire or someone with a key did, locking the door upon exiting. Only two people possessed a key to 10489 Seneca – the deceased, Randy Row, and his widow, Robin.

The defense would concentrate on portraying Randy Row as a prime suspect, distraught and unstable. But the State had three more days of testimony before the defense would get their chance. At this point, it was looking as if Gus Cahill and Amil Myshin had an uphill battle.

CHAPTER THIRTY-FIVE

The seventh day of trial started with another piece of the prosecutorial puzzle. Storage unit number 827, a 10-by-15-foot roll-up unit, was rented November 8, 1991, to Robin and Randy Row. The tracking device showed that someone from the Row family entered and exited a total of 13 times between the time the unit was rented and two days before the fire; 11 of those visits were during the month of February.

The garage-type door on the unit opened onto a cache of personal and household items: a television set, furniture, ceramic figurines neatly wrapped in tissue or newspaper, home interior decorations, kitchen appliances and utensils, a book bag, an Alf animated phone, boxes of financial records and documents, women's clothing, and collector-type dolls (mint in-the-box Barbie dolls, and a doll with a ceramic head). Everything was in new or excellent condition, no leftovers or castaways.

While sifting through the boxes that held financial records, the investigating officers discovered several insurance documents. Bingo! They had found their motive. They also discovered that the newspaper used to wrap some of the figurines was dated Friday, February 7, 1992. This was three days before the fatal fire and one day before Randy allegedly broke the figurines during a blind fury. It appeared as though Randy had been duped into moving the items Robin wanted put into storage for safekeeping, things she wanted to keep undamaged by fire.

Even more revealing were the things that were not there: no men's things, no children's things. That omission was not lost on the police or the prosecution. They made sure it was not lost on the jury.

When the next witness headed toward the witness box, a hush fell over the crowded courtroom. A young, dark-haired man strode down the center aisle. He had the kind of quiet, mysterious look that gave many women pause. The observers had anticipated this witness and watched carefully as he took his seat.

A subtle but distinct change transformed Robin now. Her characteristic stillness magnified even slight changes in her demeanor. Her face lit up; she sat taller in her chair, showing true interest for the first time since the trial had started.

Daniel Stephen McHugh carefully spelled his name for the court reporter with the same Bostonian accent as his mother and father. He stated his age as 33 years old. Somewhat nervous and embarrassed, he explained how he became acquainted with Robin Row and the nature of their relationship.

"During January and the first part of February of '92, did you and Robin Row discuss whether or not she may be divorcing from Randy?" Bourne asked.

"Yes…we would sometimes go out and talk."

"Okay. Would this be a kind of a date…or was that part of the relationship?"

"I wouldn't use the word date, but we'd go out together."

"What did she tell you on these times?"

"She basically just discussed in general terms moving away from Randy, divorcing and moving away."

"Did she tell you where she was thinking about moving to?"

"Well, the first place was Seattle."

"Were you a part of this discussion in terms of you and her going to Seattle together?"

"No, she was going up there without me."

"Was there some discussion that maybe instead of her moving to Seattle she might go to Reno?"

"Yes…we began to talk with her, we meaning my mother and father and I, of our moving to the same [city]."

The questioning turned toward the Sunday before the fire: That afternoon Danny and Robin drove just across the border into Ontario, Oregon, to play the lottery numbers and pick up a *New York Times*. They discussed Randy's alleged kidnapping of the kids and his impending commitment. They arrived back at Joan's before 6 p.m. After dinner that evening, as was his habit on Sunday night, Danny retired to his upstairs room with his son, Ryan, and watched his favorite television programs (*Book Notes, Questions Time,* and *Road to the White House*) before going to bed at 9 p.m. Robin spent the night there, but Danny had no further contact with her that evening. He remembered his father waking him up early with the horrible news of the fire and deaths.

It was time to ask the questions Danny dreaded. Bourne would elicit answers that would show the jury a second motive. In addition to coveting proceeds from seven insurance policies, Robin had an intense desire to be with Danny. Money and love, two classic motives in mothers who kill their children, also compelled Robin in her twisted scheme.

Bourne showed the witness a letter dated March 2 addressed to him from Robin Row and sent from the Ada County jail.

"Okay. Now, let's talk again about the nature of the relationship between yourself and Robin...Had you had an intimate sexual relationship with her before she was arrested?"

"Yes," Danny choked. The last thing he wanted to become public knowledge was a sexual indiscretion with this woman accused of murder. Robin covered her mouth with her hand and giggled like a schoolgirl. She appeared oblivious to the tragic circumstances that had brought her and Danny together again.

"Just what month did that occur in?"

"January." Danny's answers were clipped. He couldn't look at Robin, but she hung on his every word.

"Now, the letter that you have there seems to speak of a future together...a loving relationship, spending the rest of your lives together...Is that your view of the nature of the relationship you had with Robin Row?"

"No."

"Did you write her any letters when she was in jail?"

"I did write one letter, yes."

"Okay. What was the basic tenor of your letter to her?"

"I discussed a church I'd started going to and tried to give her some encouragement to keep her head up and –"

"Was she happy with the content of the letter – on the telephone?"

"No, she was not. Apparently she was looking for a loving emotion."

"I take it there wasn't much of that in there?"

"No."

"During the magistrate's inquiry I asked you a question, 'Would you consider that you had a romantic relationship with her,' referring to Robin? And your answer was 'No.' Correct?"

"That's correct."

"What were you thinking when I asked you about your romantic involvement and you say no?"

"Well, I interpreted that as going to my intentions. And the nature of the relationship we had was a physical one. And in my opinion...we were friends and we'd had this physical relationship, but I certainly had no romantic leanings. Obviously she liked me, but I didn't realize how intense it was."

Amil Myshin was out for blood with this witness.

"Do you use any other names besides Daniel Stephen or McHugh?" Myshin said, hinting at an undisclosed sinister motive.

"No, I don't," Danny answered truthfully.

"You don't?"

"No."

"Where does Ryan's mother live?" Myshin shot back.

"Massachusetts."

"Are you trying to conceal yourself from her?" Myshin accused.

"No. In fact, I just talked to her the other day."

"I'll just be real blunt with you...Mr. Bourne has helped you explain your perjury using this word –"

"Judge," Bourne interrupted, "I object to the form of the question."

"I'll sustain the objection, Mr. Myshin," Schwartzman answered.

"– try to explain your answer by using this word romantic as not being sexual." Myshin continued to badger. "You knew exactly what he was asking about, didn't you?"

"No. And I still say that there's a difference between a physical relationship and something else."

"Well, he used the word romantic, but you knew he was asking you about a physical relationship, don't you?"

"No. I only knew the question that he asked, and I answered it."

"I see. You also answered some questions earlier on about whether or not you'd ever seen signs of abuse on Robin Row, didn't you?"

"Yes."

"Okay. And your answer to that was none, and she always wore long clothes?"

"Uh-huh."

"Now, you'd seen her naked, hadn't you!?" Myshin's voice escalated.

"Actually, no," Danny answered calmly. "She insisted at that time on already being under the covers."

"How many times did you have sex with her?"

"A couple times."

Myshin asked for details about the Sunday night before the fire. Then he attempted to plant a seed of doubt about who was driving the silver Mazda during the early morning hours.

"Did you borrow Robin's car that night?"

"No," Danny replied simply.

"Did you have any involvement in starting this fire?" Myshin challenged.

"No. I did not."

CHAPTER THIRTY-SIX

February 22, 1993

Two weeks had passed since Joan's first experience on the witness stand. This time she would have to answer questions about her taped phone conversations with Robin. This was the testimony that could put Robin on death row. She smoked; she paced, barely noticing the fragrant flowers her victim/witness coordinator had sent to the courthouse. The chill she felt run up her spine had no connection to the snow outside or to the icy drafts that blew their way inside the courthouse.

✳ ✳ ✳

Joan was called and made her way to the front of the courtroom, where she was reminded of her oath before she sat down in the witness chair for the second time.

To end their case with a bang, the prosecution would present portions of videotaped interviews between Detective Raney and Robin and only a fraction of audiotaped conversations between Robin and Joan. But it would be enough to cause a major jolt to the defense and add the glue that might cement the prosecution's puzzle pieces into place.

Buffeted by objections, Bourne began by setting up the scenario for the most damning of the taped conversations.

"I want to direct your attention to telephone calls between yourself and the defendant on the 19th and 20th of March, 1992," Bourne said to Joan. "Now, at some point about that time did you agree to ask the defendant a question or make a statement...in connection with the things that had occurred...[in the] early morning hours of Monday or immediately before the fire?"

"I don't think that I agreed to anything. A suggestion was made to me and I thought about it," Joan responded.

"Why did this subject come up?"

"Well, through this whole thing – until these phone calls – I just couldn't believe some of the things that Gary Raney was saying to me… My attitude was 'show me'…"

"Did you believe in Robin's innocence at that point?"

"Yes, I did."

"Did you agree to make a telephone call to gain information that you thought would help the defendant?"

"Yes."

"Joan, you've got a tape there marked State's Exhibit No. 86 for identification?…"

"Yes." Joan's hand trembled when she touched the tape.

"Now, actually, before these calls started, had you already proposed a set of facts to the defendant in a call that's not contained on the tape?"

"Yes, I did."

"What did you basically tell her?"

"That I woke up, I came downstairs and she wasn't there, and I wondered where she was."

"Had she already made a response to you as to where she was or whether she remembered where she was?"

"I think she didn't remember."

"Did you call the defendant or did she call you?"

"She called me."

A small cassette tape was played. The listeners in the courtroom hung on every tinny word.

Joan's voice on the tape began, "Have you thought about what we talked about? I heard a noise…I couldn't go back to sleep…I came downstairs and you weren't here…I mean, it was like, it had to be 10, 15 minutes from the time I first heard the noise, then I went back upstairs and fell asleep and never heard you come back in."

"Yeah, but I don't have any other different answer," Robin answered cavalierly. "But, um, you know, I'm sure it will come to me if it's important."

"I mean, you know, in 10 or 15 minutes you had to have gone some-where. I mean...in the middle of the night...where did you go? I just need to know."

"Well, I can't tell you something unless you want me to make some-thing up."

"No, I don't want you to make anything up, but, you know, that's a long time to be gone, really, when you think about it."

"I don't know what you want me to do or say, so I won't say any-thing."

"No, if you don't remember, you don't remember. But I don't know; it just seems like if you leave the house in the middle of the night, there'd be a reason. Did you go out to the car?"

"No."

"Did you go for a walk around the block? I know you were really upset, apprehensive about the next morning...maybe you just stood on the porch to think?"

"Did you go outside and look?" Robin asked.

"No. I was in my nightgown."

"I do a lot of things in my life that don't make sense."

"Robin, I NEED to know."

"When I know, I'll let you know." Robin sounded haughty.

"I just can't believe that something that important you can't remem-ber what you did. I mean, there had to be a reason you left the house in the middle of the night. It bothers me a lot. I know that I've been kind of withdrawn, and I know that I've asked you a lot of questions and that didn't make you happy, but I need answers, that's all. And it's not enough to say that eventually we'll know everything, 'cause I'm sure eventually we will know everything, but there are some things we'll probably never know...I was defensive of you, and I just think I have a right to know what I was defending."

"Well, I never asked you to say anything. What you said to the police was up to you...now you have doubt in your mind."

"I have a couple of doubts, Robin, yeah. Your being in our house has involved us in something terrible. You know, I wish to God that I could say I slept the whole night through and then I wouldn't have the kind of doubts that I have. But I know that you weren't here. I know how long that you were gone. I have to settle that before I can go on with the next step. I have been carrying it around for five weeks and apparently it's not something that I can handle without asking questions. I HAVE to know."

"Well, on the same token, I have the right to know what doubts you have because this concerns my case," Robin countered.

"I have to know," Joan repeated.

"You imply I deliberately went out...to jeopardize your family."

"I don't believe you don't remember, because that's your answer to everything I ask you. You don't remember that, or you don't think that, or I'm just going to have to wait. So I'm asking specific questions about a specific thing."

"And I don't have an answer."

"Okay." Joan's voice sounded bottled and tight. "Well, if you think of an answer, why don't you call me. I'm going to hang up and have supper."

"Fine," Robin ended the conversation.

The next conversation was a taped conversation of a call from Robin to Joan at approximately 10:00 that same evening. Robin said, "I will tell you...I'll write a letter. I resent it strongly. I'd appreciate it, after you read it and found out, that you would keep it to yourself."

The next call was taped Friday the 20th. In tears, Robin claimed to Joan she had been arrested for murder (which wouldn't actually occur until the following Monday).

"Ellie says they're going to move it fast. My trial will probably be in about three months. Just thought I'd let you know."

"Did you send the letter?" Joan asked.

"No, I haven't," Robin said,

Changing subjects, Robin continued, "Channel 2 called him [Ellie] today and asked if he had comments, and he didn't even know what she was talking about...He was with him [Bourne] yesterday and he didn't say a damn word to him, and according to the computer, I was charged yesterday. Ellie thinks they're running scared because they don't have anything."

"If they don't have anything, you don't have to worry."

"A lot of circumstantial. That's what it's coming down to is circumstantial...Ellie says they're going to try to win it by publicity, adverse publicity."

"I just have to know where you went that night, that's all. And that answers everything else."

"Well, it's going to come out in the trial, so what the hell –"

"Where did you go?"

"I just sat outside your house across the street in the car. I've been seeing a psychiatrist for the last eight months, and I called her because I needed to talk to her," Robin quietly sobbed.

"I'm sorry, could you say that one more time; I didn't hear what you were saying because you were crying."

"For the last eight months I've been seeing a psychiatrist, and I called her at home and told her that I needed to see her. So she came over and we sat in the car across the street."

"Did you say that was Sue?"

"No."

"Who was it? I couldn't hear what you said."

"I said I was seeing a psychiatrist," Robin answered. "I needed to talk to her, so I called her and she came and talked to me. We were in her car outside your house across the street with it running because it was cold."

"Thank you," Joan said.

"What does it matter?"

"It matters." Joan's voice was distant, deflated.

"It wasn't even the same time as the fire, so it doesn't matter. It doesn't help ME one damn bit. It doesn't matter because during that time I don't have an alibi or one anyone can vouch for."

"Well, you were out there with her then."

"Not during the time it was set, that's why it isn't important."

"But when I thought you weren't in the house, when I knew you weren't in the house, that was like 3:30, quarter to 4:00."

"I...it...if you think about it, 'cause I have," Robin stammered, "they could easily say I had enough time to get out there and back. So it doesn't matter. That's why I didn't think it was important to tell anyone. I didn't want anyone to know," Robin whimpered. "It was real personal...I didn't think it was anyone's business."

"I understand that."

"I haven't told anyone yet, but I'm going to have to, I guess."

"I think at some point, you might."

"I don't think they'll find me guilty though. They won't find me guilty. I didn't do it, and they can't say I did! They can try, but they're not gonna – they can't. I'm ashamed. Don't tell Bernie or Danny. I just don't want to sit here all that time."

Joan quietly responded, "Robin, do me a favor."

"Huh?…What?"

"Do me a favor," Joan repeated.

"What?"

"Let me go take a deep breath."

"Joan, I need you now…I don't want to lose you too. I didn't do it! I swear!" Robin cried.

The next taped conversation occurred an hour later.

"Are you calmed down now?" Joan asked.

"Yeah."

"You have an alibi. The psychiatrist gets on the stand and says, I was with her from 3:30 to five minutes to 4:00 – or whatever the time was – when I left her she was calm; she was going back in; she was going to try to get some sleep."

"No, she told me to go in and take a shower."

"She is an excellent witness; aren't you excited?"

"I'm numb."

"But she knew that you were calm and rational; you weren't going to go someplace and set a fire and kill three people. This person can put you at this house, going inside to take a shower. You're crying a little, but you're talked out of your frustrations and hostilities or aggressions or whatever the hell the problem you were having at that particular moment in time. By the time you get out of the shower…you couldn't have done it."

"Yeah, I guess," Robin muttered, "I guess…I gotta go. They're going to book me. Bye."

The last recorded conversation between Robin and Joan was played.

"They think I'm suicidal," Robin whimpered.

"Really," Joan said blandly. "Do you feel suicidal?"

"What do you think I'll do, kill myself with my toothbrush? I knew it was coming," Robin said about the murder warrant, "but it was still a shock."

268

(Joan's phone clicked a call-waiting signal.)

"I'm not going to answer that."

"I thought it might be Danny...you didn't tell him?"

"I have something to tell you," Joan's tone sounded grave, her breathing erratic, "I have so many doubts. I had to settle them in my own mind...Robin, I never came downstairs...I know you killed them, and it's tearing me apart."

"What makes you say that, Joan?" Robin said evenly. Then, "I knew your phone was tapped."

"I KNOW you killed them. I don't know HOW you can live with that. I'm not sure I can live with that."

As she sat in the witness chair listening with the others in the courtroom to her conversations with Robin, Joan remembered how it had felt to hear Robin's responses to her questions for the first time. When Joan had asked her where she had been in the middle of the night of the fire, she had fully expected Robin to say, "You're crazy. I was sleeping right there on your couch all night." Joan had predicted she would hand a tape over to Raney that would prove once and for all Robin's innocence. When Robin didn't have an answer, Joan remembered hoping at first that Robin was just confused and had her nights mixed up. With her life hanging in the balance and other lives obliterated, how could Robin forget something as important as that night? Or maybe she had some type of amnesia from the shock.

When Robin finally told her that she was outside Joan's apartment at 3 a.m. with a psychiatrist and couldn't name the doctor, the words fell on Joan like a grand piano. It was confirmation of Robin's lies. It was confirmation of all the things Raney had been telling her. Also Joan was certain if Robin had been going to any kind of mental health professional for eight months, as she had said, she would have heard about it before now. Robin was always eager to gain Joan's approval and sympathy.

Joan was physically drained after those last conversations. In the process of trying to comprehend who her friend really was and why she hadn't seen it sooner, Joan began what would be a long process of grappling with her own anger, sadness, grief, and guilt.

* * *

Prior to trial, Cahill and Myshin had filed a motion to suppress the taped conversations between Robin and Joan based on their defendant's

Fifth and Sixth Amendment rights, claiming Joan McHugh was an "agent" of the police who deliberately elicited incriminating statements in the absence of their client's lawyer.

The motion was denied. The United States Supreme Court held that a defendant's Sixth Amendment right to counsel was violated "when there was used against him at his trial evidence of his own incriminating words, which federal agents had deliberately elicited from him after he had been indicted and in the absence of his counsel."

Robin's incriminating words were elicited before she was indicted for the murders. When the inculpatory words came voluntarily from Robin's mouth, Joan was shocked beyond belief, having expected that their conversations would completely exonerate her friend and expose the police for what she thought they were, idiots, zealots, and fools.

✳ ✳ ✳

Detective Gary Raney was sworn in as the next witness and set up the foundation for introducing edited versions of three videotaped interviews between Robin Row and detectives, including one on the day her family perished and two on the day of the memorial service two days later. References to Robin's son, Keith, who had perished in a fire in California, and to prior criminal acts, including other fires and warrants, were ordered cut from the courtroom version by Judge Schwartzman.

In an attempt to get some of Robin's relevant past actions into the record, the prosecution had earlier submitted a brief to the Court citing eight cases which applied a theory of logical relevance – "The Doctrine of Chances" – which has been used many times as the basis for the admission of evidence tending to prove intent (mens rea) or identity (actus reus) or both and how it related to the case now before the court:

"The number of fires experienced by the defendant and the number of times the defendant has gained or stood to gain financially from those fires greatly exceeds the frequency rate for those occurrences in the general population…most people do not ever experience a serious residential fire in their entire lives…a person suffering as many fires over the past 15 years as the defendant has, which caused deaths of family members on two separate occasions, is rare to the degree of being unheard of. This set of circumstances is not coincidence."

As resourceful as the brief was, Judge Schwartzman made it absolutely clear to Bourne and Swain that the fires that followed Robin Row were to be kept out of this trial. However, the tapes could be admitted in their edited versions.

The video segment of Raney's first interview with Robin showed her speak for the first time on a large monitor. The video-Robin was animated and alive, unlike the statue-like version at the defense table. Her mannerisms and inflections closely resembled someone chatting with a neighbor over coffee. The viewers saw and heard a casual and offhand Robin Row, reinforcing the image presented by witness after witness who portrayed her as cold and unemotional. They saw her inappropriate reactions, heard the disgust in her tone when she talked about Randy, and when speaking about her children, observed she was chatty one moment and perturbed by something trivial they had done the next.

Watching herself on tape telling Raney about the fire scene, finding Tabitha on the floor, and hearing about the autopsies didn't elicit a tear from the defendant's eye. But finally, when the interview reached the part about the extent of burns on the bodies of her family, what Tabitha was wearing when she died, and her explanation that she doesn't cry in public because her grandmother had taught her not to, conspicuously on cue, Robin sobbed loudly, doubled over with her head in her arms and her face covered. Gus Cahill curled his arm around Robin's spasmodic shoulders.

The detectives observed that Robin had never cried in their presence until after they had pointed out that fact to her. They also noticed that the only other times she cried was when she was talking to her friend, Joan McHugh.

CHAPTER THIRTY-SEVEN

The next day began with trial motions. Prosecutor Bourne requested a final ruling from the Court on the issue of introducing the defendant's outstanding warrant from California, the bad check charges Robin had fled the state trying to evade.

Myshin contended the prejudice to his client outweighed any probative value. The judge agreed. The jury would never hear why Robin left California nor the tarnished history that exposed a pattern of behavior: check fraud, embezzlement, fires, suspected murder, and suspected attempted murder.

"I was shown a letter here for the first time," Myshin objected, "that was written by the State to psychiatrists, I suppose. I would object to that...I want the Court to see that in advance before there's a letter flashed around here that the jury's going to wonder what the defense is trying to hide."

The letter Myshin referred to was a mailing that Detective Raney had sent to all of the approximately seventy mental health professionals in the Boise area. It simply requested that if the psychologist or psychiatrist had spent any time with Robin Row during the early morning hours of February 10, that they reply. There were no responses.

The evidence was somewhat impudent in the eyes of the judge but inventive confirmation that Robin Row's admission to Joan that she was outside in the dark, frigid morning hours with a psychiatrist was poppycock.

Myshin argued, "Well, it's hearsay...it's irrelevant...it may violate privilege. I don't know...I think it shifts the burden of proof," he finished.

"Well, Counsel," Schwartzman began to lecture, "I'm going to sustain the objection. It puts me in somewhat of an awkward position. I'm going to do it really under Rule 403 (prejudice outweighs probative value) for purposes of the State's case in chief. But really, Mr. Bourne, you know, all I can say is if the defendant wants the jury to believe that she was out with a psychiatrist at 3:30 in the morning, fine and dandy. But, Counsel, the Court's credulity is stretched to the absolute [limit] that you have to try and refute that this way…Well, I don't want to comment on the credibility."

The judge left it at that, for the time being.

Back on the stand, Detective Raney answered myriad questions on several topics. He was questioned at length about the experiment on Robin's Mazda, which he had conducted to explain why the car ran cold when Joan and Robin had driven to Seneca around 5:30 a.m. The results showed that after the car had been driven until it reached normal operating temperature, then sat for an hour and a half, it had cooled completely back down to cold. After driving only six miles in almost identical weather conditions as the night in question, the heater still did not work well enough, even with the fan on high, to be comfortable.

During cross-examination, the defense shot questions at Raney attempting to impugn his investigation, asking accusatorially about how long the scene was preserved; Robin's mail that Mrs. McHugh had received and turned over to the police (insurance policy information, checks, and letters); evidence that was seized; efforts to search for containers; and use of a laser to search for fingerprints.

"We've heard reference to a laser being used. In fact, I think you tell Ms. Row in one of your interviews that, 'We're going to take the laser out there and we're going to look for fingerprints.'"

"Yes, sir."

"Do you have such a piece of equipment?"

"No, sir."

"Did you or anyone at your direction make an effort to fingerprint the circuit breakers or the electric box located at the duplex?"

"No, sir. I attempted to evaluate fingerprinting it but found that they would have been obliterated."

NANCY WHITMORE POORE

"Is it fair to say that you got no fingerprints out of the Seneca duplex?"

"That's correct."

Taking fingerprints was a moot point since soot covered everything, including the circuit breaker box. And considering all the doors were locked and there was no sign of forced entry, there were only two sets of fingerprints to consider, Robin's and Randy's, which would be all over the house anyway.

Raney was excused and the court took a mid-morning recess. Before the jury returned from the break, the defense made another tactical motion.

"Judge, I move again for a mistrial," Gus Cahill challenged. "To coin a phrase, I think that's one of the worst examples of somebody ignoring the Court's admonition and it stinks!" he bellowed. Cahill was referring to the questions Bourne had asked Raney about the letters the detective had mailed out to mental health professionals in the Boise area, asking if any of them had seen Robin on the morning of the fire.

"You told Mr. Bourne not to get into that stuff, that you weren't letting it into evidence and then he gets right up and runs right through it again!" Cahill exploded. "And I think it's improper, and I think it's created a mistrial. I also think the testimony concerning the test of the car was improper..."

"Well, Counsel," Schwartzman sighed, "I'm going to deny the motion for mistrial. First of all, I would comment, Mr. Cahill, all you had to do was object and I would have basically sustained it...Counsel, it's a tempest in a teapot."

Perturbed, the judge went on, "If I'm forced to say it, I will. Nobody in their right mind," he continued emphatically, "is going to believe the defendant was talking to a psychiatrist at 3:30 in the morning. And the State doesn't have the negative. She could say she was talking to the Pope, and the State doesn't have to write to the Vatican asking if the Pope or some of his minions were present. It's absurd.

"If there is some direct evidence that in fact such a psychiatrist exists, number one, I'd like to know the person's name. And number two, if in fact it does exist, fine and dandy. But it's creating an illusory issue in terms of the letter and what it purports to do. The issue is almost so nonsensi-

274

cal. That was one of the reasons under Rule 403 that I didn't put it in. But technically I could have...I'm not granting a mistrial...I sustained the objection anyway, and I advised the jury to disregard it. And we're going to move on."

The battle wasn't finished as far as the defense was concerned.

"Judge, may the record reflect that I would ask this Court to recuse itself? Your attitude as you've expressed in these rulings appears to be pretty cavalier considering the nature of the case we have here. And the Court appears to have made some conclusions, and you've expressed some thoughts about the ridiculousness of what's going on here, and I think it shows the Court is not taking this seriously...with all due respect, Judge." Cahill said defiantly.

"Okay, Counsel. Fine," Schwartzman stood his ground calmly. "This is the time for motions for mistrial. I'm going to deny it, Counsel. I made my rulings on the record. They will stand...and I'm not making my comments in the presence of the jury. With that, let's bring the jury back."

✻ ✻ ✻

The prosecution called Alyce Woods as their next witness. Alyce's soft, bright-eyed charm didn't reflect her 40-something age. Her cotton-candy blonde hair, chuckle, and kind smile normally captivated children and adults alike. But on this day she was dead serious. Since the unnerving morning of February 10, she had gone through a range of emotions – shock, disbelief, anger, sadness.

Before her testimony she had been admonished by the prosecution to be very careful about what she said. The defense, she was told, was grasping at anything to get the case kicked out of court.

Alyce was somewhat of a surprise witness. She had expected Robin to break down or touch her as she brushed past the defense table, but surprise was not what she saw in Robin's face when their gazes met, Robin looked through Alyce as if she were a stranger.

Alyce answered the questions Bourne put to her. She testified that Robin had never said anything about being abused by Randy. She related what Robin had told her about Randy's condition after his motorcycle accident. Her testimony contradicted the defense's claims.

"There was one conversation," she recalled, "where the family had been forewarned that sometimes in an accident brain damage occurs, and sometimes the loved one might show signs of violence. In this particular conversation, though, the family was so happy because in actuality he seemed more gentle in the healing process – afterward."

"The first week or two into September of '91, did you receive a telephone call from Robin Row asking you to do something concerning the children?" Bourne asked.

"She was upset and she said the kids were arguing all the time and it was just getting so stressful on the family, would we consider taking the children."

That evening Robin had called back and told Alyce they had worked everything out; the kids would stay with her and Randy. Alyce was allowed to mention only this call. There were actually several calls in the same vein around the same time from the overwrought mother.

There was another call from Robin in February just four days before the fire. Robin again asked Alyce to take the children for the rest of the school year and through the summer while, Robin had said, they got back on their feet financially. As in the first call, Robin had called back and called off the plans.

"Okay. Now, when you were talking with her about 9 o'clock [the morning of the fire], did you ask her what had happened or what was going on here in Boise?"

"I remember saying, I'm afraid to ask you what's happened…She said she hadn't been home that weekend, but she got up from wherever she was staying to go get the kids up for school," Alyce wept.

"Now, when she was describing this to you initially, did she say anything about having had a premonition that there was trouble at home or having a bad feeling that there was a problem at home she needed to attend to?"

"I didn't know any – no, no."

"She just said she went home to get the kids up for school?"

"To get the kids up for school. Yeah."

That was the answer the defense dreaded. They had already successfully blocked other damaging testimony, but they couldn't stop Mrs. Woods from exposing this glaring inconsistency about why Robin had gone to the house the morning of the fire. Robin had told Joan it was because she had a bad feeling, a premonition. She told Alyce it was just to get the kids up for school.

Cahill's cross-examination was brief and gentle. This witness was likeable and credible. He couldn't risk alienating the jury by attacking her, and the sooner he could get her off the stand the better. His main point was to show that the children seemed well cared for.

"Uh-huh, they were very happy-hearted children." Alyce said.

"Did Randy seem like a gentle person to you as Robin had described?" Bourne queried on redirect.

"Yes, very much so."

"What was her [Robin's] parenting style?"

"She hollered more."

"Okay, thank you. That's all."

Randy was never abusive, Alyce was certain; if anything, Robin was abusive to him. When, a year before the fire, Randy's arm was burned by hot water, Alyce and others were told by Robin that the burn on Randy's arm was the result of a seizure. Randy had never had a seizure before nor did he have one after the supposed mishap. According to his brother, Randy had confessed that Robin had thrown a kettle of boiling water at him.

No one could understand why, after all Robin had put her through, Alyce didn't hate her. After all, she had killed two children that were as dear to Alyce as her own and had painted nasty, false scenarios about the Woods and their motives. To people in Idaho, Robin had portrayed Jack and Alyce Woods as rich and selfish, wanting the kids only because Robin gave them $500 for taking them for the summer. In reality, the Woods were not rich, and Robin gave them only $100 for three months of care.

In addition to the slander, Alyce received hateful letters from Robin that ripped her heart out. Paradoxically, Robin also sent her letters full of loving prose. "The feeling from the letters," Alyce recalled, "was that she was just mad she got caught, not sad or hurt because the kids were gone – not a reaction of a woman who had just lost her whole family."

Robin was angry that the Woods would believe she started the fire. Alyce responded, "Robin, I don't want to believe you did this, but there is a lot of circumstantial evidence, and you owe us an explanation."

The last letter Alyce received from Robin was a few days before trial. In it Robin admitted she was afraid to hear what Alyce had to say and whined, "Everybody's being so mean to me."

"With her, nothing ever jibed," Alyce remembered. "She always seemed to have money. She was going to bingo a lot, working and playing. The kids would say, 'please don't go to bingo, Mom.' From Robin's standpoint, she thought the kids didn't ever want her to do anything."

The Robin that Alyce knew before the tragedy was aloof but very charming. Yet Alyce had always sensed something malignant beneath Robin's facade in a deep, dark, unreachable place. She likened Robin to an iceberg. "The Robin that I knew in the beginning, that was my friend and the tip of the iceberg, that part of Robin is very endearing. But beneath," Alyce went on, "most of us can't imagine how deep and dark that side is."

"We were the best friends she ever had...she has burned all her bridges all her life," Alyce wagged her head in regret. "I miss the Robin that I knew. My heart wants to tell me I knew her, but that was the actor. Her own family didn't even believe her. She's so good, so excellent at her stories; she'll have you so confused. She would make me think I was in the wrong."

When she exited the courtroom, Alyce walked briskly out without looking back.

"Thank you, Judge, ladies and gentlemen, the State rests its case," Bourne finished.

✳ ✳ ✳

Court reconvened at 9:30 on Thursday, February 25, giving the defense an extra day to prepare. The prosecutors felt they had a solid case and had a pretty good idea the direction Robin's lawyers would take. But would Robin take the witness stand in her own defense?

Cahill and Myshin had few alternatives. Their client had pled not guilty. Insanity was not an option. They didn't have evidence of someone else breaking in and starting the fire. So they were left with trying to convince the jury that Randy Row was unstable – suicidal in fact – and that he had gone up to bed and gone to sleep after striking a match to the accelerant he had poured. Fortunately, they found evidence in Randy's background that would bolster their theory.

Before the jury was brought into the courtroom, Cahill began with a motion. "Judge...I would move this Court to dismiss the charges on a motion for judgment of acquittal based upon the lack of direct evidence beyond a reasonable doubt connecting the defendant to this crime, which is the standard motion to be made at this time. No further argument, I think, is necessary on that from me."

"All right, Counsel. The motion will be denied. While the evidence is clearly circumstantial, it is sufficient for the jury to return a verdict of guilty should they so find. And I will not detail it any more than your argument to raise the motion."

The defense wanted to get in testimony about Randy's dysfunctional background, including sexual and physical abuse in his childhood, and his adult psychological history, which consisted of some documented suicidal thoughts and gestures. Bourne argued that Randy's past mental state before his motorcycle accident had no bearing on the current issues stating, "It's not even talking apples and oranges, it's talking apples and camels."

"You know," Cahill insisted, "Counsel has speculated to what his theory of Robin's guilt is. And I think I'm entitled to speculate and offer evidence to show the opposite."

The defense counsel continued, "...As we heard on the tape – how many times did we hear Robin say that Randy threatened suicide all the time? We heard his voice on the tape saying, you're never going to see me again..."

The prosecutors never believed there was a nickel's worth of truth in the defense's claims that Randy was suicidal; those before 1988 were nothing more, Bourne felt, than cries for help.

"I am going to give reasonable flexibility to the defense to put on psychiatric testimony,..." Schwartzman ruled.

The jury was brought in and the defense proceeded to question several mental health professionals, extracting everything they were allowed to from Randy Row's psychological history.

A suicidal gesture was described by one witness as an attempt, and a suicidal ideation was defined as just a passing thought. It was brought out in testimony that during the recent past, Randy hadn't made any attempts. His suicidal risk assessment was listed as low.

The next psychiatric witness explained how a head injury might affect Randy's condition. "For some people, their emotional condition becomes intensified after a head injury. For other people, it's just the opposite; they become blunt..."

"On cross-examination Prosecutor Swain swerved from the subject at hand, "Doctor, did you go to Robin Row's residence on February 10 in the early morning hours between 3:30 and 4 o'clock to counsel with her?"

"No," the doctor answered, puzzled.

The further mired in psychiatric terminology the testimony became, the more heads in the courtroom began to nod and bob.

Another witness testified to a notation in the VA records indicating that the "veteran's wife" was "domineering."

One psychologist characterized Randy Row as "capable of exercising control...He impressed me as kind of a passive, dependent man. He seemed to be quite eager to please and was quite cooperative."

On cross-examination, changing the subject, Swain asked the witness, "Did you go to visit Robin Row at a residence on Bellingham Street in the early morning hours of February 10, 1992?"

"No, I did not," came the expected answer.

The last VA witness was a social worker, essentially a marriage counselor, who had seen Randy and Robin a few times in 1991. The counselor verified that there had been no allegations that Randy was physically abusing Robin or the children and that suicide was never a treatment issue. He also remembered that Robin was the spouse in control.

"Did you go to Robin Row's residence in the early morning hours of February 10, 1992, to counsel with her?" Swain asked in cross-examination.

"No."

✳ ✳ ✳

Attorney Ellison "Ellie" Matthews, Robin's first lawyer, answered questions posed by Prosecutor Bourne on cross. "You knew that Joan thought that you had gone out to the Seneca Street residence and had taken pictures of some damage that Robin said that Randy did to her property on the day before the fire. Right?"

"I don't recall precisely what Joan told me. But I know that Joan told me Robin had told her a number of things that I knew not to be true," Matthews admitted.

"I mean, you didn't go out there, right?" Bourne prodded.

"That's correct."

"And you didn't cause anybody else to go out there?"

"That's correct," Matthews replied.

"Okay. Now, in regard to talking to Robin about the divorce question, the two or three weeks before the fire, and you referring her on to another attorney, you didn't ever tell her that she should lie about anything, did you? In terms of setting up a scenario for her divorce or for child custody?"

"Of course not," Matthews snapped.

"Of course not," Bourne repeated. "And as a matter of fact, you know that she would automatically get her own children out of a divorce like that because the children weren't Randy's and he hadn't adopted them. Correct?"

"I would certainly assume that."

* * *

The defense called Bernie McHugh. As he walked down the aisle toward the witness box, his mind raced. He gave a silent prayer that he would remember whatever the lawyer would question him about.

"Good afternoon, Mr. McHugh," Cahill began.

"Good auftanoon," Bernie responded cheerfully in his cockney-like accent.

"Are you related to the Joan McHugh we've seen in this trial?"

"Yes, I am."

"All right. Do you recall what you were doing the night of February 9 last year?"

"May I interject this? I'm a recovering alcoholic and a lot of times my memory is very bad," Bernie explained.

"Were you drinking at that time?"

"No."

"Now, once again, the night of the 9th I'll tell you was a Sunday night. You remember that night at all?"

"Okay. That's the night I went to an AA meeting...I believe it was 8 o'clock; it's an hour meeting."

"When you left that evening, was she [Robin] home, do you recall that?"

"Yes."

"And what vehicle were you using?"

"The Mazda…It was Robin's."

"During the course of the evening, did there come a time when you had to go get gas for that car?"

"After I came home from the meeting…Robin asked me if I'd go get some gas."

"What did you do after you got gas in the car?"

"I just brought…the car back and parked it out back."

"Is that where you normally parked it?"

"No. I always parked it out front."

"All right. Did Robin ask you to park it back there or did you just –"

"Yes."

The back parking lot behind the McHugh's apartment complex was on the opposite end from their apartment. The probability was conspicuous that Robin had asked Bernie to park the car there to be sure it could not be seen or heard in the middle of the night.

It was Bourne's turn to cross-examine Bernie. "Did you suggest to Robin or did it come up in conversation that you wanted to go talk to Randy about this abuse thing?"

"Yes, it did." Bernie recalled, remembering the rage he had felt toward Randy when Joan told him what Robin was suffering.

"Did she tell you not to?"

"Yes."

"Why did she say not to?"

"Because it might topple him over the edge, he might get violent."

As a matter of fact, Robin had told more than one person not to bring up the subject of abuse to Randy.

Bernie testified that he had heard the washing machine running in the middle of the night and that after the Mazda sat for 20 or 30 minutes, it was cold, "cools off awfully fast."

✳ ✳ ✳

The next defense witness represented herself as Robin's "very good friend." Polly Washam had traveled from Spokane, Washington, to take the witness stand. She looked and acted like a grandmother, although she was a full-figured young woman in her 30s.

Polly, nervous at first, with her hands clasped demurely in her lap, testified about a visit with Randy and Robin she said took place in

October of 1991 and said that it had been a year and a half before that since she had seen him.

"He became angry all the – the weekend I was there; he was angry an awful lot of the time, verbally abusive. He just wasn't the Randy I knew. He was very, very depressed."

"At that time did you see anything that caused you concern in the family in terms of how Randy was acting?" Cahill prompted.

"Robin and I were upstairs and there was an enormous commotion downstairs. And when we ran downstairs, Randy had picked up a TV tray full of dishes and he threw it at Joshua, barely missing him in the head. He just totally went berserk on us."

"How was he getting along with Robin?"

"During the altercation with Joshua, Robin immediately went between Randy and Joshua to protect Joshua, and he immediately shoved her across the room – he yelled at her, he screamed at her – it was a really bad scene."

Polly became more animated.

"Did you talk to Robin after the fire?"

"Yes, I did. I called her as soon as I found out…"

"And how did she appear?"

"Well, when I talked with her, she was devastated. We cried on the phone for probably a good 20 minutes."

"Did she tell you she hadn't been home when the fire took place?"

"Yes, she did," Polly said emphatically.

"Did she tell you where she'd been staying?"

"Yes, she did."

"Did she tell you why?"

"Yes, she did."

"What did she tell you?"

Polly reared up, paused, and croaked into the microphone, "Randy had threatened to KILL her on Friday!"

"And did she tell you anything about the children –"

"Well, the children had – she told me the children had chose to stay with Randy over the weekend."

Polly didn't realize the incongruity of her last two answers and the fact that she had the dates wrong. No one else had ever heard that

Randy had threatened to kill Robin – not even Joan who had heard everything. Robin herself had told Barbara Witte on the day of the fire that the last thing Randy had said to her on the phone the night before was, "I love you."

✳ ✳ ✳

Monday, the 1st of March, marked the beginning of the fourth week of testimony and a procession of professionals and personal character witnesses for the defense. The gist of the testimony was that Randy was unhappy, depressed, possibly suicidal, and erratic in his behavior toward the children. The other common theme was that Robin kept a very neat and organized household and had very neat, happy, and well-adjusted children.

The prosecutors always finished their cross-examinations of the mental health professionals with the same question – had they met with Robin Row in the early morning hours of February 10?

After the mid-morning break, the defense rested its case. The defendant never said a word in her own behalf.

The State called a rebuttal witness, Randy Row's physical therapist, Christine Hatab. She testified that Randy helped other patients and was tolerant when he had to wait, sometimes hours, for a ride home. Even under the most trying circumstances, she didn't detect any rage or impatience in Randy.

Considering therapy can be painful and frustrating, this rebuttal testimony was important. It showed that Randy wasn't easily aggravated.

Court adjourned for lunch.

Chapter Thirty-Eight

After lunch, it was standing room only in the courtroom. People filled the seats and then lined the back and side walls. Joan and Bernie McHugh sat in front of detectives Raney and Smith and their wives. The press was out in force.

Since the burden of proof was the prosecution's, Roger Bourne would begin closing arguments, followed by attorney Gus Cahill for the defense, and finally the State again for rebuttal.

First Judge Schwartzman instructed the jury. "The law presumes the defendant to be innocent of the offense with which she is charged until she is proved guilty beyond a reasonable doubt."

"In the eyes of the law there is no distinction between direct evidence and circumstantial evidence as a means of proof, and motive is not an element of the crime charged and need not be shown. However, you may consider motive or lack of motive as a circumstance in this case."

Schwartzman advised the jury that they would be judges, and in order to support a conviction, must unanimously vote for murder in the first degree, murder in the second degree, voluntary manslaughter, or involuntary manslaughter. As to Count IV, any murder committed in the perpetration of or attempt to perpetrate arson is also murder in the first degree.

"If you have a reasonable doubt as to the guilt of the defendant, you must acquit her. But if, after going over in your minds the entire case, you have an abiding conviction to a moral certainty of the truth of the charge, then you are convinced beyond a reasonable doubt, and you should render your verdict accordingly.

"Mr. Bourne, you may proceed."

Bourne told the jury that proof beyond a reasonable doubt is not a required finding regarding collateral or side issues, such as the time the fire started or exactly how much insurance Robin Row would receive.

"The law requires you to return a guilty verdict even if you're not satisfied on that side issue. You may not know, by the end of your deliberations, whether Randy Row ever struck Robin. However, if you're convinced beyond a reasonable doubt that she committed the crime that she's charged with, the law requires you to return a guilty verdict."

Bourne recapped the major themes of the evidence.

"We know that starting in January 1992, some six weeks or there-abouts before Randy's death, that for the first time the people who knew Robin well and were close to her, in particular Joan McHugh, began to hear a story that was almost too horrible for Joan to comprehend."

Speaking softly, yet dynamically, appealing to the jurors' common sense and ability to ferret out truth, the prosecutor reexamined the different versions and inconsistencies of Robin's many stories: "A story of battery, a story of abuse, a story of rape, a story of knifing, a story of kidnapping.

"And that story got worse and worse through the month of January of '92 and up through the 10th of February 1992, to the point where her good friend and surrogate mother was nearly driven to distraction over the stories...

"And you'll recall the phone call of a night in January where Robin called Joan and said," mimicking the call, Bourne's voice dropped dramatically to a raspy whisper, his hand pressed to his ear in imitation of holding a telephone receiver. " 'He's in the next room! He's sharpening his knife! I'm afraid he's going to cut me like he's done before!' And Joan, in her fear, making Robin promise to call every ten minutes. And, of course, we know that that culminated in what the defendant told Joan was a rape...and that the sheriff's office arrived, and when they arrived, Randy broke away from them and grabbed Robin and pounded her head on the concrete before the police could take him into custody. And that Robin said later that Joan was to be proud of her because she had filed the report and had charges filed against him for this rape."

To Joan, Bourne's portrayal was uncannily accurate and an eerie reminder.

"Of course, we know about the kidnapping. That all the weekend before the fire, Joan feared for the safety of the children because she feared that they had been kidnapped."

Bourne reminded the jury that Robin told several people the kids were just fine with Randy. He reminded them of the CT scan that Robin had said showed her brain wall was bruised, a story refuted by the doctor. He reminded them of defense witness Polly Washam, "who said that after the fire she talked to the defendant and the defendant said the reason she had been gone for that weekend was because Randy had threatened to kill her, which wasn't a story that we'd heard before.

"We know, ladies and gentlemen, that the battery story is primarily not true. We know it for several reasons. First, our common sense tells us that human nature is not such that a strong, bright, independent, strong-willed person like Robin Row would stay around the house to be beaten by Randy repeatedly over a period of weeks and months...our common sense tells us that a woman who is afraid to death...isn't going to...spend a day antagonizing the bully so at night the bully will do terrible things. We know that the defendant didn't tell the battery story to people...that she should have told.

"Remember...Janet Gentry, Randy's sister? The defendant and Janet are apparently close friends, and the defendant tells Janet that she's going to divorce Randy for being childish – says nothing about battery.

"She tells Alyce Woods there's going to be a divorce, but...doesn't say anything about the abuse then. And of course, finally, a month before Randy's death, she and Randy speak to Dr. Read. They make clear that Randy has never hurt the children and he hasn't hurt Robin...If he had hurt her, that was a good time to talk about it.

"We know that the sheriff's office had never heard of either Robin or Randy Row. We know the mental health department was never there... Randy was never charged with rape or battery on police officers...The defendant didn't spend Sunday night before the fire counseling with Sue Fellen about the rape. And Mr. Washam didn't come over on Saturday afternoon to help her get her clothing out of the house. Her knickknacks were not all smashed as she claimed; they were in storage.

"There were bandages, but there were no marks. There were no broken ribs – despite her claim. And her attorney didn't go to her house to take photographs.

"She talked to Detective Raney on the 12th of February, and she said the kids don't know about the abuse – no. Randy himself wonders why there's going to be a divorce and asks Patty Coler, do you know why Robin wants a divorce? It was evident that Randy had no idea what was going on."

The prosecutor outlined the elements that proved arson, from the pour patterns on the carpet to the inside hinge latch that was found in the open position and the locked outer doors.

"We know some things about the defendant's activities on that night, don't we?" Bourne reminded, leaning into the jury box. "We know that Joan hears her up and about during the night washing her clothes and taking a shower. We know that she wakes up Joan late and says she's got a premonition and that she and Joan go to the Seneca Street residence. At first it was just something terrible, but by the time they get there, despite the fact that it's pitch black, smoky and foggy and nothing can be seen, she knows that it's fire. We know that James Brown sees a car like hers in that area about 4 o'clock.

"Next, what about her demeanor? We know that despite the fact that she told Joan and Deputy Musser that she was having a premonition, by 9 o'clock she told Alyce Woods she'd gone over to the house to get the kids ready for school...She went home from the fire and filled out a change of address...She lies repeatedly to Detective Raney about the insurance...about her relationship with Danny McHugh. And she tells a whole different story than she's been telling to Joan – there was no kidnapping. She's able to keep up her cover-up on that day despite her grief."

In terms of the law by which the jury's decision would be bound, Bourne surveyed the landscape of the crime and its perpetrator, Robin Row: her motive, her opportunity, her intent, her alibi, her cover-up, and her mistakes.

"We know several things about motive in this case," Bourne began, slowly pacing back and forth in front of the jury box, stopping occasionally to drive home a specific point. "First is the insurance motive. I see that there are four things significant about the insurance in this case that will help you decide that the defendant IS the actor. First is the amount. You know that it is extremely high, $126,000 on the children, $150,000 on Randy. Now, it's not only that the amount is high, but it's the amount in relation to the people who were being insured that's significant.

"Second, the number of policies – there's seven. These policies were the kind that you buy through the mail…they were difficult to trace. Randy probably didn't even know he was insured. It tells you that this is an anonymous way to make money on a death. If we hadn't gotten lucky with the search warrant, finding those policies in the storage unit, we would have never known. Nobody saw her face.

"The timing on the purchase of those life insurance policies. Two of them are new. One was purchased six months before the deaths and the other one was purchased sixteen days before the deaths. That's significant. In particular because she tells Detective Raney that, 'Randy has been beating on me for months.'…The end of 1990 and the first part of 1991 she was talking about divorce. That's significant that after the time that she thinks this marriage is having some trouble, she buys another life insurance policy. But even more significantly, ladies and gentlemen, is the policy that is purchased on January 24, 1992.

"That's significant, of course, because that's…right in the middle of the bruised brain wall and CT scan; it's in the very center of the rape charges; it's just a few days before the kidnapping story. You are all reasonable people, ask yourselves: If this man is so abusive, so terrible, so violent to this woman that all she wants to do is get out… the last thing she is going to do is spend some of her money to buy a new life insurance policy on a guy she's never going to see again. He's not the father of those children…that policy was purchased for one reason – because she knew she was going to collect on it within a couple weeks, and it didn't matter how much it cost.

"And, finally, the last thing that appears to be significant about the insurance policies is that the defendant lied about them. Now, she not only lied to the detective, she lied to Joan. Robin says, you keep my paycheck because the county has paid for the burial. She hides the fact that there is an insurance policy that would take care of those expenses.

"The very day that the children die, she tells Detective Raney that there is no insurance, except maybe a small one through the YWCA, and there's no policy on Randy...Why is she trying to hide that? She hides it, of course, because it shows guilty knowledge – that's the only reason.

"The next thing that is a motive to get rid of Randy, aside from the insurance, is the California warrant. The California warrant comes from the defendant. Remember, Randy calls sometime in January...and says, if you don't come home, something's going to happen that you don't want to have happen...There's only one way she can deal with that warrant...The only way she can shut him up is to get rid of him.

"Another reason a regular old divorce won't work is because of alimony. Alimony is a concern to Robin...she's worried that she's going to have to pay him if she divorces him.

"The fourth thing that tells us something about her motive is the new boyfriend. Robin has big plans for herself and Danny McHugh. Danny McHugh probably looked pretty good to her under the circumstances. I mean, he hadn't had a closed-head injury; he's...bringing in an income; he's got an education...

"Now, you have to ask yourself, how does she make the decision? I mean, we can see the decision for Randy here; she didn't like him. She was tired of him and she had a new boyfriend. What about the kids, though? How does that enter into it? How does a person make a decision to do this kind of a thing to the children? Well, you can't always judge other people by what you think yourselves. Sometimes other people's rules aren't the same as your own rules.

"But she'd made the break with the children. For one reason, the kids chose Randy over her. We know that the kids like Randy...his little shadows. They always hung on him. He spent a lot of time with them and they loved him. The kids had made the choice. And I suggest to you that that made her choice easier. If the kids were going to choose Randy, let them go with him.

"Every time she tells the story that Randy's abusing me and I had to leave town or leave the house, what does she do with the kids? She leaves them with Randy...And who does she choose over the kids? She chooses Joan and Danny McHugh...Now, don't assume that's because Randy was abusive. To begin with, we don't have any evidence or not much that he ever was. But second, if she was really concerned about that, she could have taken the kids, gone someplace else, left Randy to be abusive by himself.

"She'd made the choice, ladies and gentlemen." Looking directly into their faces, Bourne underscored his point by pressing the wooden rail between himself and the jury with his hands, as if doing so would telepathically transmit the truth of his message through the wood.

"Now I'll ask you one other thing to consider that you'll find to be significant...all Robin's things (from her storage unit)...nice furniture, clothing, knickknacks, lamps, the doll collection...What's significant about that storage unit isn't so much what's in there as what's not in there. Whose stuff isn't in storage? Whose stuff isn't boxed up ready to go to Seattle?...The kids'. The kids aren't going; the kids are staying. And that tells you what's going on right here, ladies and gentlemen." Bourne said, intently passionate.

"How does a parent make the decision to do that? I don't know. But this parent had made that decision. Only one person was leaving town and that person was Robin.

"Now, the next thing that we know about is opportunity. Robin had the opportunity to commit this crime. You know that it's only about a 20-minute drive from the Bellingham Street apartment where Joan lives out to Seneca Street. That gives her 20 minutes to get out there, 20 minutes to start a fire, 20 minutes to get back. This whole thing can be done in an hour. She's sleeping by the front door on a couch. Obviously, she comes and goes and Joan never knows it.

"Now, what about the car? When Joan checks it at 5:30 or thereabouts, whenever it was they went to drive it, it's cold. Does that mean it had never been driven that night? No. We know that car cools off fast. She had the opportunity...

"Something extremely significant is the cover-up. The cover-up applies to a variety of things. But most specifically, it could apply to washing clothes and taking a shower. You know, those things were sent off to the laboratory to see if there was any residue on them. If they're washed, there's not going to be.

"The psychiatrist story is kind of an interesting little bit of business. Joan plants the question in Robin's mind: Robin, I came down in the night Monday morning and you weren't there...Joan expected Robin to say, 'What are you talking about? I was asleep on the couch.' And, of course, Joan thought she could use that…to convince him [Raney] that Robin was innocent. Robin is confronted with an extremely difficult question now.

"You listen to the tape carefully. The defendant says: Well, are you sure? Did you check the shower? Well, I don't remember. Joan says: What do you mean, you don't remember? This is the night that your kids are killed! You're in jail! People are accusing you of murder and you don't remember where you were? Robin's in a pickle…she's got to have an explanation.

"She doesn't want Joan going to the police…that's going to blow the whole story. She calls back the next day and says: Well, I was with a psychiatrist…I was out of the house. I've been lying all along…I didn't want anybody to think bad about me for going to a psychiatrist.

"This is a woman who's been claiming to being beaten up the last six weeks, and it didn't seem to bother her much to tell that kind of a story – but she doesn't want somebody to know she's been seeing a psychiatrist?

"Now, the significant thing here is that she's telling a story to cover up…It's damage control…It's guilty knowledge. She was outside that house. She knows it, and now she knows that Joan knows it. And now you know it. That's the only explanation for why she comes up with a story like that. If she'd been in the house, folks, she would have said to Joan: You're crazy. I was in there; you were dreaming – guilty knowledge.

"Next: The battered woman. Why? You remember that I told you in my opening statement that the defendant needed a reason to be gone at 4 o'clock in the morning. She needed a reason to have her stuff out of the house. She needed an alibi that everybody would understand and nobody would question. And she concocted it from start to finish. It's the battered woman lie.

"Now why did she go through all the trouble that she did?…instead of just going to Joan's house…that night and say: Look, me and Randy are kind of having a tiff, do you mind if I sleep on your couch tonight? Because it doesn't get her stuff out of the house…All her good furniture and her doll collection and life insurance policies…would get burned up. It's to give her a reason to be gone and…an alibi.

"Well, I've talked to you about her demeanor in terms of cover-up...the way she behaved and the fact that she was able to continue to lie even when she was supposed to be grieving.

"We know that the crime scene is one that she could have entered. It was not locked with the hinge latch – she had a key. Ladies and gentlemen, I suggest to you that's proof beyond a reasonable doubt that the defendant committed the acts that she's charged with committing," Bourne paused, looking intently into the twelve captivated faces.

"Now, let's quickly look at the material allegations of the crime to determine whether that's first degree murder.

"Was the crime willful? The fire was no accident; we know that. The pour patterns clearly show the liquid accelerant on the floor. The fire was set in the most dangerous place in the house...the exits were blocked. You know that this was a willful act. I suggest proof beyond a reasonable doubt.

"Unlawful. You know that this was against the law. This wasn't in self-defense...

"Deliberately and with premeditation. That means thinking about it...When she's making up this story...rape...kidnapping...lying about any insurance – what do you think she's thinking about? It's premeditation...

"How about malice?...That is, to be decided in advance. It's the specific intent to kill. You can't set a fire in the front of the only two exits to the house and under the cold air return, under these facts, and not intend to kill the people that are inside the house. There isn't any other intention that fits these facts. Malice aforethought does not require hatred.

"You notice something else? This all had to come together by Monday morning, didn't it? Monday morning was D-day...If it didn't happen by Monday morning before 8 o'clock, the whole plan would unravel, and Joan would know the truth...When she and Robin went to pick up the kids, there'd be no sheriff's officer there, no mental health...Joan's going to know the truth.

"Causation. Kill and murder. You know that the fire is what killed these people. I suggest proof beyond a reasonable doubt.

"These people were human beings. Don't forget that fact, ladies and gentlemen," Bourne said fervently. "Randy, Tabitha, Joshua were living, breathing human beings. They can't come here and tell what really happened...but you can tell by the circumstances...YOU know that the acts...were done deliberately and with premeditation...

"Ladies and gentlemen, I suggest proof beyond a reasonable doubt that this defendant did what she's charged with doing and that by so doing is guilty of the crime of first degree murder and aggravated arson.

"Defense counsel has his opportunity next to argue the case to you. At the conclusion of that time, I'll again give you my views on his argument. I'll ask you, in the name of the People of Ada County, to return a guilty verdict against the defendant." With a figurative pound of his fist, Bourne finished as dynamically as he had started.

As he walked back to the prosecutor's table, Bourne took a deep breath, exhaling slowly. His muscles subtly and involuntarily relaxed in a way they hadn't in over three weeks. The case had been a long and intense one, for both sides. Technically it was almost over; realistically, however, the possibility existed that it would haunt everyone for years to come.

During the break, the prosecutors sat quietly. Robin gave the appearance of being calm and collected, even smiling while awaiting her advocate's closing argument.

Chapter Thirty-Nine

Attorney Gus Cahill stood in front of the jury box and held high a picture for the jurors to see. It was a portrait of Joshua and Tabitha as they had appeared in life – cheerful, carefree, smiling children.

"Ladies and gentlemen of the jury, these are the children of Robin Row. They're children she loved; they're children she cared for and nurtured for their entire lives.

"This...is what they looked like when the autopsy took place," Cahill said grimly, exposing to the jury the grisly color photographs of Robin's children in their death poses. The graphic photos were disturbing.

"Would any mother do that to her children? She was getting a divorce; she wasn't leaving the children – not with Randy Row." He laid the photos down, switched on a tape recorder full volume.

Nerves jumped when, in the tomb-like silence, Randy Row's voice echoed – loud, angry, and profane – as if from the grave. "Get her here, or I'm going to leave!" one message threatened. "Tell Robin I'm locking the front door...[tell her to] give me a call before something happens that she doesn't want to happen," was another message. "She don't have to worry about a divorce. Life's a bitch and then you die!" Randy's voice blared.

At the time she heard them, Randy's messages seemed to confirm for Joan what Robin had been telling her about his abusive, erratic behavior. She had saved them for Robin for future use in a divorce. The messages were disquieting and scored a point for the defense.

"Randy's the one who is irrational," Cahill snarled. "Randy's the one who suffers from mood swings. What is it that's going to happen if Robin doesn't 'get her fucking ass home!'?" Cahill's voice escalated to a fevered pitch. "He's going to turn her in on a warrant, tear up the house, kill the kids, kill himself. We know one thing, that Randy was alone, totally alone. And he knew he was getting a divorce. And lots of people get divorces, don't they? But Randy's not lots of people. Randy's a person whose own family has abandoned him…He's got nothing else in the world but Robin. Are those the type of stresses that you heard myriad doctors talk about that have a special impact on a head injury patient? I suggest they are.

"You heard the prosecutor in this case set up what I would call a straw man. He spent literally the first week of his case outlining all of the things that Robin Row did that were dishonest. Her lies don't mean she's guilty. We all lie…But in this trial…the lies are used as a smoke screen…designed to attack her character so that you won't do your job.

"I would suggest to you that…it is not uncommon in a divorce situation for a person to exaggerate.

"Well, who else lied in this case besides Robin Row? Well, we know the police lied. We know that Gary Raney –" when he said his name, Cahill turned and leveled a pointed finger at the detective who was sitting in the gallery, "– when he talked to Robin Row shortly after she suffered this terrible tragedy, tells her, 'Oh, well, we've got this laser technology; we'll go in there and find the killer.' But he admits to you later that's a lie.

"He's the one that sets up the lie that Joan tells…It's okay for the police to lie to get a person to make damaging statements that will help themselves. But it's not okay for a defendant…

"Joan McHugh. She lies." Again, Cahill turned to point an accusing finger, this time in Joan's direction, but he couldn't find her. Joan had left the courtroom after Bourne's closing argument. "She lies about coming down[stairs]," he continued. "She leads Robin to believe that she's Robin's friend. She's apparently funneling stuff to Gary Raney from the get-go. That's a lie…and I ask you not…to let it happen.

"My client's been charged with three counts of first degree murder. She suffered the most grievous loss that anybody could possibly imagine. And to make matters worse, she's been accused of killing…the very husband that she nurtured after that accident, alone, with very little help from anyone else – not financial, not moral, not physical help…

"I'm not here to say that the prosecutor's case is not cogent and well-prepared…but I suggest that you're the ones that are important here,"

Cahill said earnestly, looking from juror to juror. "You have to make some sense out of what's going on here.

"You decide if there's been an identification by Mr. Brown, for instance. You decide if Joan McHugh has a motive to do certain things and is therefore to be distrusted in her testimony. You decide...if at night is it possible that Robin saw from some 600 feet the top of her duplex as it was burning.

"Once again, Robin's pled not guilty. She has protested her innocence to friends, to the police. She says, I didn't do it, I didn't do it, and they can't say I did...

"How do we prove a negative?

"Don't just say, well, gosh, Robin lied a bunch of times. Gosh, she bought some insurance. You know, she's a bad person. She's guilty...

"There's an instruction that says when you hear something that points to an accused person's innocence and it's reasonable given your own experiences and your evaluation of the evidence, it is your duty to find the defendant not guilty...

"We know that the circuit breaker box is a significant point...there was no legitimate preservation of that. We know that they didn't test the front door for fingerprints...Nobody testified that they couldn't have checked fingerprints on the circuit breaker to see if Randy did turn it off...

"We know they didn't search thoroughly in the area...for containers. Once again, you can't ask them to do everything. But in a case of this magnitude, with the consequences that Robin faces, is it too much to ask? I suggest it's not.

"For all we know, the one place they took the sample where they found the heavy petroleum distillate could have been where the lamp oil, which is kerosene, that Robin talks about on the tape which may have spilled. We do know that they didn't find, of all this petroleum distillate, the light stuff that's out there on the pour patterns. They believe it's there because the pattern wouldn't get there any other way, say the experts.

"I think probably the primary thing has to do with the lack of containers...there is no evidence showing that Robin Row had any containers. There's no evidence derived from her car that they found any evidence of any accelerant at all – not containers, not spills, not anything.

"But I think the other thing that's significant is that fire is a destructive force...I would suggest to you that there is no way to know, and in fact there's been no evidence to show, that there were not plastic containers having kerosene; could have been right there and been consumed in the fire.

"Well, who is Randy?...we've played the tape; you've heard the experts. We do know one thing, he was upset about the divorce. He did suffer from mood swings. He was angry...frustrated...isolated...perfectly capable of acting out.

"Is it possible, and I suggest to you it is, that Randy...somehow starts the fire with the idea of, you know, I'll fix Robin. Comes back in and decides – he's not planning on killing the children, he's just starting a fire – is in the process of getting the children out of there and is overcome.

"The reason I offer that as a reasonable interpretation of the events of the night in question is he was dressed in his pants, his underwear, he had his wallet in his pocket and his keys. Is that consistent with a person who just went up there, went to sleep...and Robin Row or some other person comes in and they're spreading accelerant around...the fire's lit and he's consumed, you might say. Is that consistent?

"Well, let's talk about Joan McHugh. She's Robin's friend and she's, of course, right there every step of the way to support Robin...Joan is an intense person...This, well I came down there and you weren't there...I don't remember going anywhere. I've got to know. I just need to know. Well, we know now the reason she's got to know is because Gary Raney wants to know...How do you react to intense people? Well, I don't know. Lawyers are intense. Probably if you weren't sitting here you'd probably want to get up and leave now. But the point is, we do know that Robin went along with Joan.

"But Robin is very thankful that Joan has stood by her...is out there supposedly taking care of the situation while she's in jail. She's sorry: I'm sorry I've brought all this on you all. We know that Robin denies her guilt to Joan even after this psychiatrist story. And we know that Robin loves Joan McHugh. How does she end all her phone calls? I love you, Joan. I need you, Joan. And what's Joan doing?...She's taking advantage of it.

"Interestingly enough, there are a lot of things that she said that I think helped the defense, you might say. The Friday before the fire, a kidnapping or whatever, it was clear that Randy wouldn't let the kids go with her. Joan said that Randy appeared to be angry, and he physically kept one of the two [children] from getting out of the car.

"She says she saw some signs of abuse, the red marks on her [Robin's] neck. You know how they got there. She certainly believed in Robin. She believed Randy's the one that started it. She believed Robin was being abused.

"Although, interestingly enough, none of these people who heard about this did a darn thing about it. Robin and I ask you to consider all these professional people. If they believed Robin was being abused, none of them did anything...not even Joan who claims she was threatening to call the police.

"The most telling...compelling thing that Joan tells us...is that, in her opinion, Robin didn't leave the house that night. The car could not have been run that night. It was cold.

"[Robin] wasn't trying to hide that she was getting a divorce. And the fact that counsel says in his argument that she's getting a divorce and it's a problem because she's got, you know, this alimony problem, is just a red herring.

"So what do people do when they get a divorce? They divide up their property. They talk about living other places. They perhaps exaggerate to their friends their relationship to make themselves look better...People do get divorces.

"The insurance, obviously, is a significant portion of the State's case ...we had this very nice, elaborate chart up here...but it's misleading... some of these insurance policies go way back...the bulk of the insurance he [Randy] took out on himself. And he takes out insurance on Robin and on the kids. And, I would suggest, that based upon what we've heard about Randy Row, he's an accident waiting to happen...I'm sorry," Cahill feigns apology. "And probably it is wise to have accidental death insurance...It doesn't necessarily show some plan way back in '89 to do away with Randy Row February 10...both of them are taking them [policies] out.

"Is it proof beyond a reasonable doubt of motive? I suggest not.

"Well, when did the fire start? I guess we don't really know that. Mr. Dillard seemed to think it would take 15 to 20 minutes for the fire to involve the second floor...35 to 40 minutes...before it was discovered but – well, who knows? We know that the defendant was at the McHugh house at 2:30 if you believe Bernard McHugh. He says, I hear the wash going at 2:30. And Joan McHugh testified that the clock was set an hour ahead – so maybe he looked over and saw the clock said 2:30, but it should have been 3:30. We've got Mr. Healy saying he discovers the fire at 4:08 or whatever. The fire people get there about 4:30. I think that is significant...I think it is most fortuitous for the prosecutor, you might say, that Robin Row is able to slip in...spread all this accelerant around, light the fire, get out of there, leave her children up there to die, get in the car, and then get back in time for all these other things to happen that you've heard. You're the ones that have to decide: is it plausible that Robin set this fire?

"Well, to kind of sum up, I ask you to think about the testimony concerning Randy's injury. [He] has difficulty with impulse control, can't stop repeating behaviors, easily distracted, self-centered, disinhibited, he can't control his temper, he's rigid in his need for control, he acts out... [Dr.] Sanford talks about years of gestures, attempts and ideation...A number of these mental health professionals say, he's telling us he's not suicidal...It's a matter of getting attention. Is that consistent with Randy doing the acts that started this fire, but unfortunately not being able to follow through and get out with the children alive?

"And I think probably the most telling witness that the defense presented, besides the professional types, was Polly Washam. Polly Washam gives the facts and meaning to the theoretical stuff that the experts talked about. She knew he was very depressed about his relationship with his family. Little less than four months before the fire he's angry and abusive...

"Well, counsel talks in portions of his closing about how Robin acted. Her demeanor, her attitude. And he says she changed her address that day so that the insurance policies wouldn't be found – which is another red herring, by the way. What do you mean they're not going to be found?" Cahill raised his voice. "They've got her name on them!...Does that mean she's a person who's not upset at the deaths of these two children?

"What do all the paramedics say? Well, the EMT tells you she spent quite a bit of time with Robin, and Robin didn't appear to be emotional at all. You have testimony from Joan McHugh that Robin was upset. We have testimony from [EMT] Mr. Snyders about how she was...extremely upset; it took her minutes and minutes to be calmed down. I would suggest, for you to speculate that how she appears at any given time is indicative of whether she's capable of killing her children would be unfair.

"There is no physical evidence to connect Robin Row to this crime at all. She doesn't have a motive to kill her children or Randy. She's going to get a divorce...the children are going with her! And the State hasn't met its burden...

"The truth is that as many pieces of circumstantial evidence as they have mustered still doesn't undermine the underpinning of our system of justice: If the evidence is not beyond a reasonable doubt pointing to guilt, it's your duty to return a verdict of not guilty. Robin Row is not guilty of killing her family!"

Cahill appeared spent as he returned to his seat next to Robin. Body language was distant and there was no eye contact. In a room full of people, Robin Row sat alone, absently biting her nails. None of her family was in the courtroom.

CHAPTER FORTY

Prosecutor Bourne launched into his final words of rebuttal. He picked up the poster that Cahill had positioned in front of the courtroom. It screamed three bold lines: TEAR UP – KILL KIDS – HIMSELF. "Randy didn't kill himself. This isn't suicide. This is guesswork. This is speculation. There's no evidence to support it. And it's not a rational conclusion.

"Now, when counsel refers to him tearing up the house, when did that happen? October of 1990. That's the only evidence or the only occurrence that we know of where he ever broke anything.

"Now, Polly Washam says that she was there when that happened. But she's got the date wrong. She told you it was in October of '91.

"Now, what about killing the kids? What evidence is there about Randy hurting the children? There isn't any. It's never happened. Not one time from 1988 to 1992 when he died does anybody ever come into this courtroom and say Randy hurt the kids. It never happened. Now that's pretty significant when you think about it because he was with those kids day and night, from the time of his accident until the time of his death.

"What evidence do we have that Randy ever tried to kill himself?... that he was suicidal in 1992 on that Monday morning?...On Sunday afternoon he talked with his brother, Robert...about fixing the car on Monday...Does that mean he couldn't kill himself on Sunday? Doesn't mean that he couldn't, but it's an indication that he planned to live until the next day.

"He talked to his sister, Janet...He had said how pleased he was that Monday morning Robin was going to come home and they were going to work out this marriage...He was happy Sunday night because on Monday morning he was going to get back together with his wife.

"What about his relationship with the children? Every piece of evidence that you've heard from the witness stand here is that he loved the children. And they loved him. The statement from the defendant to Detective Raney: she says that the kids would rather spend time with Randy, wanted to go with Randy in the event of a divorce. If he was abusive and mean to them, that's not where they would have chosen.

"The defendant told Linda Kerr the day after the fire that she had made an agreement that the children spend the weekend with Randy. Is that an indication that she fears he's going to hurt the children?...Of course not.

"The defendant says to Detective Raney: I said just take the children to school in the morning, and I'll be over and we'll discuss this. I think he thought I meant our marriage, getting back together, but that wasn't what I wanted to discuss.

"Now, why in the world would the man kill himself that night? And where's the stress that Counsel talks about?...Where is the stress of the divorce? He's got everything to live for; Robin's coming home in the morning.

"What kinds of things can cause stress to people? Well, the breakup of a marriage or the children tearing around and making a lot of noise... what time is this when the fire starts?...3:30 in the morning, maybe a quarter to 4:00. The children up tearing around that time of night? We know that they're not. They died in their sleep. Tabitha was already on her pillow and blanket at the foot of Randy's bed. She's not up with the television set on, if that was a stressor. Everybody was sound asleep.

"Where are the stressors?...the woman that he loved had just told him, I'm coming home so we can talk about this. Now, she lied to him about that probably. She didn't have any intention of coming home and fixing up the marriage.

"Is this guy some suicidal person just walking around waiting to topple over the edge? The VA records that you have heard referred to talk about a suicide ideation in 1978 – 15 years before Randy died. And what did it amount to? He took multiple vitamins and then told his girlfriend...records show that nobody thought it was a serious attempt.

"The next thing we know about is in 1988. He comes into the VA because he's got stressors in his life. He checks himself in, and one day later he's off suicide watch.

"And what do we hear about suicide after the head injury in 1989? Nothing. Suicide is never an issue again in the marriage counseling and the other times that Randy and Robin go into the VA Hospital. But he says something extremely…important, I've never attempted it. The only time that I went into the hospital was to get attention.

"One thing that she [Robin] is consistent about when she's talking to Detective Raney is that Randy would never hurt the kids. Counsel suggests that Sue Fellen and the other women at the YWCA did nothing to help Robin when she's talking about how abusive Randy is. And yet they suggest to her, 'Come stay at the YWCA…but you've got to get those kids out of the house.' And Robin says to Sue Fellen, 'He'll never hurt the kids.'

"You know that Randy has trouble with abstract thinking…and short-term memory. Counsel suggests, out of the clear blue, that maybe he started the fire and he went upstairs and forgot he'd started it…then he was overcome by the smoke. Where does that come from? Randy, when he was talking to Dr. Read, remembered what he'd had for lunch the day before.

"But more importantly…you know that two fuels were used. One more or less as a timer and one as the powder keg underneath the stairs, the thing that would keep the fire going. That sounds like something that Randy's going to be able…to put together? This is my list of what he'd have to have done to make the crime scene look the way it does and still commit suicide.

"First, he'd have to go out and buy the fuel, two kinds because he didn't use the gasoline that was in the garage; it was still there.

"Two. He'd have to come home and pour the stuff all around, two to five gallons of alcohol or acetone on the front room carpet and then the petroleum in the closet.

"Three. He's got to gather up all the containers, go back outside and go someplace and ditch all the containers so that we can't find them… come back and…light the fire.

"Then, he's got to take off his shoes and socks and shirt because, remember…he's got [only] his pants on. He's got to get upstairs; he's got to get into bed; and he's got to get comfortable before the fire gets there. Remember what the firemen said? He appeared to be sleeping comfortably...And he's got to lay there with enough nerves of steel not to scream when he can hear the fire going down below because that's going to wake up the kids. He's got to lay there like a man of steel and wonder what it's going to be like when the flames hit him.

"Why didn't he just go out in the garage and get the two cans of gasoline, take them upstairs, pour them around in the bedroom and light them? Why go through this elaborate scheme if he's just going to commit suicide? What's the point? And we'd know, wouldn't we, because the cans would be laying right there.

"No suicide note. This is a man who had every reason to live, ladies and gentlemen.

"The evidence is that he...seems to be patient. He speaks highly of Robin; he's proud of her and he defends her. I'm not saying he doesn't have a psychiatric history...But we're dealing in realities...not some psychological abstract theoretical that maybe he could have...under the right circumstances. The circumstances weren't there.

"So now, let's look then at the Court's instruction on circumstantial evidence. It cannot be reconciled with any other rational conclusion. What other rational conclusion is there other than that Robin started this fire? Is it a rational conclusion that Randy went through all of those steps just so that he could kill himself and make it look like somebody else did it? Why would he do that? And how do you explain the insurance policies. It's not consistent and it doesn't fit.

"You heard the tape when Randy was calling up. We're not trying to play hide the ball with you. I played it to you first...because that's part of the evidence; I wanted you to hear it. Does that mean, when he says something bad is going to happen, that he's going to kill the kids or himself? Well, Robin says that he means the California arrest warrant...

"Now, Counsel characterizes the lies that Robin told as being an attack by the State on her character. That's not what we're talking about here. She's on trial because the lies are the scheme. That is the plan; that is the gravamen of the offense...The point is she made all this stuff up for a purpose...to get herself and her stuff out of the house...

"But then kind of wrapped up in that is the notion that somehow you've been lied to...by Detective Raney and by Joan and I guess by me representing the State because we somehow have hidden something from you in terms of evidence.

"Now...Joan told you what the defendant told her. You may wonder to yourself, is Joan telling the truth here...did the defendant really tell Joan all this stuff about kidnapping and rape and all that stuff? You'll find that nearly everything that the defendant told Joan, she told other people.

"[Robin tells Raney] there's no insurance. So now we know that Joan is not lying about the no insurance story. The beating story is the same. Bruised brain wall and CT scan is the same. And she admits to Detective Raney...I told Joan that I called the police, but I never really did. So we know Joan is not lying about that.

"The premonition. She tells that to Detective Raney...So what's Joan lying about? Apparently nothing.

"Well, how about the disposition of the property?...Listen to the tape again and you'll see that the defendant gives the property to Joan, and she does it for a reason...she wanted to keep Danny McHugh in town, and she says as much on the tape. Danny, I've given your mother the tax return and my paycheck; I don't want you to leave town. You're all I've got. If you leave, I'll have nobody left. I'll never see you again.

"The next thing is that the State has...destroyed evidence at the scene or we haven't done a proper job of preserving the evidence... Let's say we had tested that breaker switch and we found a fingerprint...if it's Randy's fingerprint...that's not going to give us any information we don't already have. If it's her fingerprint...that doesn't give us any information...Say there's nobody's fingerprints, does that mean that nobody touched it? No. It was shut off; we know somebody did. So what does...the fingerprinting of it, if it had been done, tell you? Nothing...talk about red herring arguments, there's one...what evidence was missed?

"We photographed nearly every inch of it. The carpet's been taken out, the hatch cover's been taken out, the panel has been taken out, the wire that burned was taken out, the floor joist was taken out. Samples were taken to see if there was any fuel on them. The thermostat was taken out, the heater was taken out, the smoke detector was taken out. Did somebody come in here and say, boy, I'll tell you if that place was still there, I could have done this whiz-bang test...prove who set that fire...Nothing was missed; it's entirely a red herring argument.

"All right. Counsel next tells you that the insurance diagram that we've created here is misleading...The diagram...gives you the dates, who bought the policy, and the amount...I haven't said that when she bought this policy on February 1, 1989, that she started to develop an intention to kill...that when she bought this add-on in February of '91 that that's the start of the intention to kill. It's the accumulation of these things that provides her with the motive...It appears pretty relevant that on January the 24th...16 days before the fire...that there is only one reason to buy that policy, and that's because the intent to kill was beginning to formulate in her mind. When you add them all together, it's a lot. A lot more than she needs, and it provides the kind of motive that she needs to be able to carry out a horrible crime.

"Finally, the reason Robin told all these stories, says Counsel, is just to exaggerate...none of this was necessary for the divorce...for the custody action...the children were her children...So what's the point?...Does it make her look better in the eyes of other people? It kind of makes her look worse. Here she is...leaving her children in the midst of this horrible thing...It's part of a plan...[that] almost worked if it hadn't been that she made some mistakes.

"She didn't quite know how to handle Joan when Joan gave her the bait question about, I know you were gone. She made a mistake there. If she'd have had the nerve to stay with it and say, 'You're wrong. You're mistaken. I was there; I don't know what you're talking about,' we wouldn't have that piece of evidence. But she gives you the look into her intentions.

"All the stories to Joan isolated Joan and Bernie and Danny McHugh from Randy. Her stories to Patty Coler did the same thing. Randy's isolated from the people who now believe that he's a killer or about to be, that he's an abuser of Robin. He can't get any information from these people about the divorce, and they can't get the truth from him about the abuse...they're afraid to talk to him, they think he's a mad man. And that's...the first thought that comes to them when the fire occurs. Randy did it...We should have gotten the kids out of there.

"But the people who he might bump into accidentally, she tells a different story...She doesn't want Anjanette to say...'Geez, you're being mean to Robin.'...She doesn't want him calling Alyce Woods...She doesn't tell Janet Gentry...she doesn't tell any therapist...Randy's walking along, happy as a clam because he doesn't know that he's being accused of all these things.

"The story's easy to believe because of the phone calls, and, of course, she's working with the women who are attuned to that. All these women at the YWCA hear these horror stories every day, and they're mostly true. So it's easy for them to believe.

"The insurance policies are perfect. There's no agent, there's no physical, they're coming through the mail, they're untraceable. We don't know if we got them all, even yet.

"The story gives her the perfect reason to be out of the house, to get her stuff out of the house...gives her somebody else to blame...[It] could blow over in a few days. It's a suicide/homicide done by a mad man. She collects the money, blows town to Seattle, and nobody asks any questions.

"But she just couldn't resist that premonition story to show off the cold car and maybe because the suspense is killing her. It's been a couple hours and nothing's happened...She's still playing the plot, though.

"She blames Joan for making her claim to call the police and disposing of the property. She blames Randy for the fire. She blames Detective Raney for not checking every garbage in town. She blames me for not preserving the house. She blames the Row family for interfering with the marriage.

"Well, ladies and gentlemen, this is an arson/murder...Two people could have possibly set that fire. One had the ability and a reason. One probably didn't have the ability and didn't have any reason. One stood to gain tremendous financial wealth and to be rid of her problems. The other stood to die a horrible death and to watch the children he loved possibly wake up during the course of it and die with him. He stood to gain nothing.

"One person created an elaborate set of lies before the fire and an equally elaborate set of cover-up lies after it. The other person went to sleep with a smile and a certain belief that on tomorrow he'd wake up and have a happier day because it would be a day of reconciliation between himself and his wife.

"One had a boyfriend and big plans with him for the future. The other believed that he and his wife had a future together. One needed a reason to be out of the house with all her belongings at 4 o'clock in the morning – a reason that everybody would understand and nobody would question. One needed an alibi that everybody would understand and nobody would question. The other person needed no alibi; he was home with the kids.

"Ladies and gentlemen, Robin Row created an alibi…and she created it out of whole cloth. She manipulated the people whom she was close to and who trusted her. Eight hours after those people had been found dead in their beds, she's still playing the story out. She is able to get through her grief and play that story on the very day that they died, right after she fills out the change of address form so the insurance policy will have a place to come to.

"She tries to tell you, through counsel, that she's just exaggerating?… This is not an innocent person who has been caught up in a nightmare. She created this nightmare. And what we have done here is present this story to you a piece at a time. [It] fits together like the pieces of a jigsaw puzzle. When you see each piece, it makes no sense to you; but when you put them all together, they interlock and you step back and you have the portrait of a crime…unexplainable in any other rational way…but that the defendant did an unthinkable thing…

"You have before you the evidence to allow you to find proof beyond a reasonable doubt that she premeditated this fire, that the containers are not in that house because she took them with her. They're not in her car because she's not an idiot…There's no flammable liquid on her clothing because she's no fool. She was washing her clothes in the middle of the night. She was taking a shower and washing her hair.

"She created this, ladies and gentlemen. As you consider it you'll find that there's no other rational explanation…but that Robin did it. Return a guilty verdict against her. Thank you." Bourne's last words were pithy and poignant.

Joan still had empathy for Robin, thinking how she must feel to have these terrible things exposed, to have to sit and listen, unable to respond.

Looking straight ahead, Robin sat rigid and still. She never looked directly at the men who were prosecuting her, and Bourne kept his mind on his job, never looking at her. Sometimes after a trial, Bourne could not even tell you what the defendant looked like. Prosecutor Swain, in second seat, watched for Robin's reactions but saw only a cold statue of stone.

Judge Schwartzman instructed the jury. He gave them the rules by which they were to make their decision. If they had any questions or needed to hear any testimony read back, they were to write it on a note and give it to the bailiff.

Even through the relief that the trial was over, the jurors felt the enormity of the task that loomed ahead. Before they had to tackle the weighty question of Robin's guilt, they hoped to have a good night's sleep at the Red Lion Downtowner, where they would be sequestered until they could reach a unanimous decision or a deadlock.

Chapter Forty-One

At 9 a.m., Wednesday, March 3, the 12 jurors entered the deliberation room. Finally, they would be able to discuss what had been foremost in their minds for weeks. They were acutely aware of the time and effort that went into a trial of this magnitude, and they walked prudently through their duties, careful not to stub a toe on a careless comment or a lackadaisical attitude toward the judge's instructions. Nobody wanted a mistrial. Judge Schwartzman's manner was stern and removed toward the jurors; he would not look at them during the trial, but they liked and respected him.

Ron, a retired high school English teacher, was elected foreman. Bonnie, a 43-year-old woman who worked for a computer chip company, acted as co-foreperson. She was a good organizer and, at first, steadfast in her opinion that Robin was innocent.

"We know she's a liar," Mark, a 37-year-old port-of-entry officer, said about Robin, "but is she a murderer?" He was vocal and played the devil's advocate. He found it hard to picture the defendant killing her family.

During their discussions, the jurors were careful to steer away from making any determinations before they had thoroughly discussed all issues. They quickly realized they would have to whittle the witness list down to key players and focus on the Saturday and Sunday before the fire.

Sifting through the mountain of exhibits was an enormous task. It took the better part of two days to pick out the pertinent evidence from the 150 pieces.

Making their decision more difficult was the lack of hard evidence linking Robin to the crime. Fortified with muffins, donuts, chips, and dips, the jurors waded through the circumstantial evidence, discussing every aspect and scrutinizing every angle or perspective of the case.

Along with Bonnie, Mark forced dissection of each issue. "She's innocent. Now, show me why she's not," was his cry.

Rich, a burly, bearded 35-year-old supervisor at TCI Cablevision, could easily picture Robin as a cold-blooded murderer because of her callous manner.

The room often grew hot with emotional debate: Was someone else involved? Did Robin purposefully disable the smoke alarms? Could she really have intended her children to die? Was it just for the money? Was it plausible that Randy started the fire?

Looking again at the videotapes of Detective Raney's interviews with the defendant, which highlighted Robin's strange detachment, the jurors realized they were full of lies and inconsistencies. "She was cool as can be," talking to Detective Raney as if it were "a walk through the park," Mark said.

"She was blatantly flirting with the detective the same day as the memorial service!" Anita exclaimed. At 29 years old, the bank secretary was the youngest jury member.

"Her demeanor was not consistent with someone who had just lost their family," Anita concluded. The others agreed.

Many of the jurors felt that Robin's brief breakdown in the courtroom while the video was played, her seemingly uncontrollable sobbing, was feigned or that seeing how she must appear to the jury, reality had hit her squarely in the face, and the tears were for herself.

"Up until that point," Bonnie said, "I think she was going to testify. Bourne would have eaten her alive! [The video] showed how hard and cold she really was. I can't imagine a person sitting for two hours and not shedding a tear or getting nervous."

The 12 jurors discussed different possibilities of how the arsonist might have gained entry. One of the men unlocked the swing lock demo easily with a credit card. Also, they knew that during their final phone call, Robin could have asked Randy to leave the swing lock open since she would be coming home in the morning. The jury felt the swing lock was not a major factor but was important to the extent that it proved the door was unlocked. Robin could have easily entered and exited, relocking the door with her key.

Some jurors looked again at the autopsy photographs. Mark studied them. He wanted the full impact of what had been done to the victims. Randy was unrecognizable, he had no face. Tabitha was on the floor wearing a T-shirt and panties. The heat had drawn her face tight and her mouth was cinched strangely into a tiny pill-sized opening. Joshua lay face-down with his arms above his head, his back burned.

The jurors didn't feel the need to spend time debating whether or not an arson had been committed. A vortex of questions and comments spun about the room. Was the time line accurate? Was Randy capable of murder? Did he have motive? Did Robin have motive? Considering the mother/son relationship, with Robin having total control of the finances and giving Randy an allowance as if he were a child, was it logical that he would initiate the purchase of any insurance policies? Were the attorneys' theories supported by the facts? Were the witnesses credible?

Some thought Robin's lawyers had some good evidence pointing toward Randy's culpability. Especially prejudicial were Randy's searing words on Joan's answering machine. They listened again to his bitter analysis, "Life's a bitch, and then you die. Unfortunately, I got the bitch end first."

There was disagreement whether or not Randy was capable of carrying out the complex process of starting the fire. Clint, a lanky construction worker, felt Randy was the fall guy for the defense. "It doesn't add up," he said. "It isn't a convincing argument, it's a textbook argument."

Most of the jurors thought the prosecution had a good case. Mark thought Bourne's closing argument "blew the defense out of the water." But it was now their job to decide whether it was good enough to overcome reasonable doubt. The defense was not required to prove anything.

Robin's psychiatrist story was a significant point for the State. If she had seen a psychiatrist that morning, wouldn't the defense have produced one? Raney's letter hadn't produced one either. But that was just one part of a two-part question.

Time frame would ultimately decide if Robin had had the opportunity to start the fire. Clint had developed a detailed timetable which conformed almost perfectly to the prosecution's case. It had only one flaw: the window of opportunity. Could they place Robin outside Joan's apartment during the time the firemen estimated the fire had started?

After they had answered all the other questions to their satisfaction, the jurors were drawn like a magnet back to one nagging point – the two-hour time period – opportunity. It HAD to be there to convict. No matter what they believed, the law said if they couldn't place her on the street during the time the fire started, they would have to acquit Robin Row. Based upon what they'd heard Joan say, they didn't think they could place Robin outside Joan's house at that time. Eleven of the jurors remembered that Joan testified that Robin woke her at 3 a.m. If Robin was with Joan from 3 a.m. on, the jurors would have reasonable doubt.

At the conclusion of the second full day, they decided they needed to listen again to Joan's testimony.

Most of the jurors dreamt about the case. In the middle of the night before they would listen again to Joan's testimony, Rich woke early, jumped from his bed and wrote down the realization that had come to him in his sleep. A parent himself, he was sure that if Randy had started the fire and had come into his room to find Tabitha sleeping on the floor, he would have picked her up and put her back in bed, making sure she was asleep before he set about to burn down his home. Also, he remembered the coroner had said that Randy was found in a relaxed sleeping pose, which indicated he was asleep when Tabitha had padded into her parents' room and laid down on the floor.

Other jurors also had difficulty sleeping. Even though Judge Schwartzman had explained that it would be his job to decide what Robin's sentencing would be, the jurors definitely thought about the possibility that their decision could send Robin Row to her death. At least half of them felt that if she had planned and executed this heinous crime, the death penalty was exactly what she deserved.

No one guessed it would be only a handful of Joan's words that would be the crux of the jury's decision. Robin Row would either walk out of the courthouse as free as anyone, be held over for a new trial if the jury was deadlocked, or be convicted of aggravated arson and murder times three.

CHAPTER FORTY-TWO

March 5, 1993

On Friday, a little more than a year after the fire took the lives of Robin Row's family, deliberations entered their third day.

After almost two hours of rereading Joan McHugh's testimony verbatim, the court reporter read the passage the jury needed to hear. Eyebrows raised. Furtive, knowing looks passed between the jurors. When they heard it, they knew it cleared up their confusion on the time frame. It confirmed whether or not Robin had a window of opportunity to be out of Joan's apartment at the time the fire was started.

After filing back into the deliberation room, the jurors listened again to some of the taped conversations, again hearing Robin say, "I'm not going to be convicted...I didn't do it, and they can't say I did."

Mark said, "turn it off." Someone else said, "I've heard enough."

"Are we ready for a vote?" the foreman asked. They all nodded in agreement.

It was after 2 p.m. The handful of people that had been hanging around the courthouse waiting for a verdict were beginning to think about going home for the day, convinced that if the jury didn't reach a decision in the next half hour, chances were a verdict would not be reached until Monday.

Melanie Threlkeld, a writer for *The Idaho Statesman*, was affixed to a hardwood bench outside the courtroom, reading a book. Kimberly Ryan, a reporter from Channel 7, popped in and out with the endurance of the Energizer bunny. The media and a handful of other interested parties, including members of Randy Row's family as well as Robin's supporters,

Polly Washam and Mary Lou Weiner, had just about given up hope of getting a verdict that day when Kimberly Ryan hollered over the balcony to those waiting below, "They've got a verdict!"

The change in the atmosphere was dramatic. Minutes that had ticked by so slowly were instantly charged. People appeared seemingly from nowhere, filling up floor space in front of the courtroom's swinging, padded doors, waiting for Robin to arrive from the Ada County jail. Joan, Bernie, and Danny were on their way. Crowding into the vestibule were members of the Row family, Detectives Raney and Smith, John Healy, fire investigators, and other witnesses previously banned from the proceedings. All waited for the doors to open on the final chapter of the trial.

The detectives had saved seats in front of them for Joan and her family. Bernie held his wife's hand and fidgeted, while Joan sat numbly contemplating the drama that would play out before them. Fear gripped her thoughts; she vacillated between sympathy for and condemnation of Robin. What if the jury lets her go because they were not allowed to know of Robin's past? What about prejudice to the State's case because they weren't allowed to present it? And would her family be safe if Robin were free? It seemed to Joan as if all the protection was for Robin.

The principals finally were in their places. Defense attorneys Cahill and Amil Myshin noticeably distanced themselves, in body language and position, from their client. Robin had been escorted in by a marshal. She wore a familiar polka-dotted polyester blouse and grey slacks, which seemed to be her dress-up attire, along with her ubiquitous black sweater, a permanent fixture on her back. Her chronic smugness was tinged with a barely discernible nervousness.

The familiar, "All rise" sounded different this time. Even though they had acted out their parts hundreds of times, the defense lawyers, the prosecutors, and the court employees were like taut strings on a fiddle waiting for a strum. Even the "civilians" seemed to be sitting on pins and needles.

On cue, everyone stood as Judge Schwartzman entered, staunch and unruffled as usual. He was the adhesive holding the courtroom together; his evenness had a calming effect.

The jurors were ushered in by the bailiff and seated as usual. There was a visible change in their deportment from their usual studious and inquisitive mien. Each juror's face reflected their herculean task – the tension, the agony, the fatigue. Yet, there was also a set determination in all twelve pairs of eyes. They sat still, awaiting the reading of the decision they had struggled with for days and which, ironically, would take the judge only seconds to read.

Dim light filtered through dust motes as Judge Schwartzman carefully explained what he was about to do. He made it imminently clear that he would tolerate no comments or outbursts. He would read the verdicts, then, one by one, he would poll each member of the jury.

Schwartzman's voice was stern and loud in the quiet room as he read the charges against the defendant in Case #18945, State of Idaho, County of Ada: three counts of murder in the first degree and one count of aggravated arson. He then received the decisions from the jury foreman.

If not for the judge's voice, those seated in Courtroom 302 probably could have heard the dust settle on the oak woodwork that surrounded them. Joan McHugh continued to fret, her heart raced, her knuckles were white. She thought: If they find her not guilty, where will we go? If they find her guilty, if she's convicted, there would be no joy.

At approximately 2:35 p.m., the judge read the verdict in his now familiar, solemn eastern cadence: "On Count I the defendant has been found guilty of willful…deliberate…premeditated murder in the first degree…beyond a reasonable doubt; Count II…guilty; Count III… guilty; and Count IV…guilty of murder in the first degree…committed in the perpetration of an arson."

In the jury box, tears spared no gender; nerves jangled and hands shook. It was the most serious decision most of the jurors had ever been asked to make. They didn't look directly at the defendant, but some took surreptitious glances to see Robin's reaction. Even though throughout the month they had seen a woman of ice, her reaction was still perplexing and unexpected. If anything was to cause her to break down, their verdict should have. Robin remained cool.

Emotion did break out in the gallery. June Row, Randy's mother, cried with relief. It was obviously a victory for Randy's family. Overwhelming sadness paralyzed Joan's body, and she couldn't stop a stream of tears. The two gun-toting marshals positioned themselves at the end of Joan's row, carefully watching her and Randy's family. She didn't understand why. She was no threat to anyone.

Schwartzman's demeanor didn't change nor did his voice falter with the serious and sensational news he was passing on. As during the trial, even now he didn't look at the jurors. He looked directly at the defendant. The jury members had convicted Robin Row of murder, of deliberately setting her house on fire to kill her husband Randy Row and her two children, Joshua and Tabitha Cornellier. All eyes were naturally riveted on Robin.

She looked straight ahead, not moving a muscle, possibly even more glacial than usual. Her brickish body language clashed conspicuously with the emotion that pervaded the courtroom. The defendant's armor cracked only slightly; her face turned a shade more pale; she briefly pressed a tissue to her nose and took a single, short breath. Gus Cahill put a comforting arm around his client, but she gave him a stiff, barely perceptible toss of her head and shoulder. Almost immediately, Robin rebuilt the impenetrable wall around herself and continued to stare straight ahead.

Judge Schwartzman asked the foreman if the verdict reflected the decisions of all members and if it were true and correct. He then polled the jury members separately, by name, asking if the verdict was true and correct. Each responded with a firm, "Yes, sir" or "Yes, your Honor."

The defense attorneys looked dejected, tired, deflated. Roger Bourne laid a comforting hand on Amil Myshin's shoulder. The prosecutor did not appear to be celebrating but was resolute and seemed confident that justice had prevailed.

It was over.

The gallery slowly shuffled out. Obviously tormented by her role as the strongest link in the chain that had led to the verdict, looking shaken, Joan McHugh was escorted out by her family.

For the first time since the trial had begun, a deputy had Robin Row stand and put her hands behind her back to be cuffed for transportation to the jail. She quietly cooperated. As she was led from the courthouse to a waiting van, her smug smirk had vanished, but she showed no emotion nor did she acknowledge a reporter who shouted: "Robin, why did you kill your kids?"

The verdict would have taken a drastically different turn if the twelfth juror, a man named Charlie, had heard Joan's testimony the same as his fellow jurors. Between the acoustics and Joan's Bostonian accent, 11 jurors had mistakenly heard and written in their notes that Joan testified that Robin woke her at 3 a.m. instead of 5:30 a.m., which would have placed Robin with Joan from 3 a.m. on through the morning. After listening to Joan's testimony again, however, they realized that the time line that they had gone over and over so painstaking did actually fit, Robin did have the time and opportunity to start the fire: "At sometime early Monday morning, the 10th, did Robin Row come into your bedroom?" court reporter Bette Storm had read Bourne's question back to the jurors.

"Yes," was Joan's answer. "...She woke me [at 5:30 a.m.] and said that at 3:00 she had this terrible feeling that there was something wrong at her house...and she thought there was something wrong, would I please go with her."

The 11 jurors had initially thought that Robin woke Joan at 3 a.m, which would have meant that Robin did not have a window of opportunity to start the fire. What Joan actually said was that Robin had had a terrible feeling at 3 a.m., but woke Joan at 5:30 a.m. to tell her about the premonition.

"[Then] we knew she could have done it," Anita said, "it fit – it all fit."

Ron, the foreperson, had gone around the table collecting votes. None of the 12 had shared their decision with the group up until that time. To arrive at their decision took one and only one vote – guilty on all counts.

The jurors discussed Robin's reaction to their verdict. They felt she'd do one of three things: "She's going to flip out, pass out, or do nothing at all, like a stone," Mark predicted.

After the verdict, Anita recalled they all felt sick to their stomachs. None took the judge up on his offer for a free dinner on the county. They just wanted to go home.

Mark said that the defense's arguments never brought out anything that made him doubt his final conclusion. He agreed with Bourne's assessment of Robin's plans. "We believed that her plan had to be stepped up."

Referring to Robin's sudden appearance at the crime scene, Mark again agreed with the prosecutor. "Bourne was correct when he said curiosity got to her – did it go out? Did it burn down?"

Mark almost cried several times during deliberations because of the brutality of the crime and Robin's lack of remorse. "She's a monster. I can't understand how a mother could bring kids into this world, disregard that mother bond – be so horrible to want to kill them – then want to witness it! We're a horrible people," he said sardonically, "a defect of humanity. If I could fix society, I would remove greed. Robin was fueled by greed.

"It upsets me to hear people say she must have been crazy." Mark went on with conviction, "The woman was never crazy. She knew what she was doing. She was crazy like a fox…really smart in one sense and really dumb in another. She told professionals about her abuse…then the psychiatrist story."

"She wanted to get ahead no matter who she stepped on," Rich concluded.

"The psychiatrist story that Robin told Joan was the big tip-off," Clint recalled. "With that statement, she put herself out of the house." He also said that her demeanor helped in making the final decision.

Clint did not believe that Robin could see her duplex that night when she and Joan approached from Five Mile. Even disregarding that it was dark and foggy, the duplex was 600 feet away and blocked by other structures.

They debated the possibility that Danny was involved. The group had mixed feelings, but Anita thought Robin would have implicated him in the beginning if he had been involved. She thought Robin was definitely obsessed with Danny. After questioning him and getting to know him better, the police and prosecutors were certain he wasn't involved. The newspaper delivery man had seen only one person in the car on Seneca that morning. And having accomplices didn't fit Robin's M.O. – she worked alone.

The jurors could not see what attracted Danny to Robin. "Her boyfriend smoked her in intelligence and appearance," Mark said.

"She really thought he was going to be her knight in shining armor; she would have done anything for him," Bonnie speculated.

320

Before they went home, Schwartzman debriefed the jurors and praised their verdict. "His debriefing was phenomenal," Mark remembered." At first the judge was somewhat intimidating, but after it was over he gave them a glimpse into his character. He outlined some of Robin's criminal history and prior fires.   •

The jurors felt that justice had been served. They were exhausted, drained mentally and physically from their experience. Serving on another jury was something none cared to do again. In payment for their service, the jurors got $10 a day plus 26 cents a mile for travel to the courthouse.

Outside the stately stone structure, the media swarmed like hungry piranha. They took their first bites out of the Row family, heading them off at the steps leading from the building. They huddled around the family as if gleaning secret plays from a football coach. "We're satisfied," June Row told the reporters. "We've got the best lawyers and detectives in town."

The defense attorneys exited next. "We are extremely disappointed," Cahill said. "Robin certainly has maintained her innocence, and we intend to continue to fight to prove that."

Myshin told reporters that the prosecutors used a "barrage of circumstantial evidence," adding, "What the State attempted to do is prove that she's a murderer because she's a bad person. This is only one phase of the war, and the war will continue, I promise you that."

The jury tried escaping surreptitiously out a side door, but a couple of media bloodhounds caught their scent. The jury foreman gave a statement: "The issues were complex, the testimony was lengthy, and the evidence was voluminous. After sifting through everything presented to us, everyone felt only one verdict was possible. We know you have many questions; the answers are all contained in the record."

With a sly smile, Detective Raney wove unobtrusively right through the media blitz.

Kimberly Ryan interviewed Joan McHugh on the courthouse steps. They were the first words Joan had uttered to the media since it had all begun. She valiantly answered the questions put to her with cameras pointed at her and microphones shoved in her face. When asked how she felt about Robin Row, Joan thought a moment then, trying unsuc-

321

cessfully to keep the quaver from her voice, answered, "I haven't even figured out how I feel. I just don't know what happened to the friend that I had…she wasn't sitting in that courtroom."

After a pause and a breath, Joan went on. "I wonder now, did I ever know Robin Row. I wrote her a letter in prison, and I asked her where is the Robin I knew that was good to me and kind to me – I don't know where she is; it wasn't that woman sitting in the courtroom.

"Now, maybe there's justice for Randy and all the children who were sacrificed so Robin could have whatever she wanted." Joan's reference was to all four of Robin's children.

After several minutes the prosecutors emerged for their command performance. They praised the jury for being conscientious and thorough. "Obviously, she is able to put together a horrible crime. We believe, and the jury agreed, that she premeditated and deliberated this crime, and she had the specific intent to kill."

Bourne praised the local fire officials and Ada County sheriff's deputies for bringing a "complicated case to justice." He said he had not yet decided whether or not to ask the court to impose the death penalty.

CHAPTER FORTY-THREE

When night fell, Ryan McHugh put off going upstairs. He was afraid to go to bed. Afraid his family's apartment would burn down like his friends Joshua's and Tabitha's had. Afraid his father Danny would die. The long fingers of Robin's victimization had reached beyond the obvious victims.

It had sounded so simple when Joan told the press she and her family wanted to get on with their lives. But reality was quite another matter. As hard as the McHughs tried to insulate Ryan from the chaos that Robin had brought into their home, they failed to recognize that if the adults were having such difficulty coping, it was even more frightening and confusing for the young boy.

The effects of Robin's actions had spread out into the community as well. She had lied and cheated individuals, which in turn had tarnished the YWCA's reputation. "She has victimized battered women everywhere," Sue Fellen said. "There are very few battered women who lie. And I will continue to believe a woman who comes in and says she's battered."

✳ ✳ ✳

After several months in solitary, Robin shuffled into the courtroom for a presentencing hearing wearing a matching two-piece, V-necked midnight blue ensemble. Courtesy of the Ada County Sheriff's Office, the outfit was artfully accessorized with silver-cuffed bracelets, one on each wrist, connected to a chain belt that clinked when she moved. Now that she had been convicted, she did not have the luxury of wearing regular street clothes.

In Idaho, for a first-degree murder conviction, Robin would receive life imprisonment or death by lethal injection. In open court and in a memorandum, Roger Bourne had asked the Court to impose the death penalty. Bourne and Swain could not help but have mixed feelings about asking a judge to have someone put to death, but they knew it was the right decision in this case. No other sentence fit the crime, legally or morally. Bourne wanted to do all he could to be certain she would not be eligible for parole at any time in the future.

Regardless of what the prosecutors asked for, the final decision would be Judge Schwartzman's. He had a reputation as a "thoughtful" judge in the sense that he would ruminate carefully before entering an order, especially one as serious as the one that was before him. Death was a sentence he had never imposed before. There were many who felt Judge Alan Schwartzman would not decide on the ultimate penalty.

To support his request, Bourne cited seven out of ten statutory aggravating circumstances: First, "At the time the murder was committed the defendant also committed another murder." This one was obvious and irrefutable.

Second, "The defendant knowingly created a great risk of death to many persons." In addition to her own family, Robin endangered the lives of her neighbors, the Healys, and the firemen who risked their lives to put out the fire.

Third, "The murder was committed for remuneration or the promise of remuneration…"

Fourth, "The murder was especially heinous, atrocious or cruel, manifesting exceptional depravity." The Idaho Supreme Court explained the meaning of this fourth circumstance as "the conscienceless or pitiless crime which is unnecessarily torturous to the victim."

The fifth aggravating circumstance read, "By the murder, or circumstances surrounding its commission, the defendant exhibited utter disregard for human life." A Supreme Court quotation defined "utter disregard" as: "…Acts or circumstances surrounding the crime which exhibit the highest, the utmost, callous disregard for human life, i.e., the cold-blooded, pitiless slayer."

The sixth circumstance was indisputable, "The murder was one defined as murder of the first degree by §18-4003, Idaho Code…any murder committed in the perpetration of ARSON...and it was accompanied with the specific intent to cause the death of a human being."

The last aggravating circumstance that the State insisted applied to Robin Row was, "The defendant, by prior conduct or conduct in the commission of the murder at hand, has exhibited a propensity to commit murder which will probably constitute a continuing threat to society."

Bourne argued, "There is no reason to think that she has any internal control that would deter her from killing again. She has become a callous, pitiless slayer. She will undoubtedly constitute a continuing threat to society."

Judge Schwartzman noted that the verdict itself established two aggravating circumstances as a matter of law: "At the time the murder was committed the defendant also committed another murder," and the murders were committed "in the perpetration of ARSON." Only one need be found to exist beyond a reasonable doubt before a sentence of death could be imposed. However, if Robin's defense lawyers could come up with enough mitigating circumstances, she would escape the death chamber.

Cahill was not through fighting. His work now focused on convincing Judge Schwartzman to impose a life sentence.

Schwartzman made it abundantly clear that a psychological evaluation would be important in sentencing and that feelings of remorse, prior criminal history, and prior involvement with possible arson-caused fires would be considered, although, he added, "The defendant does have the absolute right to refuse to answer any question therein or for that matter decline the invitation to have any psychiatric evaluation done at all pursuant to her rights under Miranda. The ball is in your court," Schwartzman reminded Cahill.

The defense had ample time in which to get their mitigating circumstances in a row. The sentencing hearing was slated for October with the judge's pronouncement scheduled for the following December. In the meantime, a presentence report would be prepared for the judge's use in making his decision. This report would outline Robin's history, including background that was initially labeled prejudicial and excluded from the trial.

On April 29, Robin requested a visit to the grave sites of her children. Cahill argued that Robin should be allowed to go to the graves and asked Judge Schwartzman to "exercise some mercy."

"The ironies of such a request are somewhat mind-boggling." Schwartzman responded. He refused "unequivocally" to force the police to allow Robin a visit to her children's graves.

* * *

On Mother's Day, Robin placed one last call to Joan asking for the title to the Mazda. Joan informed her it was in the prosecutor's hands, then took advantage of the opportunity.

"I have a lot of questions, Robin."

"I know," Robin answered. "but now is not the time; we'll talk about it later."

"I really have a lot of questions," Joan insisted.

"You'll have the answers, later."

Before she hung up, Joan resisted the urge to sarcastically wish Robin a happy Mother's Day.

Joan would get most of her factual questions answered eventually, but not by Robin. There would never be a satisfactory answer to the biggest question – WHY? Every story Joan heard or read in the media about a sociopath reminded her of Robin. In hindsight Joan realized Robin's conscience was missing; she had no remorse for what she had done or pity for her victims. She exploited people to satisfy her own selfish needs and shifted blame to cover up her lies. Joan came to realize that it would be pointless to ask Robin why she had committed the crimes. Robin would only rationalize, justify, and lie about her actions. Joan eventually reached a point in time when she had no desire to hear the answers.

* * *

Because of overcrowding, the Ada County jail had to move the women inmates to a lower-security facility. Since Robin was a high-security inmate, she was moved approximately thirty miles away to the more secure women's section in the nearby Canyon County jail. She was allowed only one hour of visitation a week. Now on the outside, Bobby, her jailhouse lover, used up her weekly allocation. In addition, weekly visits from Mary Lou Weiner, still one of Robin's few supporters, were considered clergy visits and not part of the one-hour-per-week limitation.

Robin wasn't writing to the McHughs any longer. It was too late for them to be much help to her now anyway. She had moved on. It was

326

her pattern. She used people up, then tossed them away. Robin fixated on new tasks, new scams, new people. She needed to find a way around the death penalty and worked on gaining the support of her new man. She wrote to Bobby.

Obsessively, she wrote letters to Bobby filled with tales of her past, sexually explicit passages, finger-pointing away her guilt, self-laudatory words describing her admirable mothering abilities and love for her children, even hopes for their future together and the good mother she would be for Bobby's daughter.

She wrote about falling in love with Bobby and his standing by her and selected "Unchained Melody" as their special song. Again, as it had been with Danny, Robin was more into the relationship than Bobby was; he just went along. His manner was easygoing, his voice quiet. A ragged denim jacket covered most of his tattoos and a scraggly beard covered part of his face, which was like a relief map that attested to a life on the rough side.

When Robin had a bad day, Bobby rolled with the punches. On those days, she would become as vicious as a pit bull in person and in her letters. It was as if two entirely different personalities inhabited her body, Bobby thought. Some days she verbally hammered out to him her hatred for the cops, the prosecutors, the judge, even her own attorneys. They were responsible for her predicament. Detective Raney, Bobby said, was most definitely not on Robin's Christmas list.

Several days before her sentencing, Robin "flipped out" about the outcome and about going to prison. She got special permission to see Bobby even though she'd already used her visiting hour. Robin needed a man to profess her undying love to, and Bobby was handy. She "had to get tough" he told her because she'd be "playing with the big girls" when she went to prison.

Not only did Robin have her pseudo lover, Bobby, standing by on the outside, to whom she was professing her love, she also had a lover on her side of the bars. When Robin was caught in a sex act with another female inmate, sexual misconduct was added to her file.

Bobby believed Robin when she told him that she was on some kind of drug, like Valium, on February 10, 1992, and that Danny McHugh was the one who had lit the match that sent her home and family up in flames. Bobby liked Robin; it didn't make any difference to him one way or another if she had started the fire that killed her family.

However, it would make a difference to the judge. Robin didn't have long to figure out something that would appeal to the judge's sense of mercy and keep her from death row's door.

CHAPTER FORTY-FOUR

It was Tabitha's birthday, a day before the sentencing hearing. Disregarding her counsel's advice, Robin spoke to a reporter in what some saw as a plea for sympathy. "I knew if I didn't accept it, I would be a basket case," Robin said. "I suppose when I actually hear it, it will affect me, but right now I think I'm prepared for what he's going to say.

"As I've told other people who have asked me, at least in death I know I will be with my children. I'd rather die than spend the rest of my life in prison." Since her conviction she had been trying to deal with her past, she said, including sexual abuse by a relative and emotional abandonment by her mother.

Since the guilty verdict, depression had curbed her appetite, she said, which in turn had caused a twenty-two-pound drop in body weight. Robin maintained her innocence and stated that she tired of the question: Did you kill your children?

"I have gotten to the point…where I always say, what I may or may not have done had no effect on you…and I am not going to sit here and justify anything. I have passed that point. I just tell them [cellmates] they can believe what they want to believe," Robin expounded.

If sentenced to death, Robin claimed that she would not want years of appeals. She professed to want to follow the lead of felon Keith Wells who brutally beat to death two young adults at a pub. He asked the Idaho Supreme Court to let him fire his attorneys, end all appeals, and be put to death as soon as possible. The Court agreed. His sentence was carried out January 6, 1993. It was the tenth execution in Idaho, the first since 1957, and the first to employ lethal injection; the previous nine were hangings. Public opinion seemed to be in support of capital punishment.

"I'm ready for it," Robin said in a matter-of-fact tone. "I believe in a Supreme Being. I think Hell's right here."

* * *

Since the verdict, interest in the Robin Row saga had waned. The gallery was sparsely populated. A knot of Row family members sat toward the front. Joan didn't come to the sentencing hearing but sent Bernie in her stead. On the defendant's side were the church people; Mary Lou Weiner; and Polly Washam's mother, who sat sullenly still.

"Since this is a potentially capital case, everything needs to be attended to with a microscope," Schwartzman warned. With the judge as intermediary, the attorneys wrangled over what information could be used to decide Robin's sentence.

Cahill hurled a sampling of motions in an effort to keep his client from becoming the first woman in Idaho to die on death row. He argued that Idaho was in the minority in not having sentencing by jury. His motion was denied.

Then he moved for acquittal based on the circumstantial nature of the evidence. The judge emphatically denied the motion, "No one saw or photographed Robin Lee Row actually striking the match or torch that set the apartment ablaze...The evidence was compelling if not overwhelming...[it came down to] only one person who could have and would have [committed the arson]. This is as strong a circumstantial case as I have ever seen."

Visibly frustrated, Cahill moved to disqualify the judge. The defense had been fuming over conclusions by the judge about whether the death penalty would be sought and the denial of their motion for mistrial midway through the trial, which was based on commentary Schwartzman had made about Robin's psychiatrist story: "The [psychiatrist] statements were totally unbelievable and absurd – nobody would have believed it..."

Unruffled, Judge Schwartzman responded "...The statements were not given in the presence of the jury and were totally harmless and did not qualify for grounds for a mistrial." He further interpreted that his comments about the death penalty came from the jury's conclusion, finding two aggravating circumstances – three dead people and arson.

"...Motion denied." His voice didn't require a gavel to underscore his resolve.

While her lawyer went on with more objections, Robin sat as she always did, stoic and staring.

With objections out of the way, counsel for the defense called their first witness. A slight, dark-haired woman in her early 30s nervously made her way to the front of the courtroom. She was attired in a simple white blouse and slacks. Her eyelids were dark, heavy with eyeliner, giving her a hard edge. As she made her way past Robin to the witness stand, Robin's face melted into a pleasant expression. It was a sad, crooked smile.

So quietly that the judge had to ask her to move closer to the microphone, the witness stated her full name, "Terry Cornellier." She told the court she was Robin's younger sister from New Hampshire. Up to this point, family members of the defendant's had been conspicuously absent.

Amil Myshin quickly worked up to the core of the testimony that would back up his theory that Robin's childhood was to blame for her wicked behavior. Avoiding eye contact with her sister, Terry recounted the abuse and neglect of the Cornellier children and the resulting troubles that followed all five children into adulthood. Without emotion she explained the effect of her parents' divorce on herself and her older sister, of living in an atmosphere with little or no nurturing or affection.

"I don't know how to be a mother," the witness admitted flatly.

"Did your step-grandfather have inappropriate contact?" Amil Myshin asked gently.

"Yes. It stopped when I was 13 because I wouldn't be with him alone. He touched me, my breasts and my privates, and he wanted me to touch him. He gave me money. I never told anyone until four years ago. I started getting into therapy. My sister told me she was molested by Ed, too. We talked about if he did it to our younger sister [Tammy]."

"Did it affect her?" Myshin asked.

"I think it affected her," Terry said.

Robin's unstable home life, sexual abuse, emotional neglect, and abandonment were all features of the dysfunctional setting that the defense showcased as mitigation.

"In 1979, approximately...before Robin moved to California, she was living in the same town as you were. You were living in an apartment building with your child...in New Hampshire? Does that sound about right?" Bourne began his cross-examination.

"Yes. I'm not sure of the dates," Terry replied.

"Did you take care of Keith?"

"Yes. We baby-sat each other's kids."

"Did sometimes you not know Keith was there?" Bourne probed.

"No," she answered quickly.

"Didn't you say to Deputy Sheriff Dee Pfeiffer that sometimes Robin just dropped him in front of your door without your knowledge?" Bourne asked in disbelief.

"No, she always called," Terry answered.

Bourne knew she was lying. There had been no miscommunication about what Terry had told Deputy Sheriff Pfeiffer when he interviewed her in New Hampshire before the trial. She explained to him that Robin would occasionally leave Keith on her front steps without calling; she would open the door to find Keith there without his mother. Pfeiffer had confirmed it with her again because he couldn't believe what he was hearing. In a phone conversation with Joan, Terry had recounted the same scenario.

"Sometimes Robin didn't tell the truth?" Bourne switched to a new line of questioning.

"Yes...that's true," she said hesitantly.

"Did you say to the deputy that Robin had a thing for money, for things more than she could afford?"

"Yeah," Terry responded reluctantly.

"Was she addicted to bingo; was it real important to her?"

"Yeah...she liked bingo a lot."

Bourne had squeezed as much from this witness as he could. Terry breathed a sigh of relief when she was released and walked briskly down the aisle without having given her sibling much more than a cursory glance and going back home without even one visit with Robin. Terry was the sister Robin had recently told Raney was unable to visit her at the jail because she was confined to a wheelchair. Raney had actually believed her. He had forgotten his own advice, which he had labeled Rule Number One, that sociopaths have no rules.

332

Pfeiffer was not surprised that Terry denied what she had told him for whatever reason – the axiom about the thickness of blood, or maybe she felt she needed to help keep Robin from the death penalty. From a prosecutorial standpoint, there was no point in harpooning Terry on the witness stand, questioning her about the mysterious fire in her apartment or Kristina's death. It would appear mean-spirited, and she probably would deny it.

When Pfeiffer had interviewed Terry earlier, she wasn't shy about expressing her feelings about Robin. Where her older sister was concerned, Terry was angry and, like their younger sister, Tammy, was convinced that Robin had killed her own children. Robin had once told Terry she did not want Kristina.

Terry also told Pfeiffer that Robin had a pathological need for money and got an early start on stealing. As a teenager she stole bank books and forged checks. Terry didn't believe her older sister had ever completed high school, let alone college, as Robin had claimed. Robin was often on welfare, but always got insurance on her children. She once said, "Terry, you ought to get insurance on your kids; you never know when you're gonna need it."

Pfeiffer also spoke to Robin's mother, Virginia. When they met, he saw a woman in deep denial, nice but spineless. As a teenager, Virginia had married a controlling man and had given birth to Robin when she was 16. About Robin's father, her ex-husband, she said, "Yeah, he's in prison, but I'm not sure what for." She couldn't name the fathers of any of Robin's children.

Tammy, the baby of the family, would not testify for her older sister. For that matter, she probably would not have been a good defense witness. She was angry at Robin and afraid of her. She believed Robin had planned to kill her for insurance and was convinced that her sister had murdered all of her own children.

In a small Chinese restaurant in Redding, California, Raney had talked with Tammy. She told him that for as long as she could remember, Robin had been a continuous liar. She had an obsession for money, had always been different from the rest of the family in her interpersonal relationships. Robin had no maternal instinct and was never affectionate with Joshua.

Tammy confessed to Raney that she had lied to police when Robin's car had turned up missing. She told the officers she knew nothing, which wasn't true. She remembered saying, "Robin, somebody just took off with your car!" Robin's cool response was, "Just mind your own business." And Tammy did.

About Robin's proclivity for starting fires, Tammy remembered that in 1977 Robin and Kristina were living in an apartment in New Hampshire when fire broke out in the apartment beneath Robin's, forcing her and her daughter to move into her mother's home. A few days later Kristina had died. Tammy was very suspicious about her niece's death and believed Robin murdered her.

At the end of Raney's interview with her, Tammy dropped a bombshell. "Tell me, do you think Robin could get off on this?"

"I think it looks like we're putting together enough evidence that we're going to have a pretty good case." Raney replied.

"Well, if she's gonna get off on this, will you let me know?" Tammy continued with a fierce spark of conviction in her eyes. "If she gets off on this...I'm gonna make sure she never has the chance to do it again."

Raney wasn't sure about Tammy's ability to follow through, but he read her intent as deadly serious.

CHAPTER FORTY-FIVE

There was something brewing on the fourth day of the sentencing hearing. Even the prosecutors were unsure exactly what was coming but knew it would be of some import. The defense attorneys had been in conference with Judge Schwartzman in his chambers.

Cahill began by submitting a startling request on his client's behalf. Robin wanted to present her version of the crime to which she had been found guilty in response to the presentence investigation report.

"Is this different than the defendant's right of allocution...normally in written form?" Schwartzman questioned Cahill sternly, incredulity tingeing his voice.

"Yes, sir."

"She wants to give it orally?"

"Yes, sir."

"I will permit this unorthodox and unprecedented preallocutory statement to commence. I reserve the right to cut off the testimony at any time as long as it's understood that this is not testimony. She is not under oath and not subject to probing cross-examination. She is advised that her testimony can and may be used against her. She has a Fifth Amendment right against self-incrimination," Schwartzman warned. "Go ahead, Ms. Row."

The collection of people waited. The woman they were so accustomed to seeing sit mute was going to speak. The defendant who wouldn't take the witness stand in her own defense during trial, the woman whom many, including herself, had described as a pathological liar, was finally going to give her version. Everyone leaned forward in anticipation.

335

Robin Row was speechless, her words held hostage in her dia-phragm. Three times her mouth opened then clamped shut.

Finally, dipping her head toward Cahill's, she exhaled. "I can't do it …I can't," she repeated. Cahill whispered something in her ear. Robin slowly stood. She began, quietly but steadily, reading from a paper.

"If you had asked me a year ago if I was innocent of this – this crime, I would have said, yes, that I felt I was completely innocent.

"It's been through many hours of intense interviews and hypnosis that I've come to realize differently. It was so traumatic for me that I had blocked out my involvement in it. I'm now willing to accept the responsibility for my actions that endangered the life of three people and eventually led to their death. I had remembered part of it up to a point, and then when I had blocked it is when I had gone out to the house that evening and that morning and saw the flames coming out of the house.

"I was at Joan McHugh's house and I was very agitated, very desper-ate to get out of a bad marriage. I – despite what people have said, there was abuse in the home; nobody knows exactly what went on behind our locked doors, and we didn't air it to the public. A few people knew.

"I drove out to the house that evening; I don't remember times. I think it was 3:00, 3:30, something like that. The facts that I recall are dif-ferent than what testimony was presented. I'm not saying that testimony wasn't true, it's just I don't remember it that way. I went into the house, into my home. I – I don't know exactly everything that happened because I was not in the house the whole time. I know the fire was set, I know where it was set. I myself do not recall any accelerant being used.

"I went upstairs and saw my children. The house was not intended to burn down. It was just intended to do some structural damage, enough that we would have to have left, and the children and I would have went to Joan McHugh's. And Randy, I assume, would have went to a member of his family, probably his sister. And I felt that was the only way to get him out of my life because he had told me on numerous occasions that if I tried to divorce him or if I left him he would track me down, and I firmly believe he would have…

"After the fire was set I left and went back to Joan's house. I took a shower and woke her up and asked her to go out there with me because something just didn't feel right to me. And we drove out there and we approached the street, it was all barricaded. They let us through because I told them who I was. And we walked to the house and it was on fire," Robin recounted, her voice breaking. "I remember at that point that I ran to it and then everything from that point on I had – had blocked. I remember paramedics and – talking to me, them telling me that Randy and Joshua were gone…and they couldn't find Tab – Tabitha," her voice broke again. "And the last time I had saw her she was in her bed and it didn't occur to me at the time that she would have went to the bedroom like she normally did. And I think the hardest part of this for me is knowing that she had woken up since I left. So she had to have known what was going on and I can feel her terror…That's all I have to say." She ended dramatically, steadily, her voice devoid of tremors.

The decision for Robin to speak in open court was a difficult one for Cahill and Myshin. As a general rule, it is never a good idea to put a client up to confess, which was essentially what she did. But Robin wanted to do it, and they had to find something that would show mitigation. Hiring the psychiatrist was part of the process of trying to figure out what their client was all about; the statement written by Robin, which the lawyers represented as a direct result of their client's hypnosis, was the end product of that process. They thought it would show remorse and bring out the humanity in Robin, the humanity that had not been evident during trial.

The prosecutors had mixed emotions about Robin's speech. Swain's thoughts went from one extreme to the other, from thinking he was hearing a confession, "Oh Boy! This is better than it could possibly be!" to "Oh God, right to the very end she's not going to take responsibility. She's going to try to hurt someone else, her last lashing out at Danny." Even though she didn't mention names, it was obvious that Robin thought she had found a way to have her judgment cake and eat it, too. By pointing the finger of culpability in Danny's direction, she could claim repentance without having to admit to doing the unthinkable.

The facts didn't surprise Bourne; it was what the prosecution had been saying all along. What did floor him was that Robin could bring herself to say as much as she did.

When Bourne heard the words, "I – I don't know exactly everything that happened because I was not in the house the whole time,…" he thought, Hell hath no fury like a woman scorned. Danny dumped her, and now she's going to take him down with her.

Bourne and Swain agreed that Robin's statement, what amounted to a washed-out version of a confession, was a last-ditch effort for mercy. Robin was a sympathy junkie. She couldn't resist trying to sway the judge with her words.

After the break, with her head held high, Robin took her place. The smirk, which Joan had recognized during trial as Robin's indignant mask, was pasted back on.

The defense called Carla Anderson, assistant to Dr. Arthur Norman, the defense-hired psychiatrist from Portland. Anderson testified that she believed that Robin, after receiving fifty hours of counseling time through their office, had experienced an incredible breakthrough. At first, Robin claimed she couldn't remember what had happened, denying having anything to do with the fire. Toward the end of the sessions, when her memory returned, she talked about Danny. She told the assistant she felt let down by Danny and that his testimony had helped unblock her memory.

Robin told Anderson her version of the night of the fire. She and Danny left in her car, she had said. They went inside. He asked her to go into the kitchen; he piled up stuff; she left the house before the fire was started. She said that he said it would burn out, nobody would be hurt.

Anderson believed Robin when she said money had nothing to do with what had happened. About the smoke detectors, Robin said it had to have been a coincidence they didn't go off because Danny didn't have time to go to the fuse box.

Bourne cross-examined the witness.

"Do you have notes of conversations?"

"Yes," Anderson responded.

"Where are the notes?" Bourne asked politely.

"Portland."

"What do the notes say?"

"It didn't all come out at once – basic things," Anderson said.

"Did you tape?"

"No."

"Did you make up a report?"

"No."

Anderson testified that the fifty hours in counseling sessions resulted in only three to four pages of notes. Bourne didn't believe her.

"Do you have a photographic memory?" Bourne asked.

"That depends."

"A superior memory?" Bourne wasn't hiding his repugnance at the cheap, devious method employed by the defense experts to hide the hard evidence of their interviews with the defendant.

"You knew you would be back. Why did you not bring notes?"

The witness fumbled with excuses, her answer deteriorating into a discussion about her inability to carry things because of an upper neck and back problem.

"Are four pages too many papers for you to carry?" Bourne parried.

The defense's mitigating house of cards was becoming shaky. Cahill's polite veneer was beginning to crack. They needed the next witness to pull the psychological testimony out of the fire.

After lunch, before the hearing continued, the defense's expert witness, Dr. Arthur Norman, was visibly annoyed at being kept waiting. Intermittently, he paced like a caged panther then sat in an aisle seat swinging his foot and sighing loudly. When called, Norman swaggered to the front and slouched in the witness box. His body language emanated disdain. His attitude could literally be defined as "contempt of court."

In diagnosing his client, whom he described as a "cold, aloof, frozen woman," Dr. Norman used the term alexithymia: a rare condition, he said, a severe pathology characterized by no emotion, where the person is totally out of touch with her feelings. The journal abstracts to which Dr. Norman referred were labeled defense Exhibit B.S. and entered as evidence.

Norman used his word "alexithymia" to explain Robin's familiar behavior that everyone had seen throughout the trial: "With Ms. Row, her thinking is very concrete, but she seems to be disconnected from her feelings...Even notorious serial killers cry, break down...It was...beyond denial – pathological, extreme...blocked."

Norman agreed with his assistant that Robin had blocked out what had happened and that she says it's all back, she remembers everything. She recounted for the doctor her version of February 10. "She said she went in with Danny. First thing she remembers is that Danny snapped at her in the garage." He had never done that before, and it had reminded her of her dad.

"I asked…did you go upstairs, look at the kids? She said that she went upstairs, kissed them and tucked them in like she always did. What did you feel? 'Nothing' was her response. Consciously did you think what you were doing? 'No.' Did you think about the kids while you were there? 'No.' After? 'No.'"

Bourne did believe Robin tucked her children in that night, but for the purpose of making certain they were all in place before starting the fire. That would explain her stunned expression when Joan suggested that Tabitha may have gotten out. It would explain why she knew Tabitha was wearing the diamond studs Joan had given her. Tucking in and kissing her children before she set a fire beneath them, that, in Bourne's opinion, qualified her as a monster.

Dr. Norman, too, claimed he had no notes, no reports. He did have tapes of their sessions with Robin and results of the MMPI and Milan tests. He was reluctant to turn them over.

"I have some tapes somewhere. I don't know where they are."

"How many tapes are there?" Bourne questioned.

"I don't know. They were boring, so I turned them off," Norman said.

Norman said his diagnosis was based on several things including the taped interviews that recorded Robin in an induced hypnotic state.

"It had nothing to do with a diagnosis, just had an opinion right from the beginning?" Bourne asked.

"It's the whole picture. I relied on things of yours and his," Norman answered, nodding toward the defense table.

"You formed a theory?"

"Yes. Several hypotheses."

"Well," Bourne said, frustrated with the vagueness of the doctor's conclusion, "is she psychotic, is she a sociopath?"

"No, she's not. The tests didn't show that."

❉ ❉ ❉

The State's expert witness, psychologist Dr. Robert Engle, had a much different take, for the most part, on Robin's psychological tests than Dr. Norman. "The MMPI was strongly indicative of antisocial personality, paranoid perception of the world, chronic depression, and histrionic personality," Dr. Engle said.

Engle testified that from the MMPI Robin scored 98.5 percent on sociopathic tendencies, which put her in the top 1 percent of women who have taken the test: the sociopath characterized as having a cold, withdrawn emotional style, as possessing a lack of remorse, and as being calculating and manipulating. Robin also scored high, 99 percent and in the top 1 percent, in the paranoid category, seeing the world in an adversarial way. Chronic depression was in the 85 percent range. Robin scored 82 percent in the histrionic category, which is characterized by a high need for attention and affection, possibly sought in a seductive way, and a high degree of self-centeredness, which would account for Robin's craving sympathy.

"How would therapy be used in this type of diagnosis? What about treatment?" Bourne asked.

"Not terribly responsive to verbal forms of therapy…typically incarceration, probation…something structural. This diagnosis would fit the general prison population."

"Is that a definitive diagnosis?"

"Quite definitive."

"What about alexithymia? Are you acquainted with the term?"

"Because of its lack of root, I was unable to find it anywhere [other than] a printout which had some research."

"What did you learn?"

Dr. Engle defined alexithymia as difficulty in recognizing and articulating emotion, lack of fantasy and imagination, with a relatively flat affect.

"Is that a mental disease?"

"No," Dr. Engle replied, "it's a general description of one's state…It is an adjective, not a noun."

"Is that mutually exclusive to having an antisocial personality?"

"No."

"If you knew that…she had concocted stories that weren't true…is that consistent with alexithymia?"

"No."

"Is alexithymia a mental diagnosis or a mental illness?"

"No. Oh, no."

* * *

Judge Schwartzman set the sentencing hearing arguments for November 12 and the imposition of sentence for December 16. Speaking directly to Robin, he told the defendant that at that hearing she would have the right to say anything she wanted before sentence was passed.

If Robin was ever going to, this would be a chance for her to express her sorrow or remorse for what had happened to Randy, Joshua, and Tabitha. It would be an opportunity to publicly apologize to Randy's family and the McHughs.

CHAPTER FORTY-SIX

November 12, 1993

Joan was back in the courtroom for the first time since the verdict. It had been eight months since the trial. Her hands were shaking as she and Bernie took their seats in the second row. Danny didn't come. His few minutes testifying in court was more time than he wanted to spend in Robin's company ever again.

Bourne began his closing argument to the Court by using facts he could not use in trial. "Alyce Woods took care of Joshua while Robin served time for embezzlement. Robin pled guilty to forgeries in 1987 in California, then jumped bond and came to Idaho.

"The defendant said she had bingo experience; she did, she played bingo in California...By the end of the year the YWCA [bingo] was about bankrupt...Not one penny cash had ever been deposited...Her financial situation was becoming acute.

"They died in their sleep before the flames could get to them, suffocating as they slept. In the trial, the fire was blamed on Randy, more recently on Danny McHugh.

"I find there are seven proven aggravating circumstances beyond a reasonable doubt...they all independently support the death penalty. I fear if the court picks two, even though believing seven exist, because of the unpredictable nature of the appellate court, they may be overturned.

"I haven't come across one [case] that matches the inhumanity of setting a fire beneath children...they were roasted alive. Certainly is as depraved a case as I've come across, others pale by comparison.

"She has no conscience, no pity…" Before starting a fire beneath them, "she kissed her kids good-night.

"The defendant is a greedy person, motivated by money. Her family describes her that way. Charlie [her brother] says that Robin will lie, cheat, and steal to get to bingo…anything to get to her goal. Whatever she makes isn't enough."

Bourne quoted terms from Robin's psychological history: Antisocial acting out, controlling, lack of emotional genuineness, manipulative, predatory, self-centered. Robin "fits those like they were thinking of her when they wrote the diagnosis."

Robin has a "wicked and evil nature," Bourne warned, and couldn't be trusted in this society. "No other penalty will give society retribution beyond the death penalty." Bourne finished emphatically.

"To put it mildly," Cahill launched into his closing, "this is a case that has had more problems, more emotional twists than any other case. To do these things, to be involved, to be so far out from what a mother should do, a wife should do, is a sign of a serious illness."

Cahill opened with the strongest mitigator, Robin's "catastrophic childhood, punctuated by things done to her." There was sexual abuse by her grandfather resulting in a pregnancy and abortion, he said. "She was physically and emotionally abused by her mother…Her father physically abused her mother in front of the kids. He is incarcerated now and had been for much of her childhood…The defendant acted out with sexual promiscuity and trouble with the law. Because of these things," Cahill said, "the defendant has fears of abandonment." Cahill also pointed out that Robin was institutionalized as a teenager and had two children as a teenager.

There was "no depravation [when it came to]…the kids," Cahill pointed out. "Robin did have good qualities. People said she was a good mother. She has been able to maintain employment, has acted appropriately during her incarceration, and has been helpful to others."

Despite the prosecution's evidence to the contrary, Cahill said Robin did have an abusive marriage which may have led to the crime, but it was unlikely those circumstances would be repeated.

Cahill clung to Dr. Norman's diagnosis that his client suffered from alexithymia and was so far out of normal that in her mind her children "no longer existed for her...her father was a paranoid schizophrenic...Only a person that is very ill would kill their own children," Cahill pleaded.

Challenging Bourne's aggravating circumstances, Cahill argued: First, there is no evidence to tie the defendant to a circumstantial case. Second, she did not intend to "impact" people. Third, Randy had his signature on at least one insurance policy. Also, it is very difficult to grade atrocious and heinous, Cahill argued. "The family did not suffer...'Utter Disregard,'" Cahill claimed, was language that was unconstitutionally vague. "Clearly, the defendant did not intend to kill."

Regarding the circumstance of "propensity to kill," Cahill pointed out that the crime was directed against her family – isolated. "She can have no more children, and it is unlikely she will marry again."

Cahill summed up: "The reality of sentencing someone to die is, I believe, not what society wants...not to be killers ourselves. Death is a final act. I ask the Court to leave it open until we know more about Robin. I ask the Court to impose life."

Cahill sagged, his face bore the fatigue of long hours and the responsibility of having his client's life hinge on his arguments. Robin's attorneys supported her through her stories and claims of innocence and weathered her radical turnaround as a result of therapy and her desire to read what amounted to a confession, hoping it would be viewed by the judge as remorse for a "mistake." They had given her a defense that even her appeal attorneys later had to admit was flawless.

Cahill hoped in his heart of hearts that Judge Schwartzman would not sentence Robin to death. But he acknowledged that the community seemed to want just that.

Roger Bourne had a last word of rebuttal, beginning with Robin's "catastrophic childhood."

"We don't know if we can believe the defendant beyond the general corroboration of her sister. I do point out there are other brothers and sisters. There is no evidence that those people did anything antisocial.

"No violence in her priors...I don't see that as a mitigating circumstance but rather the absence of aggravation. It doesn't outweigh aggravation."

Bourne pointed out that as far as the defendant having good qualities, yes, "she was hardworking and helpful to friends; she can be productive when she wants to be…The crux is that she is capable of making a choice."

From a back bench in the gallery, Dr. Norman sat listening, rigid and silent, to what Bourne had to say about his testimony. "Dr. Norman did psychiatric tests…He labeled her alexithymic and called the tests of no real consequence.

"First, the alexithymic description is not a diagnosis – not a mental illness. It describes the way a person reacts to others. Does the defendant even fit the description of alexithymic? Norman says she doesn't show affect…we see it on the videotape with Raney. She laughed, cried, and joked. The court has seen her cry – and in frustration. Friends say she's bright, outgoing…Norman is wrong, because he chooses or he had the wool pulled over his eyes by the defendant. He says she has no imagination. She spun tall tales; she lies about everything.

"It can't be argued that because she's alexithymic, she killed. It doesn't mean that a person who can is not sane. In addition, alexithymic or not, sociopathic or not, she can conduct herself by the dictates of the law. She chose to break the law.

"I suggest there is no mitigating substance in her profile. The defendant said she was there, but didn't mean to kill. I think that's the biggest lie of all. Who could possibly…believe that she did not intend to kill. The truth means nothing to her. She would do anything to get out from underneath, including telling Dr. Norman that she doesn't remember. [To do structural damage] she could have poured paint on the carpet for that matter. She could have gotten in her car and driven away.

"She was verbally abusive to Randy in public; she didn't fit the battered wife. If he was abusive, why would she leave the kids with him," Bourne reasoned.

"She said Randy started the fire…then Danny McHugh started it. That's the biggest lie of all." Bourne repeated fiercely, "The mitigating doesn't hold a candle to the aggravating. She is calculating, manipulative, and evil."

With conviction, Bourne asked Judge Schwartzman to "impose the death penalty…This case calls out for the death penalty. If not this case, then there is no case that this penalty applies to."

Judge Schwartzman announced he would deliver his sentence December 16. Turning his attention toward the defendant, he gave Robin the right to speak to the Court or to anyone. An opportunity to apologize. "You may sit or rise and face the Court," Schwartzman advised, looking down at Robin from the bench with the piercing eyes of an eagle.

"I don't have a statement prepared. I want to thank my attorneys for their support when I needed it," Robin said awkwardly.

"The buck stops with me," Schwartzman orated. "...The Court has two options: imposition of the death penalty or life in prison. The Court will take the two options quite seriously."

Speaking of the death penalty or fixed life with no eligibility for parole, Judge Schwartzman said sternly, fixing unblinking eyes on Robin, "You qualify, Ms. Row."

CHAPTER FORTY-SEVEN

Defense attorney Cahill was right about public opinion. *The Idaho Statesman* polled its readers: "Do you agree with the prosecutor's decision to seek the death penalty for Robin Row?" Ninety-one percent of the callers agreed with the prosecutor's bid for the death penalty. The public pendulum was swinging back toward the dispensation of harsher punishments, away from coddling criminals.

Judge Schwartzman received letters supporting aggravating circumstances from Jim Hutchings, presumably Tabitha's father; Alyce Woods; Charles and June Row; and Chris Daniels, Randy's sister.

Supporting mitigating circumstances, the judge received letters from Mrs. Washam, Mary Lou Weiner, and Mort Weiner. The letters described Robin as a good mother who missed her children and who was "framed" or treated unfairly by almost everyone. The judge also received a prolix, emotion-laden, handwritten allocution from Robin:

> "I want to talk to you about Joshua, Tabitha, Randy, and my feelings. During my trial I felt that I had to be acquitted for my children. I know now for the same reason I must be honest with myself and the court.
>
> Many people say I have no feelings or show no emotion. Most of my life, to protect myself, I learnt [sic] to hide them, but I do have feelings. I feel tremendous pain at the lose [sic] of Joshua and Tabitha. I feel the same pain all parents feel when they lose a child. I'll never be able to touch them, to hold them,

comfort them. I will miss the joy of seeing them grow into happy loving adults. I will never get to do little things like comb their hair, dress them, read to them, take walks with them...

When I look back on my childhood, I see abuse and no love. I was determined that Joshua and Tabitha would not live as I did. I broke the cycle of abuse. They knew I loved them. I do not recall my mother ever telling me she loved me. My children always felt love from me and were told often. I was a very affectionate mother. I was a good mother...

I tried to take my own life while incarcerated. Many feel I did it for attention. That was not the case. I wanted the hurt to stop – to go away.

I was a proud mother. They were bright and intelligent children. Joshua was a boy scout and Tabitha was a brownie. I feel so fortunate that the last time I spoke with them, on the telephone, we exchanged I love you's.

My life with Randy was not a happy one...There was a lot of fighting in our home. Despite what people say there was abuse. No one knows exactly what happened behind our closed doors...If I could bring him back I would...I'm truly sorry for his family's loss, sadness and sorrow.

I feel tremendous guilt for what has happened and I take full responsibility for my actions.

Once I realized the truth and that I had truly been involved and accepted it...I had the choice to continue to deny it so that my family and friends who stood by me and believed in me would never know the horrid truth as I know it or I could come forth and tell the truth regardless of the outcome. My choice was to tell the truth and face the consequences...

I do not agree with everything the prosecution said. I am not placing blame on anyone else nor did I know that my attorneys were going to disclose any of that. All I know is I told them I had to come forward with what my involvement was.

Regardless of what has happened I truly do love my children and I will feel their loss for the rest of my life…I do want you to know that whatever sentence you pass down to me it could never be more than what I am doing to myself.

Thank you, your honor, for allowing me the time to speak about what's in my heart.

* * *

December 16, 1993

In spite of her role in the prosecution's case, Joan did not want the judge to impose the death penalty. Throughout the trial, even knowing all the things she now knew about Robin, she still wondered if she had done the right thing by testifying, still wondered if there just wasn't something that everyone had missed – some obscure, elusive explanation. An inexplicable guilt had plagued her conscience. But Robin's statement in open court was the deathblow to Joan's doubt, especially when Robin implicated Danny in her murderous scheme.

Robin was now 37 years old. She had spent nearly two years in jail waiting for the moment of truth. For most of that time she had proclaimed her innocence and looked positively toward acquittal. Now, all she had left to hope for was a life in confinement over death, hinging on one man's decision.

For her sentencing, she was dressed in an orange jumpsuit with the black stenciled letters "A C JAIL" printed on the back. The pumpkin suit was not flattering and only accentuated her stubbiness. Adding to this picture was a Robin without her "cool." For once, waiting for court to begin, she seemed agitated.

Judge Alan Schwartzman looked especially solemn as he took his seat. For 39 minutes, the defendant sat expressionless while the judge read his decision, his voice reverberating gravely in the silence of the semiparalyzed courtroom.

"This Court finds that the jury verdicts are fully supported by the evidence beyond all reasonable doubt…

"The verdicts themselves establish, as a matter of law, two statutory aggravating circumstances under Idaho Code Section 19-2515(g), namely:

"'2. At the time the murder was committed the defendant also committed another murder,' and '7. The murder was one defined as murder of the first degree...'

"Based upon the evidence adduced at trial, it is beyond argument that three human beings lost their lives...All three mercifully died in their sleep as a result of carbon monoxide poisoning from the fire...

"In addition, this Court finds beyond any reasonable doubt the following set of facts:

"One, the fire was arson caused – no one disputed that at trial;

"Two, insurance policies carried on the lives of the Row family revealed...six separate policies – life and/or accidental death – were in full force and effect...benefits payable to Robin Row as a named beneficiary would potentially reach $276,500...Robin Row procured the final policy...17 days before the fatal fire;

"Three, this Court finds beyond any reasonable doubt that this alleged syndrome of physical abuse was mostly a fabrication on her part to garner sympathy and support, to place Randy in as bad a light as possible, and to provide a motive for Randy to do something totally irrational, such as take his own life;

"Four, on October 22, 1993, in open court and in the presence of her attorneys, Robin Row stated on the record...that she indeed had been present when the fire was started...that she had actually gone upstairs and seen Tabitha in her bed; and that her intent was...merely to cause some structural damage so that she could get the children away from Randy. In terms of weight and credibility, the Court finds that the defendant is and has long been a pathological liar who will bend and distort the truth and reality to suit her own purposes. At least the Court can now find, with 100 percent certainty, that the defendant was present and did set fire to the duplex apartment. Like the proverbial arsonist, she returned to the scene.

"Five, Robin Row also had a new, consuming love interest in January of 1992. Exhibit 11 is a passionate love letter written by Robin Row to D on March 2, 1992, from the Ada County jail...It reveals in intimate detail the depth of her emotional relationship to this man and their sexual liaisons during the month of January.

"It must be remembered that at the time this letter was written, Robin Row was in jail on an unrelated offense…that the memorial service for her family had occurred just two weeks earlier…and that she is now professing her love for D and promoting herself as a loving stepmother to R. The ironies of this letter are simply mind-boggling!

"Given the above factual scenario, this Court further finds…that two additional statutory aggravating circumstances have been fully proved beyond a reasonable doubt: The murder was committed for remuneration or the promise of remuneration.

"Based upon historical facts in her life (the tragic death of her son Keith in an accidental, albeit similar, type of house fire in 1980), Robin Row had every reason to expect and anticipate insurance proceeds from another accidental fire that would claim the lives of her family. While I cannot and do not ascribe this as the sole motivation for the arson-related killings, it is certainly one of the proximate causative factors leading to the triple murders, along with her new love interest and desire to eliminate family entanglements;

"By the murder, or circumstances surrounding its commission, the defendant exhibited utter disregard for human life.

"Defendant's lack of conscientious scruples against the killing of her natural-born, pre-adolescent, innocent and helpless children, along with her husband, catapult this case into the heightened dimension of utter disregard for human life…Robin Row's actions represent the final betrayal of motherhood and embody the ultimate affront to civilized notions of the maternal instinct. She professed to love her children, yet cunningly and remorselessly took their lives to meet her own needs and antisocial delusions. Maternal 'pedocide' – the killing of one's own children – is the embodiment of the cold-blooded, pitiless slayer. A descent into the blackened heart of darkness.

"In a general or descriptive sense, I have no difficulty in referring to Robin Row as mentally ill or having a mental disorder, but certainly NOT in the sense that she is psychotic, i.e., having lost touch with reality, or that she does not know the difference between right and wrong…

"I wish to focus on that aggravating circumstance which I consider the most aggravated…the defendant committed three…premeditated first-degree murders. For these capital crimes defendant shall either receive the death penalty or three fixed life sentences without the possibility of parole.

"In weighing all mitigating circumstances against this one aggravated circumstance, the scale or balance tips dramatically to that side authorizing the harshest penalty allowed by law. By any stretch of the imagination, the mitigating circumstances enumerated above pale in significance and comparison to the premeditated murders of Randy Row, Joshua Cornellier, and Tabitha Cornellier…This was no accident; there was absolutely no provocation; the murders were not committed under duress, or the heat of passion, or under some delusion that might soften moral culpability. This Court does not for one moment accept defendant's manipulative, self-serving explanation that she set the fire for the limited purpose of causing some structural damage so that she would regain custody of the children…The circumstances of the fire were such that any rational person would know and intend the logical consequences…i.e., the deaths of the sleeping victims. And Robin Row is certainly rational in that sense! Defendant's alexithymic mental condition and emotional affect may explain how she could methodically destroy her family by blocking out all human feelings of remorse – without confronting the darkness of her own soul – but it cannot come close to justify or outweigh the gravity of three murders. The horror of what she has done may also explain her coping mechanisms of emotional withdrawal, blocking, flat affect, denial, and supposed memory loss – feigned, in my opinion – Robin Row must now be confronted with the reality of what she has done; she can run from it in her mind and emotions, but she can't hide from the truth of her chosen actions.

"She has some good qualities – so do we all – and was perceived as a loving, caring mother – the ULTIMATE IRONY, I might add – and has lost touch with and blocked out her emotions. This is hardly a counterbalance on the scales of justice towards leniency, IF that is how a fixed life sentence is perceived. The murders of Randy, Joshua, and Tabitha weigh like a boulder over against the pebbles of those mitigating circumstances articulated above…the calculus tips inexorably to a sentence of death.

"I do not wish to dispose of this 'weighing' process, however, without at least considering an alternative line of thought…if the State is truly seeking the harshest sanction for Robin Row...should she not be condemned to everlasting life imprisonment? To live every day with this horror on her conscience? To live as a virtual outcast in the penitentiary, day after day, year after year, to the last breath of her allotted existence? In addition, such a sentence would obviate the necessity of costly, time-consuming appeals, federal review, and the almost incomprehensible delays that are associated with a death penalty case."

Joan exhaled. It sounded as if the judge might opt for life in prison. It would be a prolonged suffering, but at least it wouldn't be death. Maybe, Joan thought, Robin might be able to eke out some form of existence with other inmates.

"I give vent to these thoughts to be as intellectually and humanly honest as I can in the sentencing process," Judge Schwartzman continued. "That a capital case is overburdened, if not abused, with glacially slow procedural safeguards – layer upon layer – should not deter this Court from performing its heavy responsibility. While some may argue that a sentence of death represents cruel and unusual punishment, others may argue, with equal vigor, that what is cruel and unusual is only the criminal review process itself that takes so long in carrying out a judicially mandated execution. That this defendant might someday receive a commutation and be released, or even escape, is also a theoretical possibility. That Robin Row would block out her feelings of guilt and remorse; that she would disconnect from the magnitude of her crimes; that she would manipulate reality and bend the truth to soothe her conscience is, in my opinion, a foregone conclusion. A fixed life sentence would simply not achieve the theoretical punishment/retribution goals posited above.

"As a matter of law and conscience, I again find and conclude that the mitigating factors do not outweigh the aggravating circumstance of Idaho Code §19-2515(g)(2) and do not make imposition of the death penalty unjust...I would only note for the record that there is not the slightest doubt in this Court's mind, should the case ever be remanded back to me after appeal, that the death penalty would also be imposed upon the aggravating circumstance of Idaho Code §19-2515(g)(6)...by each murder, defendant exhibited utter disregard for human life.

"ROBIN LEE CORNELLIER ROW, for the crimes of MURDER IN THE FIRST DEGREE, Counts I, II and III, for the premeditated killings of Randy Row, Tabitha Cornellier, and Joshua Cornellier, I hereby sentence you to DEATH as prescribed by law. And may whatever power greater than yourself that you believe in have mercy upon your soul. SO BE IT!" Judge Schwartzman bellowed his pronouncement passionately, accompanied by an intense owlish stare. Then he swooshed from the bench and through the door to his private office.

Robin bowed her head when hearing her fate but remained stone-faced. She was handcuffed and led out. Leaning over the bench in front of her, Joan McHugh sobbed. June Row cried with relief and Robert Row let out a jubilant whoop. The rest of the observers were stunned into silence and walked stonily out of the courtroom. Gus Cahill told the press it was a tragedy and he and Amil Myshin were saddened; Roger Bourne said that justice had been served.

No one appeared untouched – with the possible exception of Robin Row.

CHAPTER FORTY-EIGHT

Robin had had her so-called 15 minutes of fame, and it was probable that any lingering celebrity would arrive for her only in death. The day after the sentencing, the front page was dominated by a shot of a man wearing a blood-splattered shirt; an attorney for a participant in a deposition regarding a dispute between brothers over a mining claim, he survived a double murder/suicide. Robin's story was relegated to an inside page. Negative or positive, she loved attention and would have relished a front-page story. But for the time being, she was locked away and would soon be forgotten, the accounts of her story long since used for wrapping fish or swaddling breakables – just as she had instructed Randy, Joshua and Tabitha to wrap her breakables for storage only days before she killed them.

* * *

In their apartment, Joan asked Bernie to pull a cardboard box down from a high shelf. It was a box of Robin's things that had come from her storage unit. Joan felt ready to look inside; it was something she felt she had to do. It represented closure.

Gently wiping the dust from the glass with her sleeve, a well of tears filled Joan's eyes as she looked at the framed pictures of Joshua and Tabitha at different ages, from baby pictures to the time of their deaths. Their dress clothes still hung in her front closet, Tabitha's pretty pink dress and Joshua's Boy Scout uniform, ready for them to wear to their aunt's wedding, a happy celebration they never made it to. She couldn't move the clothes. She didn't know why, but she just couldn't do it yet.

Joan found pictures of Keith as a baby and one of him near the age of his death wearing a charming ear-to-ear grin. At 9 months old, a big-

356

eyed Kristina Mae questioned Joan through the frame's glass with her innocent stare. Why me? In the same frame with Keith's picture was the "To Mommy" poem written in what appeared to be Robin's hand. Joan didn't have an answer for why Robin had been blessed with these beautiful children only to cruelly take them before their time.

She lightly fingered the laminated hand prints made with colored paint on construction paper that Joshua and Tabitha had given their mother on Mother's Day when they were small. The poem accompanying Tabitha's read:

> Sometimes you get discouraged because I am so small, And
> always leave my fingerprints on furniture and walls. But
> every day I'm growing – I'll be grown up someday,
> And all those tiny hand prints will surely fade away.
> So here's a final hand print just so you can recall,
> Exactly how my fingers looked when I was very small.

A sealed envelope with a tiny bump held Joshua's first lost baby tooth. Also filed away in the box were divorce papers for Robin Lee Hamilton and Wayne E. Hamilton, Jr., dated August, 1980; Robin Lee and Randy Lynn's marriage license; and birth certificates for Joshua and Tabitha.

The most ironic pieces of memorabilia were two white cards imprinted with the black-inked fingerprints of Joshua and Tabitha. In bold black letters above the prints were the words "Protect Your Child With Child Identification." Nothing, Joan thought cynically, was able to protect them from their own mother.

The mementos in this box were all that Robin had kept of four beautiful children who had been unluckily cast, born to look to Robin Lee Cornellier for their protection – for their safety – for their preservation and doomed to lives taken prematurely.

One last thing Joan picked from the box was a plain white letter-sized paper folded in thirds. When she opened it a smaller paper fluttered to the floor. With a puzzled expression, she read the typewritten poem slowly, then stiffened:

* * *

I'M SOMEONE YOU KNOW VERY WELL...! ! !
Don't be fooled by me.
Don't be fooled by the face I wear.
For I wear a mask,
  I wear a thousand masks.
Masks that I'm afraid to take off,
And none of them are me.
Pretending is an art that's second nature to me;
But don't be fooled,
  for God's sake don't be fooled.
I give the impression that I'm secure.
That all is sunny and unruffled in me,
Within as well as without,
That confidence is my name and coolness my game,
That the water's calm and I'm in command,
And that I need no one,
But don't believe me...
Who am I, you may wonder?
I'm someone you know very well...
                              – author unknown

Even though Robin had been given the death penalty – even if she were executed – Joan knew she would remain haunted by the woman who defined herself by this poem, the woman who called herself a friend. In some ways Joan felt she had become a different person because of her association with Robin. This woman had trespassed upon her life and had changed her in ways that would never again allow her to view people or situations without a certain wariness and cynicism.

When she finished the poem, Joan bent down and picked up the scrap of paper from the floor. Bernie saw the color drain from his wife's face. Joan felt as if her heart had stopped. In Robin's distinctive hand, a cross between handwriting and printing, were Joan's name and Danny's name, neatly lettered, followed by their Social Security numbers. Joan knew there was only one reason Robin would have carefully recorded and preserved those Social Security numbers. Joan and her family would have been Robin's next victims, and she trembled at the thought of how close they had come to moving away with this woman.

She had always told Robin that the truth would set her free. Initially, after finding out about the dark side to her friend's personality, Joan had thought the truth had made them both prisoners. But now, seeing her possible fate in those numbers, she realized the truth had indeed set her free – had saved her and her family – and had put Robin where she could never victimize again.

> *SURVIVORS PSALM*
> *I have been victimized.*
> *I was in a fight that was not a fair fight.*
> *I did not ask for the fight. I lost.*
> *There is no shame in losing such fights, only in winning.*
> *I have reached the stage of survivor and am no longer a slave of victim status.*
> *I look back with sadness rather than hate.*
> *I look forward with hope rather than despair.*
> *I may never forget, but I need not constantly remember.*
> *I was a victim.*
> *I am a survivor.*
>
> *– author unknown*

EPILOGUE

The Idaho Statesman's "Year in Review" for 1993 included an account of Robin Row's trial, as well as the story of Keith Wells – a convicted murderer who elected to forego his appeals and be put to death as soon as possible. His was the first execution in Idaho since 1957. Robin was quoted as saying she would follow Wells' lead and do the same thing if she received the death penalty. However, as of this printing, Robin continues to appeal her sentence.

The 2002 U.S Supreme Court ruling regarding the Ring Decision (Ring v. Arizona, in which the high court held that a death sentence where the necessary aggravating factors are decided by a judge violates a defendant's constitutional right to a trial by jury) did not benefit Robin as she had hoped. The Supreme Court declined to apply the ruling retroactively. Robin Row and 13 men also on Idaho's death row will not be able to use the absence of a jury in their sentencing as grounds to overturn their execution orders. Her case is currently under federal court review.

Robin Row continues to reside in the Pocatello Women's Correctional Center in eastern Idaho; however, she is being moved from her solitary death row cell to general population. Although Robin is allowed to see her immediate family – her mother, two brothers and two sisters – they do not visit.

The death penalty is seldom imposed on women in this country. Since the reinstatement of capital punishment in the U.S., 146 women have received the death sentence – two in Idaho. Of the nearly 50,000 women currently incarcerated, only 49 are on death row. Execution of women in the U.S. is even more rare. Since 1976, only 10 female offenders have actually been put to death. When, and if, all of her avenues for appeal are exhausted and the sentence of death is carried out, Robin Lee Row will be the first woman executed in the state of Idaho.

Where they are now:

Judge Alan Schwartzman is now retired from the Idaho Court of Appeals. It is unlikely he will have any role in Robin Row's appeal process.

Roger Bourne still prosecutes high profile criminal cases for the State of Idaho. He is currently the Chief of the Criminal Division for the Ada County Prosecutors Office.

Kevin Swain is now a magistrate court judge.

Gary Raney was formally commended for his investigation in the arson/triple murder case recounted in this book. In November 2004, he was elected Sheriff of Ada County.

Ken Smith, a 22-year veteran of the detective's section of the Ada County Sheriff's Office, continues to investigate murder, robbery and sex crime cases – including crimes perpetrated through the Internet.

June and Charles Row, Randy's parents, have both passed on since the trial. His sister, Kathy Row, was later murdered by her ex-son-in-law.

Joan and Bernie McHugh are currently living productive and happy lives. Bernie has now been clean and sober for 14 years. They enjoy their children, grandchildren, and great-grandchildren. Every item in their lives that had a connection to Robin Row has been expunged. However, Joan continues to think of the children who were lost and their missed milestones – first day of high school, learning how to drive, graduations, 21st birthdays – and wonder what they could have become.

Author's Notes

Long before I ever thought about writing any book, I was an avid true crime reader driven to understand the psychopathic or socio-pathic personality. And I have always been interested in the techniques employed by the police in their investigations to bring these slippery characters to justice. As an aspiring true crime author, I found every case a fascinating one – old and new. But it wasn't until 1992, when I read about an upcoming trial in the local newspaper, that I felt compelled to write this book.

My book became a project that would take over ten years to develop. As people were legally allowed or willing to talk about the case, access to information became available. In fact, the case continues to be an ongo-ing part of my life, as it is still pending further appeals.

It was my curiosity in the crime itself that initially attracted me to the story, but it was the sympathy I felt for the many victims of Robin Lee Row and my anger at her actions that truly motivated me. I began to outline my book by attending the trial and researching the profile of a psychopathic/sociopathic serial killer.

According to Dr. Robert D. Hare, in his book *Without Conscience – The Disturbing World of the Psychopaths Among Us*, there may be as many as 2 or 3 million psychopaths in North America. However, most psychopaths are not serial killers; rather, they are the garden-variety psychopath/sociopath – the egocentric, the manipulative, and the remorseless personality that craves instant gratification. Not evident from outward appearances, a psychopath could be anyone's next-door neighbor, friend, relative, or lover.

While I knew going into this project that psychopaths do not wear signs, I still found it hard to believe that one could not readily see through the mask of a witty and motherly looking Robin Row. It was in witnessing Joan McHugh's testimony during the trial process and through my posttrial research of Robin Row – including nearly 100 interviews spanning the country from California to New Hampshire – that I finally began to understand that the indications of a sociopath weren't as obvious as I had thought.

Robin was an accomplished manipulator whose crimes had escalated over the years as she gained confidence in her abilities. In the end I came to believe, as do law enforcement personnel who have investigated her, that the murders she was convicted of in Idaho were not the only murders she has committed – or would commit in the future if the opportunity availed itself.

I introduced myself to Joan McHugh after a sentencing hearing and began a relationship that still exists today. It wasn't an easy task to gain her trust. After several meetings, she began, reluctantly, to tell me her story. My focus quickly evolved into compassion and empathy for Joan. The moment I put myself in Joan's shoes I was shocked by the realization that her story could be mine – or anyone's. I became convinced that her story should also be told.

As for Robin Lee Row? I met Robin after her trial, while she was in the Canyon County jail, and corresponded with her during the first two years of her incarceration in the Pocatello Women's Prison. In my correspondence and in-person conversation with her, Robin failed to show any remorse or concern for her victims. Her concern was, and still is, reserved for her own needs and comforts – evidenced by her ongoing pleas for money through the Internet. Robin continues to portray herself as the victim.

Unfortunately, it is most often in retrospect that these symptoms of an emotional void are recognized as the telltale characteristics of the sociopath. It is only by exposing Robin, and telling Joan's story, that any of us can learn to avoid being sucked into a web of deception. My hope is that, after reading this book, readers will come away with a better awareness and ability to identify the red flags of the sociopathic personality – before it is too late.

– Nancy Whitmore Poore

ACKNOWLEDGMENTS

My heartfelt appreciation goes out to the individuals who gave their time and insight to help make this book a reality:

To all the dedicated firefighters from the Whitney Fire Department and the Cole-Collister Fire Station; YWCA employees Barbara Fawcett, Janice Johnson and Sue Fellen; the twelve jurors who were conscientious in their duty and contribution to our system of justice; Joshua's and Tabitha's elementary school teachers, Jane Dobson and Shirley Jackson.

To my children Cassandra, Angela, Torre, and Lexi and my grandson Jordan; my mother who attended the trial with me and read my rough drafts; and all the friends and family who supported my work with positive feedback and encouragement and put up with the long hours I spent hunched over my computer. To my literary "Booked Up" buddies who continue to encourage my literary reading beyond criminal psychology. A special thank you to Michael S. Poore and Jim Poore.

Thanks to Jean Terra, my editor, who smoothed out the rough spots, sometimes with a jackhammer, to make this account much more cohesive. And for polishing the manuscript and making this book a reality, I credit the professionalism and expertise of Jennifer McCord, Tami Taylor, and Roberta Trahan.

It is difficult to put into words what Joan and Bernie McHugh gave to this effort. They spent countless hours sharing painful memories and going over minute details to give the readers a personal, close-up understanding of the tragedy that beset them.

I would be woefully remiss if I didn't take this opportunity to applaud all the civil servants who spend countless hours working to convict and lock up the dangerous people who threaten our lives and safety. Just to name a few: Judge Alan Schwartzman, Deputy Ada County Prosecutor Roger Bourne and Judge Kevin Swain, Ada County Sheriff Gary Raney and Detective Ken Smith, the late Undersheriff H. Dee Pfeiffer, Detective Linda Scown, Lynette Porter, Coroner Erwin Sonnenberg, Lynn Bowerman, Dr. Anil Desai, Detective Chuck Sanborn, Detective Pat Tennant, Coroner George Files, and the many others behind the scenes of our justice system.

Many thanks to all the people I have not specifically named here – either because of privacy's or brevity's sake or because my memory is not what it used to be – whom I interviewed and who gave their time and personal information generously despite the sometimes painful memories attached. You are not forgotten.

Thanks to those who added pertinent information to my understanding of the sociopathic personality: William C. Anderson, author of *Lady Bluebeard – The True Story of Love and Marriage, Death and Flypaper;* John Douglas and Mark Olshaker, authors of *Obsession;* Robert Ressler and Tom Shachtman, authors of *Whoever Fights Monsters;* Dr. Robert Hare, author of *Without Conscience – The Disturbing World of the Psychopaths Among Us;* and true crime author Ann Rule, whose insightful writing about Ted Bundy, Diane Downs, and others inspired me to expose a sociopath of equal menace to society.

NANCY WHITMORE POORE

Driven to expose injustice in all forms by her innate sense of fairness, Nancy Whitmore Poore launched her own investigation into the crimes of the psychopathic serial killer, Robin Lee Row. "The scales of justice are strong in my Libran personality," Poore explains.

As an Idaho native, Nancy Whitmore Poore found the case of a Boise wife and mother accused of murdering her family particularly chilling – and provocative. Poore's passion for writing and her lifelong interest in criminal investigation combined to create this compelling account of the events surrounding Robin Row and her trial. DEADLY CONFIDANTE is the culmination of years of tireless research – including excerpts from official documents and criminal records, trial transcripts, witness testimony, and information gleaned from more than 100 interviews conducted by the author.

Nancy Whitmore Poore attended Boise State University where she studied writing and published essays and short stories. Her passions also include her family, reading, and enjoying the outdoors. Poore currently resides in Idaho where she works as a court reporter while researching her next book.

ORDER FORM

Qty.	Title	Price	Total
	Deadly Confidante by Nancy Whitmore Poore	$19.95	
	Shipping and Handling Add $5.00 for 1st book and $1.00 for every additional		
	Total Enclosed		

Method of Payment: ❏ Check or money order enclosed

❏ Visa   ❏ Mastercard   ❏ American Express

— — — — — — — — — — — — — — — —   ___/___

Card Number   Exp. Date

_____

Signature

Telephone Orders:
Call 1-800-354-5348
We accept Visa, MasterCard and American Express

Fax Orders:
1-714-545-1572
Fill out this form and fax.

Postal Orders:
Seven Locks Press
P.O. Box 25689
Santa Ana, CA 92799

Email Orders:
sevenlocks@aol.com

Name:_____
Address:_____
City:_____ State:_____ Zip:_____
Phone: (   )_____ Fax: (   )_____

Thank you for your order!

www.sevenlockspublishing.com